The People's Charter

The People's Charter

Democratic Agitation in Early Victorian Britain

Edited by Stephen Roberts

THE MERLIN PRESS

First published 2003 by The Merlin Press Ltd.
PO Box 30705
London WC2E 8QD
www.merlinpress.co.uk

ISBN: 0850365147
ISSN: 1478-7296 Chartist Studies Series

British Library Cataloguing in Publication Data
is available from the British Library

Printed in Great Britain by Antony Rowe Ltd., Chippenham

CONTENTS

For the Dodford Chartists –
whose efforts saved the cottage.

Acknowledgements

In Great Dodford in Worcestershire the National Trust has restored to its original appearance a cottage built as part of the Chartist Land Plan. This collection of essays is dedicated to the villagers whose determination brought this about (and who over the years have shown me great hospitality): Gordon and Zoe Long; Donald and Sheila McIlveen; and John and Diana Poole. My thanks to Adrian Howe and Tony Zurbrugg of Merlin Press for their support for this volume; to Robert Hall and Dorothy Thompson for their helpful comments on the introduction; to Owen Ashton for his prompt responses to my requests for material; and to Steve Farr for his expertise with computers (and for cheerfully sharing with me the teaching of Chartism to the Hagley Sixth Form).

I am grateful to the National Co-operative Archive at the Co-operative College in Manchester for permission to quote from letters in the G.J. Holyoake Collection. Crown-copyright material in the Public Record Office is reproduced by permission of the Controller of Her Majesty's Stationery Office.

To all of the contributors I am much obliged for agreeing that their essays could be included in this volume. Paul Pickering, 'Chartism and the "Trade of Agitation" in Early Victorian Britain' is reprinted from *History*, vol. 76, no. 247, 1991, pp.221-37 by permission of the Historical Association and Blackwells; Brian Harrison, 'Teetotal Chartism' is reprinted from *History*, no.58, 1973, pp.193-217 by permission of the Historical Association; Eileen Yeo, 'Christianity in the Chartist Struggle 1838-1842' is reprinted from *Past and Present*, no. 91, 1981 by permission of Oxford University Press; Cris Yelland, 'Speech and Writing in the *Northern Star*', is reprinted from *Labour History Review*, vol.65, no.1, 2000, pp.22-40 by permission of Edinburgh University Press; Philip Howell, '"Diffusing the Light of Liberty": The Geography of Political Lecturing in the Chartist Movement' is reprinted from the *Journal of Historical Geography*, vol.21, pt.1, 1995, pp.23-38 by permission of Academic Press; Stephen Roberts, 'Thomas Cooper in Leicester, 1840-1843' is reprinted from *Transactions of the Leicestershire Archaeological and Historical Society* vol.61, 1987, pp.62-76; Malcolm Chase, 'Chartism 1838-1858: Responses in Two Teesside Towns' is reprinted from *Northern History*, vol. 24, 1988, pp.146-171; Robert Hall, 'Chartism Remembered: William Aitken, Liberalism and the Politics of Memory' is reprinted from the *Journal of British Studies*, vol. 38, no.4, 1999, pp.445-470 by permission of the University of Chicago Press. Journal edited by Margot Finn. Copyright 1999 by the North American Conference on British Studies. All rights reserved.

Notes on Contributors

MALCOLM CHASE is Reader in Labour History, and Chair of the School of Continuing Education, at the University of Leeds. His publications include *The People's Farm* (1998) and *Early Trade Unionism: Fraternity, Skill and the Politics of Labour* (2000). He is currently writing a new narrative on the history of Chartism.

ROBERT HALL is an assistant professor at Ball State University in Muncie, Indiana. He has published essays on trade unionism and history and memory in Chartism, and has edited with Stephen Roberts, *William Aitken: The Writings of a Nineteenth Century Working Man* (Tameside Libraries, 1996). At present he is completing a book on work, democratic politics and the making of collective identities in the nineteenth century.

BRIAN HARRISON is based at Corpus Christi College, Oxford. His first book was *Drink and the Victorians: The Temperance Question in England 1815-1872* (1971; 2nd ed. 1994); his most recent was *The Transformation of British Politics 1860-1995* (1996). He has been Editor of the New Dictionary of National Biography since 2000, and is writing the new Oxford History of England's final volume, covering the period 1951- 1990.

PHILIP HOWELL is a lecturer in the Department of Geography at the University of Cambridge. He completed his PhD on the geography of Chartism's political culture in 1994, and has also worked on the geographies of gender and sexuality in Victorian Britain. He is currently writing a book on the regulation of prostitution in Britain and the British Empire.

PAUL PICKERING is a Queen Elizabeth II Fellow at the Humanities Research Centre, The Australian National University. His publications include: *Chartism and the Chartists in Manchester and Salford* (1995); *The People's Bread: A History of the Anti-Corn Law League* (with Alex Tyrell, 2000); and *Friends of the People* (with Owen Ashton, 2002).

STEPHEN ROBERTS is Head of History and Law at Hagley R.C. High School, Worcestershire, and a Fellow of the University of Birmingham. His publications include: *Radical Politicians and Poets in Early Victorian Britain: The Voices of Six Chartist Leaders* (1993); *Images of Chartism* (with Dorothy Thompson, 1998); and *The Victorian Working Class Writer* (with Owen Ashton, 1999). He is currently writing a monograph on the Victorian parliamentarians, Thomas Slingsby Duncombe and Charles Sibthorp.

CRIS YELLAND teaches English at the University of Teesside. His published articles involve the detailed analysis of language, and include 'The Communist Manifesto - A Linguistic Approach', in *Studies in Marxism* 4 (1998).

EILEEN YEO is Professor of Social and Cultural History at the University of Strathclyde in Glasgow. She has written extensively on Chartist culture and Chartist democracy and is currently teaching a Special Subject on Chartism, as well as extending her research for a book called 'Politics of the Public Sphere, 1750 to the Present: Class and Gender Encounters'.

Introduction

One Friday evening in early August 1886 Thomas Cooper received an unexpected visitor at his home in Portland Place, Lincoln. Cooper, eighty-one years' old and widely known as a lecturer and author on Christian apologetics, had not seen his visitor for several years and at first did not recognize him. 'But when I knew him, I cuddled him', Cooper declared.[1] The visitor was George Julian Harney, sixty-nine years' old and a resident of the United States. Cooper and Harney had first met more than half a century earlier. Both had been national leaders of the Chartist Movement. In Leicester in the early 1840s thousands of working people had pledged allegiance to Cooper's Shakespearean Chartist Association, and during his subsequent two years' imprisonment he had written an epic political poem, *The Purgatory of Suicides* (1845). If any Chartist was likely to have completed reading all ten books of Cooper's ambitious poem, it was Harney, fellow autodidact, devotee of Byron and, for five years editor of the famous Chartist newspaper, the *Northern Star*.[2] His reunion with Harney prompted Cooper to recall the radical leader who had so captivated him all those years earlier, Feargus O'Connor. 'If King Feargus, with all his faults, could step in here', he remarked, 'and … (say) he was "dying for a pinch of snuff" – as he said (& wrote from York Castle) – I would give a guinea rather than he should not have his large heart's desire'.[3]

Both Cooper and Harney looked back on their years of Chartist commitment with pride. For these two men, and for many hundreds of working men and women, involvement in the Chartist Movement had been the most momentous years of their lives. 'It was something to belong to such a movement', George Jacob Holyoake declared at a reunion of old Chartists in 1898; amongst those present was 'the last of the Manchester Chartists', W.H. Chadwick, who still wore the medal issued to commemorate O'Connor's release from prison almost sixty years earlier.[4] At the end of the nineteenth century Cooper and all these men felt their struggles to obtain a say in law making for all citizens had been vindicated.

The People's Charter was the political programme of electoral reform around which the working class campaigns of the late 1830s and 1840s coalesced. This document, signed by radical Members of Parliament and members of the London Working Men's Association, famously called for manhood suffrage, secret voting, the discontinuation of property qualifications for MPs, salaries for MPs, equal electoral districts and annual elections. This wide-ranging reform programme would have been familiar to radicals of an earlier generation – although Miles Taylor has argued that there were significant differences between what these radicals meant by parliamentary reform and what the Chartists meant by it.[5] Signed by 1,280,000 working people and backed by great meetings in the Midlands, the north of England and Scotland, the first Chartist petition was presented to Parliament in July 1839; its rejection was followed by calls for a 'national holiday' or general strike, underground preparations for a national insurrection and, finally, in November 1839 by the Newport Rising, in which soldiers shot down some twenty-two Chartists. This attempt at armed rebellion is one of the pivotal points in the Chartist story, our understanding of these events now greatly enhanced by David Jones' meticulous monograph.[6]

A number of leading Chartists were based in London. William Lovett and the booksellers and printers he worked with in the London Working Men's Association looked to education, class conciliation and peaceful propaganda spread by 'missionaries' and restrained journals such as *The Charter*. Julian Harney and Bronterre O'Brien were interested in the French Revolution, Bronterre editing a series of small journals[7]. In the North, where the provisions of the 1834 Poor Law were beginning to be implemented, Feargus O'Connor was the voice of confident, combative, class conscious radicalism. A former MP, O'Connor was at his most potent on the platform and in the columns of the widely circulating *Northern Star*, his defiant and passionate speeches and letters earning him the loyalty of thousands of working people. After more than a century of denigration O'Connor's very important role in creating and pushing forward the Chartist campaign was conclusively demonstrated by James Epstein and Dorothy Thompson.[8] By 1840 Feargus had become the embodiment of Chartism; in later years there were some personal antagonisms but no alternative leader emerged after Lovett had withdrawn.

The Chartists sought to operate according to democratic principles. The presentation of their three petitions of 1839, 1842, and 1848 were overseen by conventions or anti-parliaments of delegates elected by universal suffrage at mass outdoor meetings. Secretaries of local associations and the chairman of meetings were often elected. At the top of the National Charter Association was an elected executive; eighty-three localities took part in the election of the first executive in 1841. When O'Connor was elected to parliament in 1847 he submitted himself for re-election each year in the market place at Nottingham, regularly met deputations of electors and non-electors, and tried to arrange the payment of a salary.[9]

When a large amount of work began to appear on local Chartism (beginning in 1959 with *Chartist Studies*, a ground-breaking collection edited by Asa Briggs) the economic causes of Chartist protest were stressed. Although Gareth Stedman Jones has pointed to the political continuities between earlier radicalism and Chartism, these economic motivations remain significant.[10] The strikes of the summer of 1842 began as strikes against wage cuts, becoming strikes for the Charter. At the height of the strikes working people saw themselves involved in both political and industrial action. In the Potteries, in the largest Chartist trial ever held, 56 men were transported and 116 men and women imprisoned for up to two years; in a series of vivid and sometimes moving essays Robert Fyson has described the experiences of some of those caught up in the events of the summer of 1842.[11]

If Feargus had believed in 1839 that the events of 1831-32 would repeat themselves, there could be no doubts after the defeats of 1842 that the authorities were not going to simply bow to overwhelming popular protest. From the mid-1840s Chartism became a different sort of movement. Though manhood suffrage remained the priority, Feargus and the Chartists became inexorably linked with creating an alternative way of life to factory work. O'Connor's attempt to settle workers in independent cottage smallholdings was hugely popular. Whatever legal difficulties the Land Plan encountered, its reception amongst working people is more important; it touched deep feelings in working class communities across Britain. Alice Mary Hadfield has written a book-length study of the Land Company and five estates. Though containing much interesting detail, it lacks a basic sympathy with O'Connor and what he was trying to achieve. Malcolm Chase has provided a more rounded evaluation.[12]

The effective culmination of Chartism, and its most famous episode, was the demonstration and the final petition of 10 April 1848. Just as the Land Plan was successfully portrayed as O'Connor's enemies saw it, so down the years the Kennington Common demonstration and petition were presented as the laughable finale of O'Connor's self-delusion. The disapproving interpretation of Charles Kingsley in *Alton Locke* (1850) became rooted; one could be forgiven for thinking that Lord John Russell himself was the ghost writer of J. T. Ward's account of the events of 1848.[13] Yet there are important points to be made. At the heart of the condemnation of Chartism in 1848 were the many forged signatures on the petition. O'Connor however, was surely correct in doubting that thirteen clerks over a period of seventeen hours had been able to count 1.9 million signatures. When the Chartists asked for the petition to be returned so it could be examined, there was no response; the great petition of 1848 had been destroyed. Thomas Clark, one of the Chartists who walked alongside the cabs which delivered the petition to the House of Commons and James Watson, who attended the demonstration, looked back on the events of 1848 not with embarrassment but with pride. There were surely many other Chartists who shared these feelings; after all, two million signatures testified to an enormous level of support for the Chartist cause.[14]

The first recital of the Chartist story was given in 1854 by R. G. Gammage, himself a former Chartist. The first scholarly attempt at assessing the movement appeared more than thirty years later in the *English Historical Review*. Drawing on the papers of Francis Place, E.C.K Gonner depicted a movement led to decisive defeat by the 'unstable O'Connor' and even the 'quiet, manly' Lovett.[15] There are now scores of articles, books and theses on the subject, enough to fill two book-length bibliographies.[16] Unlikely to be superseded, the major single volume study is Dorothy Thompson's *The Chartists* (1984). The book was the culmination of a professional career dedicated to the study of Chartism, incorporating not only more than thirty years' research and reflection on the subject by the author herself but also the findings of a host of her graduate students. Of the shorter studies of the movement that have appeared, those of Richard Brown and Edward Royle are very reliable and ideal for students beginning academic work on Chartism; John K. Walton's reflective account is also helpful, providing clearly summaries of the scholarly debates.[17] The continuing vitality of Chartist studies has been confirmed not only by the appearance of these overviews, but also by the publication in 2001 of a six volume anthology of Chartist documents. Edited by Gregory Claeys, the volumes include the full texts of key and sometimes rare tracts – R.J. Richardson's *Rights of Women* (1840) or the Kirkdale prisoners' *Tracts for the Times* (1849), for example. Tracking down Chartist pamphlets in British, American and Russian archives can be an enjoyable pastime, but it is also undoubtedly time-consuming. Claeys' collection makes it even easier to write about Chartism without leaving the comforts of one's study. However, his volumes do represent the serious side of Chartism – the tract writing, conference reports and addresses to foreign democrats. The most lively and vital writing produced by the Chartists is to be found in their newspapers, particularly the *Northern Star*. It is in the *Star* more than anywhere else that it becomes clear what it was to be a Chartist. This volume includes some extracts from the Chartist press.[18]

The People's Charter seeks to gather in a single volume the most significant essays on Chartism which have appeared in scholarly journals. Stretching from 1973 to 1999, all of the essays are characterized by their fluency and understandability and by the thorough research and careful reflection which makes them more or less definitive statements on their particular themes. The book opens with Paul Pickering's account of a subject often featured in the Chartist press but not up to that point explored – the informal economy or 'trade of agitation' by which some Chartist activists made a living and helped sustain the campaign by selling such products as blacking, ink and pills to fellow Chartists. As Pickering observes in his thought-provoking essay, these men should not in the main be seen as rogues, but as full time and independent working class politicians; Peter McDouall a doctor who sold a concoction called 'McDouall's Florida Medicine', lectured for many years to Chartist audiences and topped the poll in the first election to the executive of the NCA in 1841.

Now revised and expanded for this volume, Brian Harrison's investigation of teetotal Chartism is one of the classic essays on the movement. A number of

Chartist leaders – Lovett, Henry Vincent and Arthur O'Neill – were prominently associated with the teetotal cause, arguing that political progress could only be achieved by a sober working class. Harrison examines the work of these men, but also observes that teetotalism extended beyond the leaders into the localities; teetotal Chartist societies were set up across the country and each week the names of those who had taken the teetotal pledge appeared in the *Star*. Another important facet of Chartism is considered by Eileen Yeo. If teetotalism made radicals more respectable, more single minded and fitter, appeals to religion gave their campaign legitimacy. Hymns were written and sung, political sermons delivered by the likes of the former Methodist, J. R. Stephens and the Swedenborgian editor of the *Star*, William Hill, and demonstrations organized in churches; Yeo offers an interesting account of Christian Chartism.

A movement of tens of thousands of working people, Chartism was held together by a combination of factors: its newspapers and journals, notably the *Northern Star*; by the tours of its lecturers; and by the hard work of committed local activists. Several essays in this volume consider some of the factors which made Chartism a national campaign. Published for fifteen years from 1837, the *Star* reached an enormous number of working people in its early years, often being read aloud in workshops, public houses and the open air. There is much to say about this celebrated newspaper, and Cris Yelland has produced a valuable evaluation of the language of the *Star*. Philip Howell, in his essay on Chartist lecturing, assesses another important means of national communication and co-ordination, and the Chartist localities are represented here by essays on Middlesbrough and Stockton and on Leicester. The Teesside towns were thought to have seen minimal Chartist activity; but, as Malcolm Chase demonstrates, under the leadership of men like James Maw and James Ball Owen, there was much going on. Leicester, meanwhile, under the leadership of Thomas Cooper, became a Chartist stronghold.

What became of the Chartists in their later lives? Robert Hall comments on the difficulties a Chartist autobiographer, William Aitken of Ashton-Under-Lyne, faced in telling the story of Chartism. Aitken wanted to be truthful, but, having become a Liberal, there was much he did not want to admit. Other Chartists also became Liberals. Amongst these were W. H. Chadwick of Manchester and Abraham Sharp of Bradford, both Liberal van lecturers, and the remarkable John Snowden of Halifax, who taught himself to read and (at the age of forty-one) to write and was active in reform campaigns until 1884, the year of his death. A few others became Tories, including Joshua Hobson, one of the three editors of the *Northern Star*, and Samuel Kydd, a man of outstanding qualities who became a barrister.[19] There is space to tell the later stories of only a few more Chartists. For some involvement in Chartism dramatically changed their lives. Transported at different times during the Chartist campaign, William Jones, Zepheniah Williams, William Ellis and William Cuffay all died in Australia. Amongst those who emigrated to the United States, John Campbell of Manchester became a newsagent and bookseller in Philadelphia, David Johnston of London became a photographer in Milwaukee and William Carnegie of Dunfermline died in poverty – though his son, Andrew, became a hugely wealthy steel manufacturer. When Feargus O'Connor died in 1855, 40,000 people attended his funeral. Thomas Cooper lived until 1892; this profoundly interesting man had been heard and read by hundreds of thousands of people by the time of his death.[20] Five years later Harney died; he was, his monument in Richmond declared, 'THE LAST OF THE CHARTIST LEADERS.'

Notes

[1] Manchester, National Co-operative Archive, Thomas Cooper to George Jacob Holyoake, 16 August 1886. For Cooper see: Stephen Roberts, 'Thomas Cooper (1805-92): Chartist, Lecturer and Author', in Joyce M. Bellamy and John Saville eds. *Dictionary of Labour Biography*, 9 (1993), pp. 51-7; Timothy Larsen, 'Thomas Cooper and Christian Apologetics in Victorian Britain', *Journal of Victorian Culture*, 5.2 (2000), pp. 239-59; Stephanie Kuduk, 'Sedition, Criticism and Epic Poetry in Thomas Cooper's *Purgatory of Suicides*', *Victorian Poetry*, 39, no. 2 (2001), pp. 164-86.

[2] For Harney see: David Goodway, 'George Julian Harney (1817-97): Chartist and Journalist', in Joyce M. Bellamy and John Saville eds. *Dictionary of Labour Biography*, 10 (2000), pp. 81-92; A.M. Schoyen, *The Chartist Challenge. A Portrait of George Julian Harney* (1958).

[3] Manchester, National Co-operative Archive , Thomas Cooper to George Jacob Holyoake, 16 August 1886.

[4] For a report of this reunion see Stephen Roberts, *Radical Politicians and Poets in Victorian Britain. The Voices of Six Chartist Leaders* (New York, 1993), pp. 137-8. Also see Antony Taylor, 'Commemoration, Memorialisation and Political Memory in Post-Chartist Radicalism: The 1885 Halifax Chartist Reunion in Context', in Owen Ashton, Robert Fyson and Stephen Roberts eds. *The Chartist Legacy* (1999), pp. 255-85.

[5] See ibid., pp.1-23.

[6] David Jones, *The Last Rising. The Newport Insurrection of 1839* (Oxford, 1985). Also see Ivor Wilks, *South Wales and the Rising of 1839* (1989).

[7] For O'Brien see Alfred Plummer, *Bronterre. A Political Biography of Bronterre O'Brien 1804-1864* (Toronto, 1971).

[8] James Epstein, *The Lion of Freedom. Feargus O'Connor and the Chartist Movement 1832-1842* (1982); Dorothy Thompson, *The Chartists* (1984).

[9] See Stephen Roberts, 'Feargus O'Connor in the House of Commons, 1847-1852', in Owen Ashton, Robert Fyson and Stephen Roberts eds. *The Chartist Legacy* (1999), pp. 102-18.

[10] Gareth Stedman Jones 'The Language of Chartism' in James Epstein and Dorothy Thompson eds. *The Chartist Experience: Studies in Working Class Radicalism and Culture, 1830-60*, pp. 3-58.

[11] Robert Fyson, 'The Crisis of 1842; Chartism, the Colliers' Strike and the Outbreak in the Potteries' in ibid., pp. 194-220; 'Homage to Daddy Richards' in Owen Ashton, Robert Fyson and Stephen Roberts, eds. *The Duty of Discontent. Essays for Dorothy Thompson* (1995), (1995), pp.71-96; 'The Transported Chartist: The Case of William Ellis' in Owen Ashton, Robert Fyson and Stephen Roberts, eds. *The Chartist Legacy* (1999), pp. 80-101.

[12] Alice Mary Hadfield, *The Chartist Land Company* (Newton Abbot, 1970); Malcolm Chase, 'We Wish Only To Work For Ourselves', in Malcolm Chase and Ian Dyck eds. *Learning and Living. Essays in Honour of J.F.C. Harrison* (Aldershot, 1996), pp. 133-48.

[13] J.T. Ward *Chartism* (1973), pp. 199-234. Although written in sympathy with the Chartist rank-and-file, this book offers a disapproving view of the leadership, particularly of O'Connor.

[14] See Paul Pickering, 'And Your Petitioners etc': Chartist Petitioning in Popular Politics 1838-1848, *English Historical Review*, 116, no.466 (2001), pp.368-88.

[15] R.G. Gammage, *History of the Chartist Movement 1837-1854* (1854); E.C.K. Gonner, 'The Early History of the Chartist Movement 1836-1839', *English Historical Review*, 16 (1889).

[16] J.F.C. Harrison and Dorothy Thompson eds. *Bibliography of the Chartist Movement 1837-1976* (1978); Owen Ashton, Robert Fyson and Stephen Roberts eds., *The Chartist Movement. A New Annotated Bibliography* (1995).

[17] Edward Royle, *Chartism* (1996 edn.); Richard Brown *Chartism* (1998); John K. Walton *Chartism* (1999). There are other brief histories. John Charlton *The Chartists* (1997) is a defiantly Marxist account; Asa Briggs *Chartism* (1998) is perhaps better suited to the interested general reader than the student; Harry Browne *Chartism* (1999) is very detailed; Eric Evans *Chartism* (2000) is sceptical about recent scholarly interpretations, particularly with regard to O'Connor (and misidentifies certain illustrations).

[18] Gregory Claeys, ed. *The Chartist Movement in Britain 1838-1850* (2001). Also see Dorothy Thompson ed. *Chartism: Working Class Politics in the Industrial Revolution* (1986). This 22 volume facsimile series includes some lively autobiographical writing as well as tracts and manifestos. Reprints of Chartist journals such as *the McDouall's Chartist and Republican Journal* (1841) and the *Red Republican* (1850) should be available in some of the larger public libraries.

[19] For Kydd see Stephen Roberts, *Radical Politicians and Poets in Early Victorian Britain. The Voices of Six Chartist Leaders* (New York, 1993), pp. 107-27.

[20] Cooper was a tireless lecturer. He embarked on regular summer lecturing tours from the mid 1840s onwards, talking to large audiences about historical, literary and theological subjects. The second half of his life was spent as an itinerant Christian preacher; he delivered thousands of lectures and preached thousands of sermons in hundreds of towns and cities. These lecture tours were accompanied by publications; in the fourteen or so years after they appeared, his autobiography had sold 14,000 copies and one theological book had sold 24,000 copies.

A CHRONOLOGY OF THE CHARTIST MOVEMENT

1836   London Working Men's Association established. William Lovett is secretary (June).

1837   East London Democratic Association established (January); Birmingham Political Union re-established (May); First issue of *Northern Star* appears in Leeds. Feargus O'Connor is proprietor and William Hill editor (November).

1838   Great Northern Union established in Leeds by O'Connor (January); The People's Charter, in the main the work of Lovett, published in London. National Petition launched in Birmingham (May); Northern Political Union established in Newcastle (June); Great meetings in Birmingham (August) and on Kersal Moor, Manchester, (September) emphasize emergence of national protest movement.

1839   National Convention of 53 delegates meets in London (February); Re-locates to Birmingham (May); Bull Ring riots lead to arrest of Lovett and others. House of Commons refuses to consider by 235 votes to 46 National Petition of 1,280,000 signatures. Sales of *Star* reach 50,000 a week (July); A 'sacred month' of strikes abandoned amid arrests (August). Newport Rising results in some 22 deaths and 125 arrests (November).

1840   Small scale risings in Sheffield and Bradford (January); Newport leaders transported (February); O'Connor imprisoned for seditious libel (May); National Charter Association established as organizing force of the movement (July).

1841   National Association established by Lovett and denounced in the *Star* (April); Chartist candidates appear on hustings in general election (July); O'Connor released from prison (August).

1842   Launch of Complete Suffrage Union in Birmingham (January); National Convention meets in London (April); House of Commons refuses to consider by 287 votes 49 National Petition of 3,317,752 signatures (May); Strikes against wage cuts and in support of People's Charter widely supported in industrial districts. Many of Chartist leaders arrested (August); CSU conference in Birmingham encounters hostility from Chartists (December).

1843   Trial of O'Connor and other Chartists at Lancaster. Not sentenced, but others tried elsewhere, including Thomas Cooper, imprisoned (March); Joshua Hobson becomes editor of the *Northern Star* (August); Land question discussed at Chartist Convention in Birmingham (September).

1844   Lecture tours maintained by O'Connor and other leaders such as Thomas Clark (January-March); Land question discussed at Chartist Convention in Manchester (April).

1845   Chartist Co-operative Land Society established (April); Fraternal Democrats established in London. George Julian Harney is secretary of this internationalist organization (September); Harney becomes editor of the *Northern Star* (October); Land Plan considered by special conference in Manchester (December).

1846   Heronsgate, the first Land Plan estate, acquired (March); Cooper's arguments with O'Connor culminate in his expulsion from Chartist Convention at Leeds (August); National Land Company created (December).

1847   Land Plan journal, the *Labourer*, edited by Ernest Jones, appears. Land Bank opens (January); Heronsgate opens as O'Connorville (May); O'Connor elected MP for Nottingham (July); Chartist estate of Lowbands opens (August).

1848   National Convention meets in London; Kennington Common demonstration; Committee of House of Commons examines National Petition and reports far fewer signatures than claimed (April); National Assembly meets; Arming and drilling in the north (May); Chartist estates of Snigs End and Minster Lovell opened. Committee of House of Commons considers Land Company. Plots in London. Jones and other leaders arrested (June-August).

1849   National Parliamentary and Financial Reform Association established (January); O'Connor's motion in House of Commons for the People's Charter defeated. Chartist estate of Dodford opened (July).

1850	National Charter League, led by Clark, established (April); *Red Republican,* edited by Harney, appears (June); Jones released from prison (July).
1851	O'Connor opposes alliance with NPFRA at Chartist Conference in Manchester (January); Chartist Conference in London adopts socialist programme (March); *Notes to the People,* edited by Jones, appears (May); Act of Parliament to wind up Land Company (August); *Northern Star* is sold (December).
1852	*Northern Star* re-emerges as Harney's *Star of Freedom* (April); *People's Paper* is launched by Jones (May); O'Connor arrested in House of Commons and taken to Tuke's asylum (June).
1855	40,000 attend O'Connor's funeral (September).
1857	O'Connorville sold (May).
1858	Last Chartist Convention (February).

CHARTIST PROFILES

WILLIAM AITKEN (1814?-69). A schoolmaster who was active in the militant 'physical force' centre of Ashton-under-Lyne, Aitken spent most of 1840 in prison and, after the collapse of the strikes of 1842, emigrated briefly to the United States. He published verse, and subsequently became an uneasy supporter of the Liberal Party. He committed suicide during the writing of his autobiography.

THOMAS ATTWOOD (1783-1856). Founder of the Birmingham Political Union in 1830 and, after the passing of the Reform Bill, elected as one of the town's MPs, 'King Tom' presented the Chartist petition of 1839 to the House of Commons. He split soon after with the Chartists, resuming his interest in currency reform.

JONATHAN BAIRSTOW (dates unknown). An energetic and effective lecturer and editor of the *Chartist Pilot* in 1843-4, Bairstow became embroiled in quarrels with Thomas Cooper, eventually vanishing from sight.

GEORGE BINNS (1815-47). The composer of a long poem called the *Doom of Toil* (1841), Binns formed a close political partnership with James Williams. The two men ran a bookshop in Sunderland, enabling Binns to travel as an agitator throughout the Durham coalfield. They were imprisoned in 1840 and

Binns later emigrated to New Zealand, where he died.

PATRICK BREWSTER (1788-1859). A Scottish minister and moderate Chartist, associating himself with teetotalism and class collaboration. Well known as a public speaker, he debated with Feargus O'Connor in 1839 and 1841.

PETER BUSSEY (1805-69). 'Fat Peter' was a Bradford publican and highly committed radical, who was almost certainly involved in underground planning for a national rising in late 1839. He escaped to the United States after the Newport Rising, not returning home for fourteen years.

JOHN CAMPBELL (1810-74). Elected to the executive of the National Charter Association in 1841, Campbell was an active lecturer. He made his living as a bookseller, an activity he continued after his emigration to the United States in 1843.

WILLIAM HENRY CHADWICK (1829-1908). Known as 'last of the Manchester Chartists', Chadwick was active in 1848 and was imprisoned. A campaigner for the Liberals in later life, he remained immensely proud of his Chartist past.

THOMAS CLARK (1821?-56). 'Paddy' Clark began his Chartist career in Stockport, and became a close associate of Feargus O'Connor. He was elected to the executive of the NCA in 1843 and subsequently managed the affairs of the Land Company. A powerful lecturer, he repeatedly urged the Chartists and the Irish repealers to make common cause. His support for an alliance with middle-class reformers after 1848 eventually led to rows with other Chartist leaders, including O'Connor.

JOHN COLLINS (1802-52). A Birmingham Chartist, who worked closely with William Lovett. Imprisoned in 1839-40, the two men produced *Chartism. A New Organisation of the People* (1840).

SAMUEL COOK (1786-1861). Active in the radical cause in Dudley for some thirty years, Cook was imprisoned on several occasions, including in 1839 and 1842. If not campaigning on local issues of prices and public health, this highly committed working class politician was raising money for Garibaldi.

THOMAS COOPER (1805-92). With Cooper as their 'General', the working people of Leicester rallied to the Chartist cause in the early 1840s. Incarcerated for two years, Cooper composed his ambitious political poem, the *Purgatory* *of Suicides* (1845). Though he subsequently quarrelled with O'Connor, he continued to espouse radical opinions, editing two interesting journals in 1849-50. His autobiography (1872) eloquently recounts his radical, literary and religious activities.

WILLIAM CUFFAY (1788-1870). Transported in 1848, Cuffay was the son of a Caribbean slave and a prominent London Chartist. He died in Australia.

THOMAS AINGE DEVYR (1805-87). A radical journalist in the north of England, Devyr became involved in insurrectionary plotting in 1839-40. He fled to the United States, where he continued to write, editing a series of journals and eventually producing a volume of reminiscences (1882).

CHRISTOPHER DOYLE (1811-?). Having made his name as a Chartist lecturer, Doyle worked full time as a director of the Land Company. He was a close friend of fellow Irishman, Thomas Clark, eventually supporting his breach with O'Connor.

JAMES DUFFY (1794?-1843). Involved in the Chartist rising in Sheffield in January 1840, Duffy was imprisoned for three years. He supported himself by lecturing to Chartist audiences after his early release because of ill health.

THOMAS SLINGSBY DUNCOMBE (1796-1861). Radical MP for Finsbury, Duncombe presented the Chartist petition of 1842 to the House of Commons and took up the cases of imprisoned Chartists.

WILLIAM ELLIS (1809-71). One of the Chartist 'martyrs', Ellis died in Tasmania after being transported for an act of arson he did not commit. The story of the life of this talented man in Australia after 1843 is very tragic: he was often convicted of drunkenness and other offences.

JOHN FROST (1784-1877). The most famous of the Chartist 'martyrs', Frost was transported for his involvement in the Newport Rising of 1839. He was very well known as a Chartist before the Rising, and also greatly respected locally, having been a magistrate and mayor of Newport. He returned to Britain in 1856, still a radical but mostly devoting his later years to spiritualism.

ROBERT GAMMAGE (1815-88). Author of the first history of the Chartist Movement (1854), Gammage was a national leader in the early 1850s. His admiration for Bronterre O'Brien is reflected in his book.

GEORGE JULIAN HARNEY (1817-97). A superb journalist, editor of the *Northern Star* (1845-50) and his own periodicals, Harney was one of the outstanding leaders of the Chartist Movement. Clearly associating himself with physical force (he brandished a dagger), he worked in London and Sheffield but also travelled extensively as a lecturer. He knew Marx and Engels well, and in 1845 founded a society which supported European revolution, the Fraternal Democrats. He spent much of his later life in the United States, finally returning to Britain in 1888; the journalism of his final years includes affectionate reminiscences of his Chartist colleagues.

HENRY HETHERINGTON (1792-1849). A London radical and newspaper publisher, Hetherington signed the People's Charter and worked closely with William Lovett.

WILLIAM HILL (1806?-67). The first editor of the *Northern Star* (1837-41), Hill was a Swedenborgian minister.

JOSHUA HOBSON (1810-76). The second editor of the *Northern Star* (1843-5) and also its publisher for six years, Hobson later became a Tory journalist.

SAMUEL HOLBERRY (1814-42). One of the Chartist 'martyrs', Holberry led the Chartist rising in Sheffield in January 1840 and died in prison in June 1842. 50,000 lined the route of his funeral procession.

SUSANNA INGE (dates unknown). A London Chartist lecturer, Inge contributed briefly to the *Northern Star*.

ERNEST JONES (1819-69). The last of the Chartist leaders, Jones entered the movement as a poet, lecturer and denouncer of Feargus O'Connor's critic, Thomas Cooper, in 1846. Very prominent in 1848, he went to prison. He edited a series of journals, keeping the Chartist cause alive in the 1850s with the *People's Paper*. The final phase of his political career was spent building bridges towards popular Liberalism.

WILLIAM JONES (1809-73). One of the Chartist 'martyrs', Jones was transported for his involvement in the Newport Rising of 1839. He died in poverty in Australia.

SAMUEL KYDD (1815-92). A very able man who became a successful barrister, Kydd worked as an anti-free trade Chartist lecturer in Scotland and the north of England and, in 1848-9, was one of the movement's key national agitators. By the 1850s he had clearly adopted the radical Tory views of his friend, Richard Oastler.

JAMES LEACH (1806-69). A well known Manchester Chartist, Leach was imprisoned in 1848. As a pamphleteer, he wrote about the factory system and the need for an alliance with the middle class.

JOSEPH LINNEY (1808-87). Operating from Manchester and then the Black Country, Linney was imprisoned in 1842-4. He remained a working class politician after his release, eventually supporting the Liberal Party.

WILLIAM LOVETT (1800-77). The author of an autobiography (1877) which greatly shaped early writing about the movement, Lovett is seen as the voice of moderate moral force Chartism. Though he drafted the People's Charter and remained steadfast in his support for manhood suffrage, he never joined the National Charter Association. His influence on the movement was considerably less than that of Feargus O'Connor. Imprisoned in 1839-40, he subsequently developed his ideas through the National Association for the Political and Social Improvement of the People.

ROBERT LOWERY (1809-63). An eloquent missionary for teetotal Chartism and later the owner of a temperance hotel, Lowery's political allegiances moved from the middle class reformer, Joseph Sturge, to the Liberal Party.

PETER MURRAY McDOUALL (1814-54). A surgeon who became involved in Chartism in 1838, McDouall was soon very well known as a lecturer. He edited one of the movement's best periodicals, *McDouall's Chartist and Republican Journal* (1841). Imprisoned in 1839-40 and 1848-50, he died in Australia.

GERALD MASSEY (1828-1907). Active in late Chartism, Massey produced poetry for the movement's journals. He later published volumes of verse; his volume on spiritualism (1871) was described by Thomas Cooper as 'the craziest stuff I ever saw in print'.

JOHN MITCHELL (1806?-45). An admirer of Wiliam Lovett, Mitchell promoted teetotalism and moral force views amongst the Aberdeen Chartists. He was a prolific poet.

JAMES MOIR (1806-80). A supporter of the radical cause in Glasgow for many years, Moir lent his support to Christian Chartism, middle class reform organisations and eventually the Liberal Party.

JAMES BRONTERRE O'BRIEN (1804-64). A man with a theoretical mind (but probably also an alcoholic), O'Brien was described as 'the schoolmaster of Chartism' by Feargus O'Connor. His talents as a journalist were clear to the readers of the *Northern Star*, but his contributions ended with his quarrel with O'Connor. It was an embittered break and never mended: Bronterre subsequently ran a series of his own small journals which were read by a very loyal but small band of followers.

FEARGUS O'CONNOR (1794-1855). Greatly underrated for more than a century, O'Connor was the most important of the Chartist leaders. A superb orator, powerful, defiant, humorous, his arrival in each town on lecturing tours was a major event. O'Connor's leadership was highly personalised – he often referred to the sacrifices he made – but there can be no doubt that he provoked strong loyalties. Working people rallied around him at times of dissension, and some of them named their children after him. He founded the *Northern Star* in 1837, which soon established itself as the voice of a national protest movement. O'Connor more than any other single individual held the Chartist Movement together. He was responsible for setting up the National Charter Association in 1840 and the Land Company in 1845. He was the only Chartist elected an MP.

ARTHUR O'NEILL (1819-96). Pastor of Birmingham's Christian Chartist Church, O'Neill was imprisoned after the strikes of 1842. He formed his life-long friendship with Thomas Cooper during his incarceration.

ROBERT PEDDIE (1803-?). The leader of the Chartist rising in Bradford in January 1840, Peddie was imprisoned for three years. A romantic revolutionary, he published a volume of poetry.

LAWRENCE PITKEITHLY (1801-58). A well known West Riding Chartist, Pitkeithly was an advocate of emigration.

JOHN RICHARDS (1772?-1856). Imprisoned at the age of 70, 'Daddy' Richards was a dedicated advocate of the Chartist cause in the Potteries: he attended the National Convention at 1839 and was still addressing meetings in 1848.

REGINALD JOHN RICHARDSON (1808-61). Author of one of the most interesting Chartist pamphlets, the *Rights of Women* (1840), Richardson was a Manchester activist. He contributed regularly to the Chartist press, aligning himself in the early 1840s with O'Brien.

WILLIAM PROWTING ROBERTS (1806-71). Active in Wiltshire, 'Black Jack' was a solicitor who became the legal champion of both the miners and the Chartists. He was treasurer of the Chartist Land Society, fittingly dying at a house he had acquired at Heronsgate.

HENRY SOLLY (1813-1903). A Somerset Unitarian minister, Solly lent his support to Chartism and the Complete Suffrage Union. He wrote a great deal, including two volumes of interesting memoirs (1893).

JOSEPH RAYNER STEPHENS (1805-79). In the late 1830s Stephens joined forces with O'Connor to fiercely condemn the 1834 Poor Law to meetings throughout the north of England. A former Methodist minister, he was imprisoned in 1839-41. Hugely popular in the early years of Chartism, he remained a public figure, opposing teetotalism and the Sunday closing of public houses for the rest of his life.

JOSEPH STURGE (1793-1859). A Birmingham Dissenter, Sturge launched the Complete Suffrage Union. In 1842 Chartists attended this middle class organisation's conferences. Sturge also campaigned for corn law repeal, teetotalism and peace.

JAMES SWEET (1804-79). Determined organizer of Nottingham Chartism for more than a decade, Sweet was a close associate of O'Connor, who became the town's MP. He later addressed meetings of the Reform League.

JOHN TAYLOR (1805-42). Flamboyant in his dress and the user of insurrectionary language, Taylor was one of the movement's romantic revolutionaries. He was arrested on two occasions, but not imprisoned.

HENRY VINCENT (1813-78). An energetic and effective Chartist lecturer, Vincent championed teetotalism and, in due course, an alliance with middle class reformers. He became O'Connor's 'little renegade'.

MARY ANN WALKER (dates unknown). For *Punch* a hilarious figure, Walker was a London Chartist lecturer.

CAROLINE MARIA WILLIAMS (dates unknown). From a middle class background and a schoolteacher, Williams contributed periodically to the *Northern Star* in the early 1840s.

JOHN WATKINS (1809-50). From an upper middle class background, Watkins led the Chartists of Whitby. He was perhaps initially drawn to Chartism as an act of rebellion against his family. His brief imprisonment in 1840 greatly pleased his neighbours. He wrote a great deal, including poetry and eventually an attack on O'Connor.

JAMES WATSON (1799-1874). A London printer and publisher, Watson worked closely with Lovett throughout the 1830s and 1840s. He published smaller Chartist periodicals, including the *Cause of the People* (1848) and *Cooper's Journal* (1850).

JOHN WEST (1811-87). One of the most determined of the Chartist lecturers, West was an Irishman. He was imprisoned in 1848-9; decades later old Chartists were raising money to relieve his poverty.

THOMAS MARTIN WHEELER (1811-62). Author of a Chartist novel, Wheeler worked closely with O'Connor. He attended every Chartist Convention between 1839 and 1851 and served as secretary of the Land Company.

GEORGE WHITE (1812-68). A remarkable man who, defying arrests and imprisonments, fought for the suffrage for the whole of his adult life. An Irish woolcomber active in Leeds, Birmingham and Bradford, White was imprisoned in 1840, 1843-4 and 1849. Very suspicious of middle class radicals, he wrote a great deal, including political pamphlets and verse. At his second trial he refused to continue unless he was provided with a glass of wine and a sandwich.

JAMES WILLIAMS (1811-68). Imprisoned with his political ally, George Binns, in 1840, Williams later supported an alliance with middle class radicals. He was a well known figure in Sunderland all his life, working as a councillor and newspaper editor.

ZEPHENIAH WILLIAMS (1784-1877). One of the Chartist 'martyrs', Williams was transported for his involvement in the Newport Rising of 1839. In Australia he eventually became a wealthy mine owner.

Chartism and the 'Trade of Agitation' in Early Victorian Britain

Paul A. Pickering

The Charter has been fruitful in many things – much honesty, much patience, much usefulness and much quackery. There is a number of degraded men attached to the noble army of Chartists, who think how they can best live by the Charter. They invent blacking, and call it Chartist blacking; they make broadcloth, and appeal to the patriotism of Chartists to clothe their nakedness in none but Chartist materials. I have no doubt that we shall have every trade in the country hoisting the Charter for the sake of self.

Nemo, *National Association Gazette,* 26 March 1842

Nemo's comments highlight a phenomenon that has largely escaped the attention of the Chartist historian: the plethora of goods and all manner of paraphernalia that were paraded under the banner of Chartism during the early 1840s. His criticism points to one reason for this inattention – Chartist products are easily dismissed as blatant profiteering. Nor was Nemo alone in voicing this criticism: even the *Northern Star,* which became a veritable catch-all for Chartist merchandise, had cause to suspect the 'patriotism' of some entrepreneurs seeking to use Chartism as a vehicle for profit. After the highly successful Chartist blacking business was established by Roger Pinder, a Hull merchant, the *Star* complained of such an onslaught of 'communications from parties seeking to catch customers' that the editors felt obliged to offer a blunt warning that they would not 'fill the *Star* with gratuitous advertisements for blacking makers and other traders ...'[1] The social historian should not, however, follow Nemo or the *Star* in dismissing Chartist products as either crass exploitation or harmless entrepreneurship. The range of Chartist products was extensive enough to be an important feature of Chartist life and, placed in context, provides the historian with an insight into the culture of mutuality that underpinned the Chartist struggle. This essay is based on two propositions: first, that Chartist products should be seen in the context of an informal Chartist economy, sustained by notions of exclusive dealing and co-operation, and, second, that as a consequence they were a legitimate part of the 'trade of agitation', a term that was used disparagingly at a time when the leisured gentleman provided the model for public life and the modern concept of paid political service had not yet won acceptance.

The sale of seemingly unrelated products in connection with radicalism was not something peculiar to the Chartist experience. E. P. Thompson has suggested that, in the years after the conclusion of the French wars, radicalism became a profession for the first time – the successful radical periodical provided a living for editors, regional agents, booksellers and even itinerant hawkers.[2] The point that needs to be made is that many of these individuals who broke new ground as professional agitators in conventional occupations also dabbled in products. One such professional radical, Thomas Wooler, editor of the highly successful *Black Dwarf,* promoted the sale of radical brand tea and coffee as early as 1819.[3] William Cobbett, the most prominent radical journalist of the age, not only sold his tracts, books and newspapers from his home in Kensington but also plants and seeds including 'Cobbett's Corn' which was actually maize imported from North America. Cobbett hailed the virtues of his corn in his *Cottage Economy* (1822) and in the pages of his famous *Political Register.*[4] The other leading radical of that generation, Henry Hunt, became a radical entrepreneur *par excellence.* Hunt was a manufacturer before he became a radical; his first appearance in public life was as the brewer of 'Hunt's Genuine Beer' in 1807.[5] By the early 1820s, at the height of his popularity, as he informed the radicals of Great Britain, he was promoting the 'salubrious and invigorating qualities' of 'Hunt's Breakfast Powder'. Samuel Bamford, the Middleton radical, found this 'corn coffee' unpalatable, but Hunt reported numerous offers from agents willing to participate and it was sufficiently successful to remain on the market for at least a decade.[6] Ever resourceful, later in the 1820s he embarked on a succession of commercial ventures including 'Hunt's never fading Writing Ink' and 'Hunt's Matchless Blacking'. His reputation as a radical blacking merchant grew to such an extent that it joined his famous white hat of liberty as part of his public personality, at least in the minds of contemporary political cartoonists.[7] As late as 1831, during Hunt's term as MP for Preston, the Manchester radicals resolved that 'all radical reformers in Great Britain and Ireland, and throughout the world, be recommended to use and promote the sale of Hunt's Blacking', and the product continued to be advertised in radical journals well into the 1830s.[8]

Nor was the phenomenon peculiar to political radicals. In 1840 the followers of the socialist Robert Owen were informed in the columns of their journal the *New Moral World* that they could purchase medals of Robert Owen which were 'peculiarly appropriate ornaments to be worn at annual festivals', or, better still, they could buy busts of the great man at 5*s.* for plain cast, 6*s.* for painted and 7*s.* 6*d.* for bronzed.[9] As Norman Longmate has shown, the Temperance movement also generated a collection of products from 'Temperance Wallpaper' to 'Temperance Pills', which were guaranteed to ward off the craving for drink and provide an 'efficacious remedy for ... sickness, acidity or heartburn, spasms and flatulent distensions, giddiness, headache, drowsiness and dimness of sight'.[10] Supporters of the Anti-Corn-Law League were offered Anti-Corn-Law scarves, medals and prints; could take tea and breakfast off 'Anti-Corn-Law Crockery'; and, reflecting the predominantly literate middle-class composition of the movement, were encouraged to seal their private correspondence with stickers or wafers displaying Anti-Corn-Law slogans. John Gadsby, publisher of the *Anti-Corn Law Circular* and principal sticker-merchant, claimed to have sold in excess of 3,000,000 sheets (six stickers per sheet) at about 8d per 100 between February 1840 and March 1842. This was despite the fact that, true to the principles of free trade, Gadsby was heavily under-cut by the Glasgow Anti-Corn-Law Association who offered wafers at 5,000 for 2s.[11] The anti-slavery movement which pioneered so many of the strategies of public agitation in the early nineteenth century was also involved in the sale of products; some of them ('slave-free' sugar and cloth manufactured with 'slave-free' cotton) were directly related to its crusade and others, such as Wedgwood crockery, were made so by being inscribed with the anti-slavery motto, 'am I not a man and a brother'.[12]

As a mass movement Chartism generated an extensive range of products. Some appeared as nothing more than revivals of earlier radical products. The recipes for breakfast powder were dusted off and a 'Chartist Breakfast Powder' or 'Chartist Beverage' appeared for sale in many parts of the country: in Leicester by Crow and Tyrrell, in Halifax by the Thompson Brothers and in Manchester by William Atkinson. The idea of radical blacking was revived as 'Chartist Blacking' by Pinder and others including Wilson, the Leeds Chartist, J. T. Smith of Plymouth and William Anderson of Dundee.[13] Another entrepreneur with an eye for historical precedents, 'A Chartist (from his infancy)', offered 'to supply his brother Chartists with ink, to be called Chartist Ink'. Other products showed a little more initiative. In Bradford it was 'GOOD NEWS FOR THE NAKED' when the prominent Barnsley Chartist, Joseph Crabtree, announced that he would visit with a 'large assortment' of clothing for his Chartist friends. Yet another 'sincere Chartist', John Hague of Little Horton, hawked his wares – 'valuable RECIPES for various disorders' – around the towns and villages of Yorkshire and Lancashire. Hague faced stiff competition from at least two sources: the famous 'Chartist Pills', which were guaranteed to 'avert much of the illness usually affecting the working classes' and had as their principal agent Joshua Hobson, publisher of the *Northern Star;* and 'McDouall's Florida Medicine' which was peddled by Peter McDouall, 'the little doctor' who was one of the most prominent national figures in the Chartist movement. Finally, for those whom this range of medicines failed to help, the 'Chaplain of the Manchester Chartists', the Revd James Scholefield, offered Chartist funerals.[14]

To justify their association with the cause of Chartism or the use of the name Chartist, many of these entrepreneurs devoted a proportion of the profits to the coffers of the movement. Crow and Tyrrell, for example, contributed '3 shillings out of the receipts for every 100 lbs' of their powder to the Executive of the National Charter Association (NCA) and 'Chartist Ink' yielded 'one penny in every shilling' to the same source.'[15] The anticipated results were considerable: in the three months after March 1842, Pinder's Blacking was expected to accrue one hundred pounds for the Executive and a thousand for 'local sources' while Pinder himself anticipated a return of 6*d*. or 8*d*. per gross.[16]

Some of the Chartist products were of an overtly political character. A Manchester radical, for example, developed a range of 'CHARTIST ADHESIVES, OR STICKERS':

> On one is printed the sentence – 'Remember Frost, Williams and Jones'; and on the other – 'The Charter, and No Surrender'. They are neatly engraved on green paper, ready for pasting, and we would recommend the use of them as a good mode of calling attention to the Chartist victims and the People's Charter.'[17]

In January 1842, another enterprising Mancunian presented complimentary samples of his new 'splendid Tri-colour Silk Scarves' to the members of the NCA Executive, whose numerous public appearances guaranteed him a roaring trade. By April, a report of a meeting in Manchester noted that of several thousands assembled, many were distinguished 'by an Executive Scarf' which had been sold to local Chartist Associations at £2.10*s*. per dozen. Another venture that was similarly aimed at the Chartist tradition of symbolism and public theatre was the sale of 'Chartist Satin Rosettes' that were manufactured by a London Chartist for use at public meetings.[18] The *Northern Star* itself indulged in the business of radical products in the form of an enormously successful series of portraits that were given away at regular intervals to boost the sales of the newspaper. Along with the champions of the Chartist agitation, an extensive range of political heroes from Andrew Marvell to William Cobbett were honoured in this way. The multitude of reports of meetings, halls and parades embellished by this 'Portrait Gallery of the People's Friends' testify to their popularity among the rank and file of Chartism.[19]

With the portraits grew another small industry: to protect portraits used as decoration for the home or Chartist Association Rooms, the Edinburgh agent for the *Northern Star* and others 'made arrangements with a brother Chartist for supplying frames'. Tom Carlile (son of the notorious London radical publisher) issued his own series of portraits and offered a selection of gilt and rosewood frames for the same from his bookshop in Deansgate, Manchester.[20] There were many other occasions when individual Chartists exhibited a keen eye for business. In May 1841 a report from Salford noted that 'the fashion for White Hats is again being brought up to distinguish the friends of truth and justice from those of class legislation.' The report went on to note that Mr Smithhurst of Oldham has set up as a 'Chartist Hat manufacturer' to cater for this revival of Huntite pageantry. And so the list goes on: over a year later, in August 1842, those Chartists who planned to attend the unveiling of the massive monument to Henry Hunt that stood in Revd Scholefield's church yard in Manchester were informed that a 'number of very neat China models of the Monument ... will be exposed for sale on the day.'[21]

It is quite probable that some of these ventures represented nothing more than naked self-interest and crass exploitation; amongst the extraordinary range of pamphlets, books and tracts that peppered the advertising columns of the Chartist press there were also some of extremely dubious value. As the editor of the *Northern Star* commented in relation to a printed version of a speech by O'Connor: 'The good people of Bolton paid their £2. for their report of this meeting and as Mr Cobbett would say, "a precious bargain they have for their money": it is as much like Mr O'Connor's speech as a pig is to a wheelbarrow.'[22] But the point must be made that Chartism drew much of its strength from this flourishing 'trade of agitation'. Activists for the most part could only be paid by what they could make from the movement. In the early 1840s, for example, the Manchester district alone sustained twenty-one lecturers who were organized and paid according to a comprehensive plan plundered from the Methodist Circuit system.[23] To the army of lecturers must be added a host of Chartist activists who supported themselves as journalists, publicists, news vendors and editors. The proliferation of these occupations both reflected the sheer size of Chartism and helped to create it by placing the movement on a firmer organizational base. The contrast with the Anti-Corn-Law League which at this time was developing into 'a political machine' is instructive.[24] The largely middle-class League, which was able to finance its agitation from the independent wealth of its supporters, had a team of directly paid men, such as Alexander Somerville, to perform as lecturers and agents. It could easily afford to do so: in his *History of the Anti-Corn Law League* Archibald Prentice stated that the seventy-odd individuals who sat with him at the inaugural meeting of the Manchester Anti-Corn-Law Association in October 1838 contributed by themselves in excess of £10,000 of the estimated quarter of a million pounds that accrued in the coffers of the League. By contrast Chartists across Britain subscribed a mere £1,700 to finance the first great Chartist National Convention (an indicator of the social composition of the movement rather than enthusiasm). This left many of the full-time leaders of Chartism to make a living as best they could in the 'trade of agitation'.[25] The line between those who earned a living from the sale of Chartist products and those who lived as Chartist publicists, editors, journalists and lecturers was not hard and fast; indeed many survived by a combination of these pursuits. William Sumner, for example, a shoemaker who took over the clientele of John Campbell's Salford news agency after the latter's ascendancy to the post of NCA Secretary, supplemented his meagre income by becoming the Manchester agent for Pinder's Chartist Blacking; James Leach's bookshop in Tib Street was the Manchester agency for Chartist scarves; Thomas Cooper, of the Shakespearean Chartists of Leicester, ran a news agency, edited a series of smallish Chartist periodicals, kept a school, served as a public lecturer and was also the local agent for Crow and Tyrrell's Chartist breakfast powder. William Benbow, a prominent figure in radicalism since the Blanketeers' march of 1817, wandered from town to town in a cart from which he sold his tracts, pamphlets and books and which doubled as a platform for his firebrand speeches.[26]

In some cases persecution left Chartists with little choice other than to make a living from the movement. As James Leach, the first President of the NCA, recalled, his move from the cotton industry into the world of politics came after he had led the resistance to wage reduction and was thereby no longer 'considered a fit person to enter a factory'. William Butterworth, another Manchester radical, emerged from prison in 1840 to find that he could not obtain employment in his trade of spinning. 'The fact is', lamented Campbell in a public appeal on Butterworth's behalf, 'the factory tyrants of Manchester will not employ him under any consideration whatever'.[27] The abrasive class values of Manchester were reflected in the unequivocal editorial of the Tory *Manchester Courier*. 'We do not hesitate to pronounce our deliberate opinion that the mill owner and employer of any class who knowingly tolerates an Owenite or Chartist is guilty of treason to society and of suicide towards himself'.[28] In this atmosphere of fear and persecution a notorious Chartist like Butterworth had no option but to look to the Chartist community for succour. Butterworth went on to establish himself as one of many Manchester agents for the *Northern Star* and as a lecturer on the South Lancashire circuit. He might just as easily, however, have turned to selling Chartist products, as was the case with Wilson, the Leeds Chartist, whose plight was summarized by the *Northern Star*:

> WILSON, THE NATIONAL RENT COLLECTOR – This person who suffered so much scandalous treatment from Whig officials in this borough, is, we understand, now seeking to obtain a livelihood as a dealer in blacking; we sincerely hope that no working man in Leeds will go to Church or Chapel on Sundays with his understandings blackened by any other material than Wilson's blacking. We think the support of this man a duty which the working men of Leeds owe to themselves.[29]

The response to Wilson's plight points to an important part of the context in which we must seek to understand Chartist products: the Chartists had created their own 'informal economy',[30] or network of goods and services provided by members and sympathizers for each other. At the local level this 'informal economy' extended from obvious centres such as radical news agencies and bookshops to a network of printers, coffee shops, pubs, hairdressers, tobacconists and other traders who were known for their association with the cause of radicalism. Most Chartist localities could boast at least one shopkeeper, publican or small tradesman. In Bradford, for example, it was Peter Bussey whose public house, the Roebuck Inn, was the local Chartist headquarters; in Halifax it was James Haigh Hill, 'the Chartist butcher'.[31]

In a district the size of Manchester and Salford the Chartist 'informal economy' was extensive. The bookshops-cum-news agencies ranged from long-established and well-patronized landmarks to small, often ephemeral concerns. By far the most successful was the news agency and publishing business established by Abel Heywood in Oldham Road, Manchester, in 1831. So successful was this venture that it has left enough evidence for the historian to cross the threshold of the shop and browse the shelves of a business conducted on an impressive scale. In 1839 Heywood sold a staggering thirty to forty thousand newspapers, pamphlets and books per week. A considerable part of this was Chartist material: during 1839-40 he sold an estimated 18,000 copies of the *Northern Star* alone each week.[32] Like Chartism itself, the Chartist stock on Heywood's shelves was mingled with a wealth of literature that reflected a mosaic of other causes. Heywood was the publisher and/or agent of well over a dozen periodicals ranging from the *Manchester and Salford Temperance Journal* to the *Social Pioneer*.[33] In a deposition to the Home Office Heywood claimed that, in addition to selling 'many thousands of religious, scientific, literary and other books', he had also sold 1,500 Bibles, 2,000 Common Prayer Books and 1,500 Testaments in 1839. The sales of Christian literature did not reassure the ever-vigilant Bishop of Exeter, who denounced Heywood in the House of Lords as a 'habitual vendor of blasphemous literature' put out by the Owenites.[34] The Bishop had a point: a single edition of the *New Moral World* listed no less than 74 books and pamphlets for sale at Heywood's including a dozen or more works by Owen himself.[35]

Later in the 1840s a reporter from the *Morning Chronicle* found the shelves of Heywood's shop 'a literary chaos,' crammed with 'masses of penny novels and comic song and recitation books' 'jumbled with sectarian pamphlets and democratic essays':

> Educational books abound in every variety. Loads of cheap reprints of American authors, seldom or never heard of amid the upper reading classes here, are mingled with editions of the early Puritan divines. Double-columned translations from Sue, Dumas, Sand, Paul Feval and Frederic Soubtie jostle with dream-books, scriptural commentaries, Pinnock's Guides, and quantities of cheap music, Sacred Melodists and Little Warblers.[36]

A reporter interested in other facets of working-class life would have found that Heywood's shop had far more to offer than even this extensive range of books and periodicals. Tickets to practically every function in the working-class calendar from Chartist *soirées* and Operative Anti-Corn-Law Association dinners to Owenite festivals and Temperance tea parties were to be had at Heywood's. The counter would have seldom been without a subscription box or two: for the Chartist National Rent; for the defence fund to aid John Frost and the other Welsh Chartists facing treason charges; for the Chartist Victim Fund (of which Heywood was national Treasurer); or for the relief of the victims of some local disaster.[37] Our reporter would have seen Crow and Tyrrell's breakfast powder on sale, and he might even have found a few left-over bottles of Hunt's Blacking, for which Heywood was the agent earlier in the 1830s.[38]

At any one time during the Chartist years there were well over a dozen shops dealing in radical publications in Manchester and Salford[39] but not all were anywhere near the magnitude of Heywood's. William Willis, radical bookseller of Hanging Ditch, boasted a stock of over 50,000 volumes; R. J. Richardson sold 300 *Northern Stars* every Saturday morning from his shop in Chapel Street, Salford; and at the most modest end of the spectrum there were the small establishments like William Sumner's in Addersley Street, Salford, which survived from week to week on the sale of a modest number of fifty *Stars*.[40] In addition to these bookshops and news agencies, the 'informal economy' included a network of other shopkeepers such as Appleton's hairdressers in Bank Top, Owen's tobacconists in London Road and Williams's provision shop in Willmot Street, Hulme. It also included a number of taverns and beer houses such as the Mitre Inn, in the Old Church Yard, where the Manchester Political Union regularly met; the Hop Pole Inn in Deansgate, the home of many of Manchester's trade unions; the Queen's Stores in Whittle Street with its comfortable and private 'snug' near the Chartist Rooms in Tib Street; and the General Abercrombie, a tap room in Great Ancoats Street where the publican was Edward Nightingale, a notorious Chartist known as the 'dictator of New Cross' for his involvement in roughhouse tactics at public meetings.[41] Supplementing this network were Chartist lecturers, hawkers and vendors of Chartist merchandise, and Chartist tradesmen such as John Holdens, a tailor, who gave the movement 1s 3d. for every £1 he made.[42]

This informal economy was related to general patterns of interaction in popular culture which E. P. Thompson has described as the 'rituals of mutuality' – the notion of a community with an emphasis on duty and mutual obligation.[43] Those Chartists in the 1840s who advocated trading within an informal economy asked no more of their members and supporters than did the leaders of the neighbouring temperance Rechabite Tent or than had John Wesley a century before when he argued that Methodists should demonstrate a desire for salvation by 'doing good especially to them that are of the household of faith, or groaning to be so; employing them preferably to others, buying one of another, helping each other in business....'[44] Beyond this general cultural pattern which saw benefit societies, sick clubs and trade unions flourish, the Chartist community ethos was permeated with the assumptions and rhetoric of Owenism, reflecting, in many cases, active experience of the co-operative movement during the early 1830s. In Manchester and Salford where the roots of the co-operative movement were strong[45] the Chartists undertook a range of co-operative enterprises which formed part of the informal economy. In Salford the Chartists developed a 'plan of practical co-operation'. This involved a weekly meeting at which money was pooled and produce purchased in bulk:

But our friends go beyond a mere distribution of wealth among themselves, they are also, as far as is practicable, carrying out the operative production of it themselves, by employing each other. Messrs Millington and Yates have been appointed shoemakers, Mr Roberts, clock maker, and Mr Campbell, news vendor to the Salford Chartists. This is the way to bring the shopocracy to their senses.[46]

A similar intent was evident when a group of Chartists in East Manchester resolved 'to raise funds, for the truly philanthropic purpose of enabling the working man to lay out his little money in purchasing his provisions of the best quality, and at a lower price than could be obtained under the old system of competition.' In this case their resolve led to the opening of a store in Travis Street close to the Chartist Association Rooms in Brown Street.[47] Other stores were opened in London Road, Deansgate and Whittle Street, and, in May 1840, at 32 Clarendon Street, Chorlton, the Chartists of West Manchester established the Hulme and Chorlton Joint Stock Provision Company.[48] Rapidly the latter became a successful venture: in October of that year the healthy trade led the co-operative parties to relocate to larger premises a few doors down Clarendon Street and, a month later, to establish a second store in Melbourne Street, Hulme.[49] It was claimed that the presence of the Clarendon Street Store had a notable impact on the price of bread in Chorlton and, as the defiant announcement of the opening of the second store warned: 'We are determined to make the shopkeepers of the above township [Hulme] sell their bread at the same price we have made them in Chorlton ... working men come forward and assist us in keeping down the profit mongers.'[50] Apart from a warning to beware of 'jobbing or self-interest friends', the Chartist press was quick to declare co-operatives to be 'a powerful accelerator of the public good'.[51]

The other side of the co-operative coin was exclusive dealing – the practice of 'boycotting and patronising tradesmen according to their political persuasion'. A better understanding of how such a system was conducted can be gained by following one of its notorious practitioners, William Tillman, Secretary of the Manchester Political Union and first Secretary of the Provisional NCA Executive, as he toured the business establishments in Deansgate in August 1839. In each shop the pattern was the same. After reading a political address calling for (financial) assistance, Tillman produced the 'Black Book' which was drawn up into three columns: 'favourable', 'scoundrel' and 'call again'. Tillman's effectiveness can be measured in more than subscriptions of shillings and pence: when he was dragged before the local magistrates for his actions not a single shopkeeper could be found who was prepared to appear for the prosecution.[52] Once identified, the 'enemies' of the cause were exposed to the wider Chartist community, as was the case in Dewsbury when the walls of the town were placarded with the names of all publicans and shopkeepers who refused to contribute to the National Rent.[53] Chartists recognized that the effective implementation of this tactic depended largely on the 'patriotic spirit of the women'; the fact that it was widely employed bears testimony to their contribution and to the importance of the family unit to the structure of the movement.[54]

Exclusive dealing was a powerful weapon in the local struggle for the Charter and afforded at least some measure of retaliation against the wholesale persecution of known Chartists. The front line of the 'shopocracy' — those dependent on working-class patronage – were most susceptible to economic coercion. A report from the village of Coxhoe in Scotland in November 1839, headed 'Power to the People', for example, told of a local shopkeeper who had doggedly refused to make the necessary contribution to Chartist funds and had been forced out of business for his stand. Presumably many others, like those 'afraid of appearing' against Tillman, considered more carefully.[55] Like co-operation, exclusive dealing was a longstanding practice in the popular radical movement. During the first parliamentary election in Manchester in 1832, the strategy was used extensively in an attempt to persuade the newly enfranchised shopocrats that a vote for William Cobbett was in their interest. No sooner was the cry for universal suffrage raised, as was the case in early 1837 in Manchester, than a plan of exclusive dealing was proposed to facilitate its success.[56] This prominence in the tactical repertoire of Chartism was reflected by its inclusion among the 'Ulterior Measures' prescribed by the General Convention of 1839.

For all that the 'trade of agitation' in this wide sense developed within Chartist cultural patterns, those Chartists who practised it faced constant suspicion and criticism. Stemming not only from the misrepresentations of their opponents but also from a traditional notion of politics as the province of the independently wealthy and, it seems, from a grim view of human nature, the criticisms of paid agitators were legion. As the Manchester radical and trade unionist, John Doherty, pointed out in 1832: 'there is the common – a sort of standing notion, in the public mind, which is carefully fostered and propagated by all the arts and influence of the rich – that every man who becomes a leader among the poor has some design upon their purse.'[57] So prevalent was the critique of professional politicians that it found its way into a guide-book; in 1839 Benjamin Love stated in his *Handbook of Manchester* that when trade is bad and the operatives have 'an inclination to grow disorderly', 'there is never wanting a "leading spirit", more intellectual than the mass, who knows how to "direct the storm" especially if he sees a pecuniary emolument to himself, though it be at the expense of the poor.'[58] Nor did this critique come solely from the avowed enemies of the movement; there were many radicals of the 'old school' who frowned upon paid agitators. In his *Passages in the Life of a Radical*, Samuel Bamford recalled that good orators 'left their work or their business, for a more profitable and flattering employment; tramping from place to place hawking their new jingles, and guzzling, fattening and replenishing themselves, at the expense of the simple and credulous multitude'. Writing in the Chartist years, Bamford went on to argue that the payment of speakers was 'a bad practice … and gave rise to a set of orators who made a trade of speechifying, and the race has not become extinct'.[59] Despite the fact that point four of the People's Charter echoed the longstanding radical call for the payment of MPs so that working men could enter politics on a full-time basis,[60] 'disinterestedness' and 'independence' were still powerful virtues in Chartist circles. The 'gentleman' leaders of radicalism owed much of their popularity to this factor. The monument erected by the Manchester Chartists to Henry Hunt, for example, was raised 'to perpetuate the name and fame of one of the most bold, most strenuous, most disinterested and most able advocates of LABOUR'S CAUSE'. As for O'Connor, 'Hunt's successor', Thomas Cooper recalled:

> The immense majority of Chartists of Leicester, as well as in many other towns, regarded him as the only really disinterested and incorruptible leader – As I knew no reason for doubting the political honesty and disinterestedness which O'Connor ever asserted for himself, and in which the people believed, I stuck by O'Connor, and would have gone through fire and water for him.[61]

The practical needs of the movement coupled with the growing working-class self-awareness that characterized Chartism during the early 1840s did not sit well with the virtues of 'disinterestedness' and 'independence' which, in practical terms, made politics an avocation of the wealthy. This growing contradiction was no more evident than in the controversy that erupted between William Hill, editor of the *Northern Star,* and the NCA Executive, after the publication of the NCA Balance Sheet in late 1842. Concerned over numerous items such as high travelling expenses, Hill penned a scathing editorial accusing Campbell, and later Leach and McDouall, of 'gross and plain jobbing'. Subsequently Hill broadened his attack, first by describing those local leaders who had defended the Executive as 'job seekers ... fraternising with the jobbers' and 'money fingerers', 'who look anxiously for the Executive's cast slippers', and secondly by issuing an extremely provocative call for an 'unpaid executive': 'the inherent selfishness of human nature renders the best men unfit for an undue amount of confidence.'[62]

On one level the NCA controversy brought the credibility of the incumbent leadership into question. For James Leach the affair provoked 'a great deal of noise about the shop that he kept' – a subject about which he felt compelled to speak to the Manchester Chartists. In his defence at a public meeting in Carpenters' Hall, Leach reiterated the reason for his entry into politics and with it the necessity that he undertake a business reliant upon politically based patronage: 'Three years ago he worked in a factory not more than three stones throw from the place he now stood ... he lost that situation for daring to expose the Factory System ...'[63] While Hill continued to pursue the matter, eventually branding Leach and McDouall as liars and scoundrels, the worst excesses of the controversy were quelled with Campbell's resignation as Secretary and subsequent emigration to North America. On another and more important level the contradiction between Hill's call for an 'unpaid Executive' and its implications for the leadership of a movement which demanded payment of parliamentarians, continued to haunt the Chartists into 1843. Ever the perceptive leader, O'Connor summed the dilemma up succinctly in February 1843:

> If you have an unpaid Executive you must have a purely middle class Executive because you cannot get working men to live without wages and the very moment you elected working men as your officials that moment every door is closed against them and at once they are marked and if in work dismissed.

It was not until several months later, in September 1843, after a revision of the NCA rules and the establishment of an unpaid Annual Delegate Convention to watch over the affairs of the paid Executive that the matter was resolved.[64] Throughout, however, many Chartists, from news vendors and journalists to the humblest pedlar of Chartist merchandise, continued to take the only practical resolution to the problem that confronted the first independent, nationwide movement of the working classes – they supported themselves by the 'trade of agitation'.

In large part their efforts have failed to make an impression on historians. On the one hand, contemporary commentators and historians of Chartism, from Frederick Engels to James Epstein, who have afforded a special place to the NCA as the first working-class party in history, have rarely broached the question of how this organization was financed and how working men subsisted as full-time cadres.[65] Nor has the 'trade of agitation' been examined by more general historians of nineteenth-century British politics. Even H. J. Hanham, who describes the development of a 'fashionable' and increasingly respectable occupation of election agent in the late 1860s, goes no further than referring vaguely to individuals 'further down the social scale' who lived a shadowy 'disreputable' existence as lecturers and part-time election canvassers-cum-political hacks on the fringe of this political world. Undoubtedly some of them were the former Chartists who are known to have drifted into the liberal movement of the mid-century.[66] For the rest, full-time working-class agitators of this earlier period have suffered the sort of treatment meted out in Henry Jephson's late nineteenth-century treatise on the development of the platform. Despite a recognition that money was the 'sinews of agitation', Jephson merely copied into the record the contemporary suspicion of the motives of those who made it a trade.[67]

Although Chartist Peter McDouall was surely correct when he conceded that 'every agitation has, and will be more or less cursed by the company of selfish or designing men',[68] on the whole those who hawked Chartist products should not be condemned or dismissed in this way. Many who turned to the sale of Chartist products did so in the face of oppression and persecution in an atmosphere pervaded by class hostility and confrontation. Chartist products – manufactured and sold within a Chartist community – formed part of an 'informal economy' that was sustained by the twin concepts of co-operation and exclusive dealing and reflected the culture of mutuality that underlay the struggle. Equally, the prolific growth of the 'trade of agitation' in the Chartist years highlighted the changing requirements of working-class agitation. In keeping with the tradition which saw politics as a distraction of the rich, the leadership of radicals had generally fallen to 'gentlemen': Major Cartwright, Henry Hunt, William Cobbett and Feargus O'Connor were all bearers of this mantle. By the 1840s this model was becoming well and truly superseded as growing working-class self-awareness fostered a determination among Chartists to place confidence in 'men of their own order'.[69] Those individuals who sought to eke out a living within the Chartist community represented an attempt to translate this rhetoric into reality. The prejudice against paid working-class agitators died hard. According to the Webbs, it was the mid-1870s before trade union officials were not automatically dismissed as 'pothouse agitators, unscrupulous men, leading a half idle life, fattening on the contributions of their dupes'.[70] The need for resourcefulness and initiative to survive in the 'trade of agitation' did not die with the prejudice. As the political sociologist R. T. McKenzie has pointed out, the Labour party agents of the 1950s spent a 'considerable' part of their time 'raising their own salaries by means of specially organised football pools and other money-making devices'.[71] Although misrepresented and misunderstood, the development of the 'trade of agitation' in the Chartist era must be seen as a formative and crucial phase in the transition to the modern system of paid servants of political causes.

Notes

[1] *Northern Star,* 29 Jan. 1842, p. 5. This essay is based principally on Manchester and Salford sources. I would like to thank Alex Tyrrell for his comments and suggestions during the preparation of it. The phrase 'trade of agitation' was widely used by the late 1830s; I am unaware of its origin.

[2] E. P. Thompson, *The Making of the English Working Class* (1980), pp. 740, 789f.

[3] I. J. Prothero, *Artisans and Politics in Early Nineteenth Century London: John Gast and his Times* (1979), p. 133. John Brewer has pointed out that the followers of John Wilkes could select from 'thirty-one different engraved portraits, coffee and tea pots, spoons, jugs, figurines, snuff boxes, pipes, tobacco papers, buttons and twenty-six different coins and medals...', *Party Ideology and Popular Politics at the Accession of George III* (Cambridge, 1976), p. 185.

[4] W. Cobbett, *Cottage Economy* (1822; Oxford, 1979), pp. 195-200; *Cobbett's Weekly Political Register,* 17 Feb. 1821, p. 483; 3 Mar. 1821, pp. 597-8. See also G. D. H. Cole, *The Life of William Cobbett* (1924), pp. 245, 272, 311.

[5] H. Hunt, *Memoirs of Henry Hunt Esq.* (1820; New York, 1970), vol. I, pp. 104-5, 112-13; R. Walmsley, *Peterloo: The Case Re-opened* (Manchester, 1969), p. 118.

[6] H. Hunt, *Letters to the Reformers of England, Scotland and Ireland,* Aug. 1821, pp. 28-9; Dec. 1822, p. 16; S. Bamford, *Passages in the Life of a Radical* (1839-41; 1984), p. 294.

[7] See 'The Blacking Merchant', 'Preston to Wit' and 'Matchless Eloquence', Victorian State Library, *Mf English Cartoons and Satirical Prints,* Reel 19, no. 15150; Reel 21, nos. 16539, 16575. See also M.D. George, *Catalogue of Political and Personal Satires Preserved in the Department of Prints and Drawings in the British Museum* (1952), pp. x, xi.

[8] *Poor Man's Guardian,* 9 July 1831, p. 8; 21 Jan. 1832, p. 256; 16 Feb. 1833, p. 56; 16 Nov. 1833, p. 372; 26 July 1834, p. 200.

[9] *New Moral World,* 21 Mar. 1840, p. 1192; 2 May 1840, p. 1286; 9 May 1840, p. 1296.

[10] N. Longmate, *The Waterdrinkers* (1968), pp. 201-2; see also *English Chartist Circular and Temperance Record,* 30 Apr. 1843, p. 279.

[11] *Anti-Corn-Law Circular,* 6 Feb. 1840, p. 4; 20 Feb. 1840, p. 8; 21 May 1840, p. 7; 5 May 1841, p. 12; 30 Dec. 1841, p. 92; 10 Mar. 1842, p. 112; *Manchester Times,* 18 Feb. 1843,

[12] A. Tyrrell, 'Women's Mission and Pressure Group Politics in Britain 1825-60', *Bulletin of the John Rylands University Library of Manchester,* lxiii, no. 1, (Autumn 1980), p. 209 n. See also A. Tyrrell, *Joseph Sturge and the Moral Radical Party in Early Victorian Britain* (1987), pp. 141-2.

[13] *Northern Star,* 18 Jan. 1842, p. 1; 29 Jan. 1842, p. 5; 5 Mar. 1842, p. 2; 23 Apr. 1842, p.8; 7 May 1842, p. 1; 3 Dec. 1842, p. 2.

[14] *Northern Star,* 26 Jan. 1839, p. 5; 5 Dec. 1840, p. 5; 24 Dec. 1841, p. 5; 5 Mar. 1842, p. 2; 12 Mar. 1842, p. 2; 16 Apr. 1842, p. 5. See also *Poor Man's Guardian,* 24 Nov. 1832, p. 624.

[15] *Northern Star,* 5 Mar. 1842, p. 2; 16 Apr. 1842, p. 4. See also *British Statesman,* 13 Aug. 1842, p.6.

[16] *Northern Star,* 26 Mar. 1842, p. 3. The editors of the *Star* estimated that the sale of Crow and Tyrrell's powder and 'Pinder's blacking ought, if properly supported, to produce abundantly sufficient to pay the Executive, the Convention, and all the public lecturers', 30 Apr. 1842, p.4.

[17] *Northern Star,* 30 Jan. 1842, p. 5.

[18] *Northern Star,* 22 Jan. 1842, p. 1; 5 Mar. 1842, p. 5; 2 Apr. 1842, pp. 6-7; 23 Apr. 1842, p.8.

[19] *Northern Star,* 6 Jan. 1838, p. 4; 26 May 1838, p. 4; 4 Aug. 1838, p. 3; 14 Nov. 1840, p. 8. See also J. A. Epstein, 'Feargus O'Connor and the Northern Star', *International Review of Social History,* xxi, pt 1 (1976), pp. 74-5; J. A. Epstein, *The Lion of Freedom* (1982), pp. 71-2.

[20] *Northern Star,* 12 May 1838, p. 1; 6 July 1839, p. 1; 3 Aug. 1839, p. 2; *Regenerator and Advocate for the Unrepresented,* 3 Nov. 1839, p. 20.

[21] *Northern Star,* 29 May 1841, p. 2; F. O'Connor (ed.), *The Trial of Feargus O'Connor Esq. and Fifty-eight Others at Lancaster on a Charge of Sedition, Conspiracy, Tumult and Riot* (1843; New York, 1970), p. 108.

[22] *Northern Star,* 24 Feb. 1838, p. 6.

[23] Home Office 45/46, f. 3, 'Chartist Plan of Lecturers for South Lancashire, 1841'.

[24] N. McCord, *The Anti-Corn Law League* (1968), pp. 163f.

[25] A. Prentice, *History of the Anti-Corn Law League* (1853), vol. I, pp. 73-4; R. G. Gammage, *History of the Chartist Movement* (1854; 1976), p. 91. See also K. Judge, 'Early Chartist Organisation and the Convention of 1839', *International Review of Social History,* xx, pt 5 (1975) pp. 38 1-2.

[26] *Northern Star,* 29 Jan. 1842, p. 5; 5 Mar. 1842, pp. 2, 5; 16 Apr. 1842, p. 2; 3 Dec. 1842, p. 5; Cole, *Cobbett,* p. 246; T. Cooper, *The Life of Thomas Cooper* (1872; Leicester, 1971) , pp. 143-77. See also A. R. Schoyen, *The Chartist Challenge: The Life of George Julian Harney* (1958), p. 105. Benbow had also dabbled in the publication and sale of pornographic literature – see I. McCalman, 'Unrespectable Radicalism: Infidels and Pornography in Early Nineteenth Century London,' *Past and Present,* civ (Aug. 1984), p. 77f

[27] *Northern Star,* 29 May 1841, p. 1; 3 Dec. 1842, p. 6. The problem confronted many working-class radicals. See, for example, *Poor Man's Guardian,* 30 Mar. 1833, p. 96; *Northern Star,* 23 Apr. 1842, p. 8.

[28] Cited in *Manchester and Salford Advertiser,* 18 May 1839, p. 3.

[29] *Northern Star,* 21 Sept. 1839, p. 4.

[30] I am grateful to Professor Peter Bailey, University of Manitoba, for introducing me to the concept of an 'informal economy'.

[31] For Bussey see A. J. Peacock, *Bradford Chartism* (York, 1969), p. 13; for Haigh see B. Wilson, 'Struggles of an Old Chartist' (1887), reprinted in D. Vincent (ed.), *Testaments of Radicalism* (1977), p. 205.

[32] HO 44/35 (1840 Misc.), 'Memorial from Abel Heywood to Marquis of Normanby,' Apr. 1840; F. Leary, *MS History of the Manchester Periodical Press* (Manchester, 1889), p. 212.

[33] Periodicals which Heywood published and/or sold during the 1 830s and early 1840s included

inter alia: Poor Man's Guardian, Poor Man's Advocate, Regenerator and Chartist Circular, English Chartist Circular and Temperance Advocate, Northern Star, Social Pioneer, New Moral World, Manchester and Salford Temperance Journal, Trades' Journal, Herald of the Rights of Industry, Rational Religionist and Independent Inquirer, National Association Gazette, and *McDouall's Chartist and Republican Journal.* Later in the 1840s Heywood detailed a similarly extensive range of periodicals in evidence before Milner Gibson's Select Committee on Newspaper Stamps, *British Parliamentary Papers,* 1851 (588) vol. XVII, pp. 371-89.

[34] HO 44/35 'Memorial'; *Hansard* [Lords], 4 Aug. 1840, col. 1233. See also the dossier against Heywood compiled by a Manchester anti-socialist society which described him as 'the principal printer and publisher of the blasphemous, profane and immoral publications coming from this town', HO 44/35, Maude to Normanby, Apr. 1840.

[35] *New Moral World,* 18 July 1840, p. 48.

[36] Reprinted in P. E. Razzell and R. W. Wainwright (eds), *The Victorian Working Class: Selections from Letters to the Morning Chronicle* (1973), pp. 175-6.

[37] For examples see *Anti-Corn Law Circular,* 7 Jan. 1840, p. 7; *New Moral World,* 30 May 1840, p. 1266; *Northern Star,* 25 Apr. 1840, p. 7; 10 Oct. 1840, p. 8; *Manchester and Salford Advertiser,* 4 Feb. 1837, p. 2; 12 May 1838, p. 1; *Manchester Times,* 17 July 1841, p. 2.

[38] *Poor Man's Guardian,* 16 Feb. 1833, p. 56; *Northern Star,* 11 June 1842, p. 7.

[39] Apart from Heywood's, Manchester outlets included James Wroe's in Great Ancoats Street, John Doherty's in Shudehill, James Leach's in Tib Street, Arthur O'Neill's at 354 Oldham Road on the way to Mills Platting, Isaac Gleave's in Liverpool Road, George Jacques' in Oldham Road, Tom Paine Carlile's in Deansgate, James Cooper's in Bridge Street, Joseph Linney's in Garret Road and William Willis's in Hanging Ditch. A report in Oct. 1840 referred to 'seven or eight' vendors of the *Northern Star* in Salford. These included R. J. Richardson's in Chapel Street and John Campbell's (later William Sumner's) in Addersley Street, *Northern Star,* 17 Oct. 1840, p. 2.

[40] *Manchester and Salford Advertiser,* 16 Feb. 1839, p. 2; HO 40/53 f. 927, intercepted letter (Feb. 1839), C. E. Hulme to R. J. Richardson; *Northern Star,* 17 Oct. 1840, p. 2. According to the figure provided in this report Richardson's weekly sales had evidently dropped to 100.

[41] See *Manchester and Salford Advertiser,* 10 Aug. 1839, p. 2; 9 Nov. 1839, p. 2; 28 Mar. 1840, p. 4; *Champion and Weekly Herald,* 6 Jan. 1839, pp. 3-4; *Manchester Times,* 2 Mar. 1839, p. 3; 26 Jan. 1843, p. 4; *Northern Star,* 24 Sept. 1842, p. 1; 0' Connor, *Trial,* pp.117f.

[42] *Northern Star,* 5 Nov. 1841, p. 1.

[43] Thompson, *English Working Class,* pp. 456-89.

[44] Cited in L. F. Church, *The Early Methodist People,* @@@ p. 187. I am grateful to Alex Tyrrell for bringing this reference to my attention.

[45] A report in the *United Trades' Co-operative Journal,* 1 May 1830, pp. 68-9, referred to eleven co-operatives in Manchester and Salford.

[46] *Northern Star,* 13 Mar. 1841, p. 8; 20 Mar. 1841, p. 1. See also 21 Dec. 1839, p. 8.

[47] *Northern Star,* 21 Mar. 1840, p. 2.

[48] *Manchester and Salford Advertiser,* 9 Nov. 1839, p. 2; 14 Mar. 1840, p. 3; *Northern Star,* 29 Feb. 1840, p. 5; 30 May 1840, p. 4.

[49] *Northern Star,* 29 Aug. 1840, p. 1; 10 Oct. 1840, p. 5; 7 Nov. 1840, p. 2.

[50] *Northern Star,* 7 Nov. 1840, p. 2. These claims were not uncommon. See, e.g. *Northern Star,* 12 Nov. 1842, p. 5; 19 Nov. 1842, p.1.

[51] *Regenerator and Chartist Circular,* 4 Jan. 1840, p. 4; *English Chartist Circular,* 29 Aug. 1841, p.1.

[52] *Manchester Times,* 27 July 1839, p. 2; *Northern Star,* 3 Aug. 1839, p. 5. See also *Northern Star,* 29 June 1839, p. 7.

[53] *Northern Star,* 20 July 1839, p. 5.

[54] *Northern Star,* 29 June 1839, p. 4; 27 July 1839, p. 5; *Manchester and Salford Advertiser,* 29 June 1839, p.4. See also D. Jones, 'Women and Chartism', *History,* lxviii, no.222 (February 1983), 15-16.

[55] *Northern Star*, 30 Nov. 1839, p. 7. See also 25 June 1842, p. 5.

[56] *Poor Man's Advocate*, 8 Sept. 1832, pp. 3-4; 17 Nov. 1832, p. 4; *Manchester and Salford Advertiser*, 29 Apr. 1837, p. 4. See also *Poor Man's Guardian*, 21 Sept. 1833, p. 304; 5 Oct. 1833, pp. 323-4. The tactic continues to be employed in British politics. See the 'Boycott Apartheid 89' campaign, *Morning Star*, 18 Mar. 1989, p. 1.

[57] *Poor Man's Advocate*, 10 Nov. 1832, p. 1.

[58] B. Love, *Handbook of Manchester* (Manchester, 1842), p. 102. See also *Manchester Times*, 17 Sept. 1842, p. 2; HO 40/37, Egerton to HO, Dec. 1838; HO 40/54, f. 889, Shaw to Phillips, 20 Dec. 1840; A. Prentice, *History of the Anti-Corn Law League*, vol. 1, p. 193; Judge, 'Early Chartist Organisation', p. 382.

[59] Bamford, *Passages*, pp. 35-6. See also D. Ross, *The State of the Country* (Manchester, 1842), p. 6. As Dorothy Thompson has noted, so-called 'interested agitators' often earned less than in the trade they had forgone: *The Chartists* (1984), p. 163.

[60] Point four of the Charter called for the payment of MPs to the tune of £400 per year; when parliamentary salaries were finally enacted in 1911 £400 a year was agreed to. See W. Lovett, *Life and Struggles of William Lovett* (1876; 1967), p. 314; F. Williams, *Fifty Years March* (1950), p. 189.

[61] *Northern Star*, 2 Apr. 1842, pp. 6-7; Cooper, *Life*, p. 179. For a balanced discussion of O'Connor's leadership see J. Epstein, *The Lion of Freedom* (1982), pp. 90f. Part of the reputation of Richard Oastler, the 'King of the Factory Children', stemmed from his standing as a 'volunteer Champion'. See C. Driver, *Tory Radical: The Life of Richard Oastler* (New York, 1946), p. 443.

[62] *Northern Star*, 26 Nov. 1842, p. 7; 3 Dec. 1842, pp. 6, 7; 17 Dec. 1842, p. 4; 24 Dec. 1842, pp.. 1, 4. Bronterre O'Brien, editor of the *British Statesman*, weighed into the dispute against his former protégé, John Campbell, and provided a further outlet for criticism. See *British Statesman*, 19 Nov. 1842, pp. 6, 9; 26 Nov. 1842, p. 6; 3 Dec. 1842, pp. 1, 7; 10 Dec. 1842, p. 4. For a discussion of the NCA crisis and the general issue of accountability see E. Yeo, 'Some Practices and Problems of Chartist Democracy,' in J. Epstein and D. Thompson (eds), *The Chartist Experience* (1982) , pp. 354-60.

[63] *Northern Star*, 3 Dec. 1842, p. 6. McDouall claimed that 'I never put one penny of profit in my pocket arising from anything in which I have been engaged since I joined the Chartist movement – neither from pills, pamphlets or politics', *British Statesman*, 3 Dec. 1842, p.7.

[64] *Northern Star*, 4 Feb. 1843, p. 1; Yeo, 'Chartist Democracy', p. 357.

[65] F. Engels, 'A Working Man's Party' (1881), reprinted in K. Marx and F. Engels, *Articles on Britain* (Moscow, 1978), p. 376; Epstein, *Lion of Freedom*, pp. 220f. See also T. Rothstein, *From Chartism to Labourism* (1929; 1983), p. 68; N. Stewart, *The Fight for the Charter* (1937), pp. 147-8.

[66] H. J. Hanham, *Elections and Party Management. Politics in the Time of Disraeli and Gladstone* (Sussex, 1979), pp. 238f. See also N. Gash, *Politics in the Age of Peel: A Study in the Technique of Parliamentary Representation* (1953), pp. 105-36.

[67] H. Jephson, *The Platform*, vol. ii, pp. 354, 379.

[68] *Manchester and Salford Advertiser*, 5 Oct. 1839, p. 3.

[69] For a discussion of this issue see my article, 'Class Without Words: Symbolic Communication in the Chartist Movement,' *Past and Present*, cxii (August 1986), 144-62.

[70] Cited in Hanham, *Elections*, pp. 323-4.

[71] R. T. McKenzie, *British Political Parties* (1963), pp. 542-3. See also G. O. Comfort, *Professional Politicians: A Study of British Party Agents* (Washington DC, 1958), p. 60.

Teetotal Chartism

Brian Harrison

The nineteenth-century radical's exhilarating and energetic attack on aristocratic and Anglican privilege and monopoly came spontaneously and often simultaneously from many directions, but the besieged Establishment had the advantage of remaining united against a divided enemy. To draw the reformers together into what became the Gladstonian Liberal Party, changes were needed at three levels: their ideas needed to be welded together into a coherent reforming 'package', new constituency machinery was required to focus the package upon the voter, and the reformers had to integrated into a cohesive party of the left. The gradual break-up of Chartism in the 1840s assisted the first,[1] the National Charter Association anticipated the second with its complex set of interlocking structures devised (with some effect) for democratic participation and local control,[2] and with the bid for a teetotal alliance Chartism was foreshadowing the third, for in the form of local option and franchise extension these were two among several radical components of the Gladstonian late-Victorian Liberal crusade.

The advantages of coalescence were not always obvious at the time: fragmented but independent reforming effort could be specialized, single-minded, energetic and uncompromising. Yet the Chartist journalist Thomas Cooper, confronted at Leicester in 1841 with a split between Corn Law repealers and Chartists, 'often wished that some influential person ... would offer a compromise' whereby both causes would coalesce on the basis of taking 'anything that could be got first'; he found no local spirit of compromise,[3] and no national party machine existed to impose one. There was a second drawback of reforming fragmentation: reforming pressure needed to be steady but was episodic. Already by 1840 this had evoked concern from the Chartist leaders William Lovett and John Collins.[4] By 1847 Lovett wanted 'a GENERAL ASSOCIATION OF PROGRESS' to co-ordinate the campaigns for franchise reform, disestablishment, free trade, lower taxation, direct taxation of property, cheap law and justice, better education and housing and temperance, and against privilege, taxes on knowledge, and war. 'I still entertain the hope', he wrote many years later, 'that the day is not distant when some such general organization of the friends of progress will take place'.[5] His proposal in some ways foreshadows the National Liberal Federation of 1877, but in the 1840s extra-parliamentary radical movements had yet to be bolted on to the Whig/Liberal parliamentary grouping so as to create the Gladstonian Liberal crusade.

Radical critics of the Establishment felt as yet little affection for party as such, and many saw the Liberal Party's Whig leaders not as the solution but as part of the problem. For the Chartist leader Robert Lowery in 1841 there was little to choose between the parties: 'if they disliked the tiger, was that any reason for falling in love with the jackal or the fox?'[6] Nonetheless, the affinities between the radicals' separate crusades, movements, causes and campaigns were already becoming apparent. The *National Temperance Chronicle* in 1851 drew attention not only to a 'circle of the sciences' but also to 'a *circle of moral and philanthropic movements*; so that he who begins in seeking the welfare of his fellow-men in one thing is led step by step to seek it also in other things'[7]. These reforming affinities were not only horizontal – between reforming contemporaries – but also verti-cal, between radical reformers in different generations. For the early-Victorian radical, agitation was beneficial in itself, and the formal excuse for it came later, so when one agitation came to an end, another tended to be born. Hence the origins of the London Working Men's Association [L.W.M.A.], which the Char-tist leader William Lovett described as growing out of the agitation against the newspaper tax: 'we found...that we had collected together a goodly number of active and influential working men, persons who had principally done the work of our late committee; and the question arose among us, whether we could form and maintain a union formed exclusively of this class and of such men'.[8] So there was a pedigree of reform, less formalized than Establishment pedigrees, but no less influential for that: success in one crusade was cited, and its supporters were recruited, in the anticipation of further success in another[9].

The long-term solution to fragmented campaigning was to arrange the reformers' separate demands in the programme for a Liberal Party whose leaders could assign the timing and scale of response to each. But an intermediate stage on the way to this was for reformers spontaneously to seek bilateral alliances independently of party, with varying degrees of formality. Obvious candidates for such alliances were sub-sections or extensions of the same movement: feminists operating in the political and sexual spheres, for example; temperance reformers advocating moral suasion and/or prohibition; opponents of vivisection and animal cruelty. But there were also repeated attempts at alliance between kindred movements: peace and free trade after 1846 were drawn together by Richard Cobden, for instance, just as pacifism and feminism drew together after 1914. The brief life of Teetotal Chartism is another such alliance, and its history illustrates the awkwardness but also the potential of the transition from Chartism to Liberalism.

Although the Chartist and temperance movements have not lacked his-torians, Teetotal Chartism is now forgotten. Late-Victorian teetotalers wanted to stress their movement's political and religious respectability, but also to play down its disagreements with the organized working class. So the temperance movement's official historians never uncovered its early Chartist connections, and temperance reformers had even at the time been wary of them for fear of alienating middle-class and religious groups. As for the socialist intellectuals who wrote the first histories of Chartism – their prime concern was to submerge the Liberal Party and provide twentieth-century socialism with a popular pedigree. So they focused on the Chartist role in enhancing working-class consciousness, and were less interested in the Chartists' Liberal affinities. Repudiating the Liberal's individualist moralism, the socialist historian of Chartism was less interested in Teetotal Chartism than Liberal historians might have been. Yet it is only a twentieth-century socialist perspective that requires the Chartist and teetotal roads to diverge: at the time, Chartists were – as Charles Kingsley emphasized –'the great preachers and practisers of temperance, thrift, charity, self-respect, and education'.[10]

I

Fusion between Chartism and temperance in the 1840s was far from inevitable. To begin with, if 'temperance' meant water-drinking, as it did after the teetotalers in the mid-1830s had defeated the anti-spirits movement,[11] a whole new set of drink-free social institutions and attitudes needed to be created, for as Lovett and Collins pointed out, the entire working-class environment made sobriety difficult.[12] Chartists found it no easier than most early-Victorian working men to dispense with the publican. Respectability and abstinence were not yet firmly aligned, and Nottingham and London Chartists in the 1840s frequently met in the several drinking places whose names they often also applied to their branches; such places often housed cultural activities, if only because – in Nottingham, at least – their radical clientele had often established in them libraries for working men that were supplemented by their Chartist successors.[13] Drinksellers lodged itinerant lecturers, took in radical newspapers, and provided a meeting-place for radicals excluded from schools, town-halls and chapels. 'I have pretty generally found a good deal of compassion for the poor people to prevail amongst publicans and their wives', William Cobbett had written.[14] The publican's 'large room' could be hired cheaply, and his catering facilities were valued. The L.W.M.A. held its first public meeting in the Crown and Anchor, the Chartist convention of 1839 eventually had to move into Johnson's Tavern because the British Coffee House was too expensive, and when drink was excluded from the dinner organized for Collins and McDouall at Manchester in 1840 the Chartists had to do their own cooking.[15] Chartists gathered at drinking places immediately before the Newport rising, and the case of James Allen shows how easily a publican could be caught up in his customers' politics.[16] So governments preferred radicals to meet at places where the licensing system gave the authorities some hold over the proprietor. Several London public-houses were threatened with losing their licence in 1839, and in that year Mr. Taylor, publican of the Mason's Arms, Monmouth, was allegedly 'summoned to appear before his great and mighty highness the Mayor to shew cause why he allowed Men calling themselves Chartists to frequent his house'; the town clerk threatened penalties unless he refused them beer.[17]

Predictably there were several drinksellers among leading local Chartists – at Barnsley, Peter Hoey; at Bradford, Peter Bussey; at Tyneside, Martin Jude, John Blakey and Richard Ayre.[18] Also predictably, the temperance question soon became controversial – among radicals in the *Poor Man's Guardian* by 1831, for example. J. S. Buckingham's parliamentary inquiry into drunkenness in 1834 saw Lovett and Francis Place taking opposite sides. For three further reasons Chartists found a temperance alignment difficult. First, it cut across the sociability that helped the movement to cohere. Even a strong-minded Chartist was tempted to drink with a political friend who had travelled from afar; while lecturing at Witney in June 1842, the Chartist John Cluer allegedly accompanied two other Chartists to the Britannia public-house, where they 'spent the night merrily, frequently singing the well-known glee "When shall we three meet again – in thunder, lightning or hail"'.[19] The story is, to say the least, *ben trovato*, and Chartists could not afford to repudiate too frontally their movement's groundswell of semi-conscious, semi-hedonistic socialism. The zest for good living that pervades J. R. Stephens's speeches or G. J. Harney's correspondence was perhaps best articulated by the Trowbridge Chartist who promised his audience 'plenty of roast beef, plum pudding and strong beer by working three hours a day'. Harney may have taken the pledge in 1841, but he was drinking again by 1846.[20]

Religion caused more difficulty. Enthusiasm for sobriety must be distinguished from enthusiasm for the movement claiming to promote it; many Chartist leaders, children of the Enlightenment, disliked the temperance movement's religious connections. The anti-spirits movement originated among evangelicals and dissenters in the late 1820s, and although the teetotal movement in the mid-1830s attracted more working men and appealed to more secular motives, it still seemed to Peter McDouall, unsympathetic at the Chartist national convention of 1842, 'more of a religious than a political body'.[21] The attack on 'Gothic' superstition runs consistently through Lovett's autobiography, and towards its conclusion he urged working men to 'remember, that *ignorance and superstition* are the two chief crutches which prop up and support every species of despotism, corruption, and error in every part of the world'.[22] The serious-minded radical artisan needed to decide whether reason was more at risk from alcoholic drinks than from the religiosity of the movement which attacked them. Radicals and secularists by no means always enjoyed free speech at temperance meetings, and there seemed something hypocritical about sabbatarian temperance reformers who discouraged sober secular Sunday recreations. As early as 1829 Lovett's petition for the Sunday opening of museums had claimed that 'the best remedy for drunkenness ... is to divert and inform the mind', and in *Chartism* he and Collins blamed drunkenness partly on parliament's hostility to harmless recreations,[23] yet teetotalers were by no means united behind such causes. For most evangelical teetotalers, moral reform reflected conversion to a particular set of religious beliefs, and in August 1839 Banbury teetotalers were embarrassed when local Chartists signed the pledge solely to deny the government revenue; such a motive was 'sadly lowering the standard and principles of the Society, which does not seek to embarrass the Government, but rather to extricate poor unhappy sinners from the awful course which they are pursuing, and preventing others from becoming drunkards'.[24] Temperance organizations were politically too quietist even for Christian Chartist tastes.

Class loyalties offered a third obstacle to teetotal Chartist union. The springs of middle- and working-class moralism overlapped but were not the same. Whereas secular well-being and individual and collective self-respect were central to working-class aspirations, more central to middle-class hopes were social leadership and religious self-cultivation. For some Chartists the teetotaler's stress on individual conversion risked subordinating the convert. 'There is an ascendancy to be gained over the person committed to our care,' wrote Dr. Trotter, discussing the reclamation of drunkards in 1804, 'which, when accomplished, brings him entirely under our control'.[25] Far from strengthening a working man's self-respect, public confessions of drunkenness might merely advertise middle-class sobriety and philanthropic virtue. There was also the need to defend working men against collective depreciation. The former Chartist Henry Solly recalled in 1893 'the prevalent horror and disgust attaching to the name of Chartist' after the Newport rising. Lovett recalled a conversation on a bus about mineralogy with a Wesleyan minister who expressed astonishment on learning who he was: '"What! William Lovett, the Chartist?" "Yes, I replied, the same individual." "Why," said he, scrutinizing me very earnestly, "*you don't look like one*," evidently believing that a Chartist was something monstrous'.[26] For the sake of their class image, respectable artisans – whatever they might say in other contexts – were wary of advertising a working-class drunkenness that was well enough known already; as Lowery complained in 1838, 'the aristocrat can swill his wine and brandy and no one know it; but the poor man who drinks in the public house is immoral.'[27] Such sentiments prompted disruption at the New British and Foreign Temperance Society's anniversary meeting at Exeter Hall in May 1838 when 'a person named WIGHTMAN' tried, amid much interruption, to substitute six to eight working men for as many dissenting ministers and gentlemen on the committee. The chairman, Earl Stanhope, replied that the committee's duties were burdensome 'and it was necessary that, without any wish to disparage others, the persons who filled it should be those who by their leisure, and other qualifications, were enabled fully to attend to its duties'.[28] Working men staged similar hostile demonstrations at sabbatarian, anti-spirits and anti-slavery meetings during these years.

II

Important growth-points in both movements were, however, driving them closer together. No nineteenth-century working-class movement could flourish with drunken members: they not only damaged the movement's image but might abscond with the funds; from this, working men had difficulty in obtaining legal redress, as the Christian Socialist workshops painfully illustrate. So Robert Owen's socialism did not prevent him from promoting sober 'social festivals'; unsober Owenite branches might be unharmonious. Owen wanted drinkshops banned from New Lanark, drink taxes raised and spirit licences gradually withdrawn. In 1834 he pronounced Buckingham's demand for a parliamentary inquiry into drunkenness 'most excellent and valuable', and early teetotalism owed much to his disciple John Finch. For Owenites, radicals and Chartists – as for members of the early Labour Party – sobriety and political integrity went together.[29]

These long-standing radical attitudes and pragmatic necessities were carried forward into Chartism by the London craftsmen who founded the new movement. In the 1830s radical attitudes to abstinence changed in only two respects: first, teetotalers taught some Chartists that total abstinence from beer and wine as well as from spirits was feasible for working men; and, second, some working-class radicals adapted this perception for their own (largely secular and political) purposes. Lovett struggled to solve all political and personal problems through exercising reason, later claiming that the phrenologist George Combe's *Constitution of Man* (1828) had 'opened up to me the first clear ideas of my own nature, and taught me how much my future conduct would depend on my own exertions'.[30] He learned by experience that an individual could lever himself out of an unfavourable environment, and so waged a lifetime's assault on drunkenness. Furthermore, respectable artisans saw teetotalism as a self-denying self-cure. Like vegetarianism, it could deliver in bodily well-being the same self-reliance that reason delivered in the sphere of belief: the doctor, like the clergyman, could be cast aside as a redundant crutch. Lovett advocated temperance throughout the 1830s, defended Buckingham against Place in 1834, and in 1837 was even ready to disfranchise drunkards. He never joined the official teetotal movement, but in 1842 was quite prepared to become a teetotaler if this would promote the Chartist cause.[31]

He wanted education conducted through small groups of serious-minded working men: the sober, if banded together, might eventually pervade the entire working class. The LWMA, of which he was secretary, wanted radical leadership in morality as well as in politics; radicals must therefore exclude 'the drunken and immoral' from their ranks. The LWMA did not pursue mere numbers; its aim was 'to draw into one bond of UNITY the *intelligent* and *influential* portion of the working classes in town and country'. Drunkards neglected their families, muddled their brains, and made themselves 'the ready tools and victims of corruption, or slaves of unprincipled governors'. A rigorous training in self-discipline would achieve more than mere radical talk.[32] Hetherington and Cleave, Lovett's two prominent colleagues in the LWMA, were both abstainers; indeed, apart from its exclusively working-class membership and political concern, the LWMA's aims did not in practice diverge significantly from those of the early teetotalers. Its *Address and Rules* wished that 'the teachers of temperance and preachers of morality would unite like us, and direct their attention to the source of the evil' – poverty and overwork – 'instead of nibbling at the effects and seldom speaking of the cause', but in the absence of political reform to tackle the root cause, it agreed on the need for temperance propaganda.[33] The new poor law was never unanimously condemned by Chartist leaders, whose remarks sometimes anticipate the outlook of the Charity Organisation Society. The Chartist Henry Vincent, on the point of joining the Complete Suffrage Union in April 1842, declared that 'no man was fit to be a leader of the people unless he would tell them of their own errors, as well as proclaim those of their rulers'. The same thought informs his remark of 1871: there were two classes of hereditary pauper in Britain, 'one at the top and the other at the bottom of the social scale'.[34]

From the mid-1830s onwards, loosely-affiliated, non-religious, and only half-acknowledged working men's temperance groups and individuals clustered on the fringe of organized teetotalism, and by the late 1830s some Chartists were publicizing affinities between Chartism and temperance. John Fraser in 1838 linked them in his *True Scotsman*, and early in 1840 thought it 'a revolting spectacle' to see 'pot-house politicians hiccuping for liberty, while they make themselves degraded slaves'.[35] Several Teetotal Chartist societies were formed early in 1840, the year when temperance moved to the centre of Lovett's political scheme. Hoping that radicals now saw 'the necessity of substituting reason, argument, and legitimate efforts, for invective and menace, threats and violence', he and Collins in *Chartism* recommended drink-free district-halls (financed by mass levy) to foster self-improvement and drink-free recreation. They claimed that for every working man unable to pay the penny-a-week subscription there were 'hundreds who waste twice that amount daily'.[36] Joseph Sturge, the *Morning Chronicle* and many Chartists welcomed Lovett's 'new move', which at first promised to broaden out Chartist support considerably.[37]

Henry Vincent was among the scheme's supporters in spring 1841. He was the eldest son of a radical gold- and silver-smith from Holborn. When Henry was aged eight, his father's business failed, and the impoverished family went to Hull, where Henry was apprenticed to a printer in 1828. He was attracted into politics during the Catholic emancipation crisis and the July revolution, and became vice-president of a Hull Paineite young men's discussion group. In 1833 he returned to London, met Lovett, and in November 1836 joined the L.W.M.A. He became a political missionary, popular in the West of England and South Wales. In 1839 he launched the *Western Vindicator*, and his language grew increasingly excited. In May he was arrested for participating in a 'riotous assemblage' during April, and in August he was tried and imprisoned at Monmouth. He refused to warn his fellow Chartists against violence or to discontinue his *Vindicator*, thus sacrificing the chance of better conditions and early release. Tried again in March 1840 for conspiring with Frost, he ably defended himself, but was imprisoned for a further year. Vincent had abstained since 1836, and had often advocated self-improvement and sobriety. But with him as with Lovett, prison sharpened temperance zeal. By 28 February 1840 Vincent was envisaging 'a *moral combination* of the people that will achieve our every desire', and during September he envisaged an educational lecture-tour after his release. In October he warned Northampton Chartists against destroying reason 'by inundating it *with poison*': a drunkard could never be a good radical. 'I am a real down, upright, slanting, and octagonal Tea-totaller,' he told his friend John Miniken on 1 December, and in that month – together with Neesom, Cleave, Hill and Hetherington – he signed an address which argued that a tyrannous aristocracy governed only through the vices of the poor, and that Chartists must therefore become teetotalers[38]. The *Morning Chronicle* on 2 December sympathetically proclaimed Chartist teetotalism a 'better pledge of the coming franchise than the loaded musket'. Moral-force Chartists also welcomed the manifesto, and Vincent enthusiastically sent a copy to Place.

Judging by its signatories, Teetotal Chartism was strongest in the North of England. One hundred and thirty of the 135 signatories are known; of these, 48 came from Yorkshire, 26 from Lancashire, 20 from the Midlands, 13 from the Potteries, nine from London, four from Scotland, three from Ireland, two from Sunderland, two from Wotton-under-Edge and one from Brighton. London had at least five Teetotal Chartist societies – at Bermondsey, Lambeth, Cheapside, Beak Street and East London[39] – and of these perhaps the most lively was the East London Chartist Temperance Association. Its committee of ten met weekly, and general meetings were held monthly. A library and employment register were established, lectures and discussions were held, and before being admitted members had to abstain for a week from all intoxicants and tobacco. By February 1841 the members of its female section were enthusiastically hearing female testimonies to the blessings of teetotalism, and were promoting 'the singing of patriotic and sentimental ballads, and the delivery of excellent recitations'. The Association's leading personalities were C. H. Neesom and his wife. A feminist and freethinking Spencean, Neesom had campaigned for a free press, had joined the East London Democratic Association by 1836, and was briefly a member of the L.W.M.A. His revolutionary connections led him to be imprisoned twice in 1840, and in October 1840 he vowed to take no more sugar till the Charter had become law. He was among those who drafted the Teetotal Chartist manifesto in December, backed Lovett's new move in 1841 and the Complete Suffrage Union in 1842. His secularist loyalties persisted till his death in 1861. He was among the most courageous and principled of Chartists, convinced that Chartism could flourish only through popular education: a fitting representative of the rationalist strain in Teetotal Chartism.[40]

Why did Teetotal Chartism prosper at this time? Unfavourable economic circumstances accentuated the Chartists' continuing concern with poverty, and the evils associated with drunkenness were so patent that many Victorian reformers were tempted to exaggerate its salience among poverty's causes. Poverty certainly preoccupied Henry Vincent during the months when he adopted Teetotal Chartism. His prison letters denounced 'the System', and he was easily moved by suffering: by the starving button-maker who died in Oakham gaol during 1840 after stealing some spoons to secure the arrest that would save him from starvation, and by the unemployed whom he watched through a Nottingham window in July 1842, walking two abreast through the streets without work or food. 'What scenes of wretchedness, poverty, drunkenness, debauchery, and prostitution are to be traced in our Manufacturing Districts,' he exclaimed to Place in August 1840, after reading Gaskell on *The Manufacturing Population of England*: 'how have these things been produced – or how can they be remedied?'[41]

Teetotal Chartists found in drink the reason why their movement had crumbled before government repression during 1839: governments, they claimed, drugged their potential critics into political timidity. The theory was not so very absurd in a society whose army was recruited with drink bribes, whose police were often dismissed for drunkenness, and whose M.P.s 'treated' their way into parliamentary seats;[42] sober working men would, it was thought, soon 'see straight' politically and end such abuses. The *Northern Star* pointed out on 5 September 1840 how 'teetotalism leads to knowledge – knowledge leads to thinking – thinking leads to a discontent of things as they are, and then, as a matter of course, comes Chartism'. When he described the temperance evangelist Father Mathew as the oculist of the Irish people, O'Connor even gave a hint of the potential in temperance for that elusive alliance between Irish and English reformers which would so have alarmed the Establishment.[43] Furthermore, at a time when at least a third of government's revenue came from drink taxes, and when direct taxation was so unpopular that the money could hardly have been raised in any other way, universal sobriety might deny government the pay for its soldiers and police. Cobbett and Hunt had earlier from similar motives recommended abstinence from all excised articles, including tea and coffee.

And, at a time when at least half the national revenue went to the fundholder and at least a fifth to the armed forces, extensive moral reform might provoke a fundholder's panic while simultaneously denying the government physical force. Brougham himself privately described non-payment of taxes at this time as 'a thing utterly beyond all power of law – and even of force – and wholly impossible to be put down. This it is that makes it so formidable.'[44]

When Chartists went further, and argued that 'no government can long withstand the just claims of a people who have had the courage to conquer their own vices' – they were moving towards political fantasy; J. S. Mill later dismissed notions about truth's inherent power to prevail as 'idle sentimentality',[45] and the alarming experience of government repression in 1839-40 clarified minds on this point. Chartist mobilization in 1839, like the General Strike in 1926, gave at least a hint of working-class potential by showing 'what we could do'. Yet in the short term, the failure was complete. A few families obeyed the national convention's recommendation of universal abstinence during the sacred month of 1839, but Chartist leaders had exaggerated the people's readiness while underestimating the power of the ready cash which a government supported by the rich can always deploy: it is when unemployment and distress are at their worst that policemen and soldiers can be most readily recruited. In guiding the Anti-Corn Law League, Cobden wisely avoided tax avoidance: 'as though Government would not lay a tax on something else if it lost its revenue,' said Ernest Jones in 1855, scotching the revival of such strategies.[46]

Teetotal Chartism flourished after 1839 largely because the events of that year highlighted the need for a middle-class radical alliance. No early-Victorian argument against extending the franchise was more often deployed than the claim that drunkenness was rife among the lowest grades of elector; de Tocqueville even maintained that English election saturnalias, by disgusting the middle class with democracy, kept privilege politically intact. In February 1840 Vincent privately admitted that the government prosecutions would 'suppress foolish talk' in the Chartist movement. His aim now was to attract middle-class radical support; as he told Miniken on 1 December, 'I'll make a slap in that quarter some day'. On 31 December he told Place that 'the late movement has taught me a few useful lessons which I shall not fail to profit by'. He intended to adopt new tactics which would dispel old prejudices, win converts, '*and place my own character high above reproach*'; at the start of his temperance tour, he announced that 'the days of idle bombast and rant are gone by'.[47] Both Cooper and Vincent claimed to believe that the Frost rising had begun as a demonstration, and had become a rebellion only because spies urged the Chartists to drink. 'No riot was intended,' wrote Vincent in January 1842, 'until some drunken men madly and wickedly fired upon the Westgate Inn.'[48]

A sober Chartist movement might also recruit more women. Their enfranchisement had been ruled out from the Charter for the same reason that

Gladstone ruled women out of the third Reform Bill in 1884: it might overload the reforming package.[49] But this did not preclude special Chartist approaches to women. From the first, the L.W.M.A. advocated female suffrage, and Lovett thought that pothouse radicals disgusted women with working-class politics. O'Connor may have specialized in the unshorn chins, but Vincent had always enjoyed addressing female audiences. In November 1838 he told the Banbury women that they were 'the most important portion of the human race, because the character and conduct of the people depends much on your intellect and your exertion'. He courted female support at Banbury in June-July 1841 with some success. His poster on 14 June invited 'the ladies of Banbury' to a special ladies' meeting at the Theatre: 'I offer myself to represent Banbury as the friend of your sex.'[50]

Vincent's new tactics may have been reinforced by reading William Godwin, whose *Political Justice* emphasized that only ignorance kept middle and working classes apart. In a better society, said Godwin, the working man would 'no longer spend the surplus of his earnings in that dissipation, which is at present one of the principal of those causes that subject him to the arbitrary pleasure of a superior'.[51] Vincent's new move coincided with the Godwinite correspondence-course that Place was laying on for him. On 29 August 1840 Vincent told Place that he was 'much pleased' with Godwin's *Inquirer,* which he had just been reading, and expressed a 'strong desire' to read *Political Justice.* Place sent him a copy on 9 September. Vincent's temperance zeal first appears in his letter to the Northampton Chartists on the same day. By 5 October Vincent was determined when free to 'recommence my career on an improved mode of action', which would involve educating the people out of their superstitions and inculcating sobriety. He was already composing an article on teetotalism, and intended to take the teetotal pledge. On 10 November he told Place that he had read *Political Justice* 'carefully', and that 'on the whole' he had 'never read a book I liked so well'. He approved Godwin's scheme for promoting reform through educating the people and setting them a good example. Sobriety, he told Miniken on 1 December, 'will lead to *thinking* and *reading*'. His temperance manifesto was published before 2 December.[52]

Whatever Godwin's influence on Vincent, teetotalers – whose movement was growing fast in the late 1830s – furnished him with a template. Chartists and teetotalers had for some time been competing for the same type of recruit, and the friction between them reflected the similarity of their aims and appeal. The Chartist delegates Lowery and Duncan found it difficult to promote Chartism in Cornwall during 1839 because teetotalism had absorbed 'a considerable amount of enterprise and talent', and because elite working men saw it as the only remedy for social problems. Yet this did not prevent rank-and-file Cornish teetotalers from approaching the Chartist lecturers secretly for information, or from attending Chartist meetings. This reforming rivalry is epitomized in the somewhat undignified scramble for an audience between the Chartist and temperance orators whose meetings accidentally coincided at Kennington Common on Whit-Monday in 1839.[53] Teetotal Chartism offered some hope of eliminating such regrettable disputes within the party of progress. Sponsored by several of the earliest London Chartist leaders, allied with rank-and-file from both temperance and Chartist movements, Teetotal Chartism might inject into Chartism some of the teetotalers' moral and organizational energy.

Vincent was impressed by the temperance successes of Father Mathew (fully reported in the *Northern Star)* towards the end of 1839, and in December 1840 Vincent fully expected Mathew to uproot drunkenness among the London Irish.[54] The movement suggested new ways of associating 'men whose sober habits will have a powerful tendency to morally improve the whole population', but it conflicted with Godwin's recommendations in one important respect. When launching his campaign in the press, Vincent admitted the need to avoid appealing to 'the brute passions of the multitude... in wicked imitation of our rulers', but he diverged from both Place and Godwin by seeking political progress through public lectures and popular agitation. Place therefore ignored Vincent's requests for money while contesting Banbury in summer 1841: 'leave off running about the country your wife with you,' he wrote on 4 June, 'learning nothing which can ever be of any use to either of you, but much which is likely to tell in the contrary direction. Go to your own business and become a man of business, for the next ten years, you may perhaps at the end of that time, be in a condition to do some public service.'[55] Yet in his ultimate strategy Vincent did not diverge from Place, for Vincent was now seeking middle-class goodwill: he was taking middle-class fears of franchise extension at their face value and seeking to remove them. During his lecture-tours from 1841 onwards, much less was heard about teetotalism rapidly overturning the government. Working people should prove themselves to the middle class; they should 'forsake the gin palace, and so shew the aristocracy that they were a people worthy to be entrusted with the power they claimed'.[56]

Vincent's temperance manifesto produced a second wave of Teetotal Chartist societies early in 1841. Precocious in both Chartist and temperance activity, Scotland was naturally prominent in a movement that united them. In England, Teetotal Chartist societies existed at Leeds and Birmingham; by 16 January 1841 at Dewsbury; by 20 February at Hawick, holding social meetings with songs, recitations and addresses; and by 6 March at Bradford. There was also a society at Hull, and a society with both moderation and teetotal pledges at Bristol. Some weeks before Vincent's visit, societies were formed at Leicester and Loughborough, the latter with a newsroom and library.[57] His teetotal lecture-tour during March and April took him through Oxford, Banbury, Northampton, Leicester, Kettering, Nottingham, Cheltenham, Stroud and Gloucester. It served a double purpose, for he wanted to publicize his newspaper, discontinued in December

1839, but now revived as the *National Vindicator*. His speeches advocated class harmony, and concluded with signing a pledge, promising to abstain and 'to use all lawful and constitutional means to cause the People's Charter to become the law of the land'. Vincent's tour secularized and politicized the temperance lecture-tour which the Preston teetotalers had pioneered in the mid-1830s.[58] His teetotalism ensured that water was available at his radical dinner in Banbury during March, and local radicals decided to form a Teetotal Chartist society. Thomas Cooper was advocating a Teetotal Chartist pledge before Vincent reached Leicester, where Vincent administered the pledge to 63 Chartists, including Thomas Cooper, who himself later administered it locally to 'several hundreds'. Cooper kept his pledge for four years, abandoned it only for medical reasons, and re-signed it in 1861.[59] Vincent followed a similar plan elsewhere. At Nottingham he spoke against physical force, but argued that 'the only way to obtain anything from men who rule us, is to make them very uneasy'. He urged Chartists to petition parliament, to support only Chartist candidates at elections, and to take the teetotal pledge. The *English Chartist Circular* claimed that Vincent bid fair 'for some of the laurels of Father Mathew'.[60] Many leading Chartists now favoured teetotalism, even including G. J. Harney. Also at about this time some Aberdeen teetotalers persuaded Robert Lowery, who had often attacked pothouse politicians but was still ignorant of teetotal arguments, to sign the pledge.[61] So 1841 saw a Teetotal Chartist spring.

Then, on 13 March and 3 April in the *Northern Star* O'Connor denounced the quadruple alliance of church, teetotal, knowledge and household suffrage Chartism as 'trick, farce, cheat, or humbug'. He saw these separate developments as potentially divisive weapons of the London philosophic radicals whose influence he so detested. Teetotal Chartists might soon want the franchise confined to Chartists willing to take the pledge; there might then be 'washing and cleansing Chartists declaring you are too dirty for enfranchisement'. O'Connor used similar arguments in 1842.[62] Chartists in the North were now hanging on O'Connor's every word. In March his warnings prevented a Teetotal Chartist society from being formed at Warrington, though local teetotalers were invited to join the local Chartists for weekly discussions. Bradford Teetotal Chartists rejected O'Connor's arguments, but in May their society branded Lovett's supporters as 'enemies to the Chartist cause'. The Leeds Teetotal Chartists in the same month announced that, rather than aid the hated Whigs, they would vote Tory at the coming election. William Hill, editor of the *Northern Star* and connected with Hull teetotalism, doubted whether O'Connor had displayed 'his usual acumen' in the matter.[63] Thomas Cooper, O'Connor's eager Leicester disciple, admitted that O'Connor's remarks had 'fallen like electric sparks among us', but felt that Teetotal Chartism was 'advancing gloriously' locally. He therefore imported new and politically naive rules from Nottingham: the pledge was to be voluntary, and failure to take it should not be allowed to diminish a

Chartist's local standing. The pledged Chartists were to hold weekly meetings, as a section of the Leicester Chartist Society, with their own minute-book.[64]

The *Northern Star* was soon filled with the names of 'rats escaping from the trap' – that is, withdrawing their support from Lovett's scheme. C. H. Neesom was 'threatened and entreated by turns' to retract, and was disturbed during the night at his London house by O'Connorites threatening 'to drag him out of bed and do for him'. Neesom's loyalty to Lovett forced him to close his shop, and his wife her school. G. D. H. Cole rightly accused Lovett's scheme of 'massive simplicity'.[65] It ignored the legal obstacles and also the administrative expense of raising large sums from small subscriptions. Lovett established only one drink-free working men's meeting-place – the National Hall, Holborn – where meetings were held till 1857. He never lost his hatred of drink, which became in his old age a scapegoat to explain the human imperfections to which he was never reconciled, and to account for the apparent failure of the radical ideals which he never betrayed.[66]

Vincent wavered in his loyalty to Lovett. On 26 April he explained in a public letter that he had supported Lovett's scheme because based on his 'admirable pamphlet', though he had always anticipated failure 'in consequence of the general poverty and slavery of the people'. On 1 May the *Northern Star* rejoiced at his 'retractation' before the men of Derby with his claim that the middle classes would merely legislate Lovett's funds away from Chartist purposes. The Bristol Chartists later squeezed Vincent into admitting that Lovett's scheme, unless endorsed by the National Charter Association, was divisive and 'impracticable when opposed by the majority of the Chartist body'. Vincent received his reward in June 1841 when O'Connor praised him as 'the Benjamin Franklin of Chartism', 'brave and gallant', and 'one of the most exciting and animating speakers belonging to our ranks'.[67] Vincent needed such support, for during May and June he was at Banbury, fighting the first of his eight election campaigns.

During the contest he bid strongly for middle-class support, but made little of his teetotalism, perhaps because Barnes Austin, his leading local backer, was a brewer. After a plucky fight, Vincent was defeated on polling day, 30 June. In July he was still privately confessing himself 'an out-and-out Teetotaller', but he abandoned his Teetotal Chartist pledge-signing. The *English Chartist Circular* was soon complaining in vain about lack of news from Teetotal Chartist societies. The paper's subtitle 'Temperance Record for England and Wales' was, for the rest of its life, a misnomer. Teetotal Chartist societies were still active in Hull and Bradford in May 1841, and in July there were still many teetotalers among the Tavistock Chartists; in October the Leeds Chartist Total Abstinence Society welcomed O'Connor's release from prison. Nevertheless by 1842 even the London moral-force Chartists had begun to doubt the political potential of teetotalism, nor were there any further moves to form Teetotal Chartist societies.[68]

Temperance still had its advocates at the Chartist national convention of April

1842, though O'Connor opposed a motion that it should recommend total abstinence policies.[69] But Vincent's influence in the Chartist movement was waning. His debts were piling up, and his suspicions of O'Connor (privately expressed as early as August 1838[70]) were ripening; in April 1842 he became a lecturer for the Complete Suffrage Union and wound up his *National Vindicator* for good. In its last number, on 23 April 1842, he claimed that the Birmingham CSU conference 'proved the existence of virtue and talent in the persons of men who have hitherto feared or disliked each other', and advertised the strength of middle-class radicalism. Chartists, he said, should retain their distinctive title and organization, but they should welcome converts from every rank. In the *British Statesman* for 8 May the traces were cut: Vincent branded O'Connor as 'a fair and palpable mixture of knavery and folly', and O'Connor retaliated in the *Northern Star* on 4 June. In a scorching indictment of 'the political pedlar', he tore Vincent to shreds; four years later, after Vincent had been lecturing throughout the country for the CSU, O'Connor described him as 'the last arrow in hypocrisy's quiver'. Cooper denounced 'that little renegade Vincent', and never forgave him for his stance in 1842.[71] For some years Vincent faced Chartist heckling, yet he retained his temperance and radical ideals. What he did not retain was what for him had become an outmoded political strategy: henceforward he continued to recommend mutual improvement, temperance, franchise extension, religious liberty and an undying hostility to Toryism – but as a freelance political lecturer.

III

What does the Teetotal Chartist episode signify? It highlights the difficulty of co-ordinating nineteenth-century radical reformers through pragmatic bipartite alliances. The attempt at union, far from drawing the reformers together, divided them still further. For without superseding the temperance or Chartist movements, it simply added a third (intermediate and ephemeral) movement to the other two. Attempts at Methodist reunion in modern times had a similar outcome. Furthermore, the attempt at union fostered Chartist disunity at both local and national levels. In March 1841 Leeds Teetotal Chartists tried to form a National Teetotal Charter Association, and there were teetotal squabbles among Leicester Chartists.[72] Only under much firmer and subtler leadership, from politicians with far more assets to deploy against sectarians than Lovett or Vincent could wield, could faddists be welded into a reforming yet governmental party.

The episode also reveals the prevalence within Chartism of attitudes ripe for absorption into a reconstituted Liberal Party, for both sides in the episode were Liberals at heart. O'Connor argued in the *Northern Star* for 6 February 1841 that 'until the master is as much dependant upon the workman, for an augmentation of his capital, as the man is upon the master for employment in the pursuit, no union can be formed upon anything like equality.' Yet his occasional excursions into a proto-Marxian analysis did not preclude a middle-class affiliation; his objection to it was not principled but tactical, affiliation being seen as worthwhile only on his own terms. O'Connor believed that socialism 'must inevitably end in a war of the industrious against the idle', and his Chartist settlements were more like a temperance housing estate or a middle-class suburb than an Owenite community. He would have shared Vincent's view, expressed privately to Place in January 1841, that 'society would not progress if our heads (or rather our desires) were all planed down to one level. Competition, with all its evils, seems best adapted for developing the energies and talents of the human race.' Vincent believed that Owenism would lead to over-population; he had little faith in free trade as a complete remedy for poverty, but at that time his alternative (which he never publicized) was not socialism but birth-control.[73] There were several public controversies between Chartists and Owenites, but on socialism teetotalers and Chartists were often in agreement. Two teetotal leaders, F. R. Lees and Mrs. C. L. Balfour, wrote pamphlets against socialism; socialists who distributed tracts at a teetotal festival near London in 1840 were expelled, 'and to show their detestation of their detestable principles the teetotalers tore up their tracts and threw them to the winds'.[74]

Nor did O'Connor repudiate teetotalism. Much of Chartist history has been written by his enemies – from Lovett's autobiography, from the *Place Papers,* and by the early-twentieth-century WEA lecturers whom Lovett (O'Connor's archenemy) is said to have resembled. Mark Hovell wrongly attributed O'Connor's conduct in 1841 to the fact that 'knowledge and temperance were alike alien' to him. 'He cared neither for education nor morals,' wrote Hugh Gaitskell; 'having neither in great measure himself, he was not likely to wish to see them in others.'[75] This is not only to ignore O'Connor's explicit rebuttal of such a view: it also misunderstands the tactical problem he faced and ignores the shrewdness of his political response. Disputes over affiliation with other progressive causes bedevilled many nineteenth-century reforming movements, and any intelligent pressure-group leader in the 1840s avoided entangling his cause with temperance. Cobden, despite his loathing of O'Connor, acted likewise when confronted (in the Anti-Corn Law League) with Joseph Sturge's teetotal zeal. 'Once make nonconformity ground for exclusion,' O'Connor wrote, 'and you establish sects and sections, instead of one universal corps of regenerators.'[76] O'Connor's aim was also of course to weaken his Chartist enemies, some of whom used Teetotal Chartism as a weapon against him, for he rightly suspected that its advocates – Brewster, Lowery, Lovett and later Vincent, to name only four – were not his friends. Furthermore, a national movement could hardly have survived under revived dominance by L.W.M.A. elitism: a tiny group of refined gradualists could never have run a mass movement, nor could they ever like O'Connor have mobilized the 'unshorn chins'.

The Hovell/Gaitskell interpretation also neglects O'Connor's subsequent attitudes. True, O'Connor's personal example was inconsistent. At first he argued that he needed no pledge to strengthen his willpower. Nor did his promise in 1847 to abstain from all exciseable articles till victory was complete later prevent him from consuming fifteen glasses of brandy a day during the three months before his committal by the Speaker.[77] Nevertheless, unlike O'Connell, he did not embrace teetotalism in its hour of triumph and attack it during its time of trial. Quite the reverse. He had always been sceptical of abstinence tactics ('chippings of the Excise, and ... attacks on the tea-pot'), and in 1839 he was understandably wary of abstinence policies recommended to working men by people not themselves tempted to consume. Of course if working men abstained from excised articles for three weeks 'Spring Rice would not have a sixpence in his coffers', but were working men yet ready for effective self-denial?[78] He turned against Teetotal Chartism at the time when Father Mathew was achieving his greatest successes, and stood out for teetotalism during the movement's trough-period after 1843. He deplored drunken Chartist lecturers who ought to have been setting an example; Father Mathew, 'the real liberator of his country', seemed to be preparing for the accomplishment of O'Connor's dearest wish: the union of Irish repealers with English Chartists. He ridiculed the threat that a *Northern Star* which advocated abstinence would be thrown out of the drinkshops: nothing, he said, could do him greater honour.[79]

Nor were these mere words: the Land Scheme's history shows O'Connor's temperance views influencing his practice. He sought in the scheme's Chartist communities the sort of vice-free society he had envisaged in 1840, where 'every man's character was of value to his neighbour'. Temperance would be feasible, he said, only in a society where working people were not wage-slaves, and where they could fall back in a crisis on their own allotments. Like any contemporary rent-conscious landowner, O'Connor valued a sober tenantry, and like several other landowners at the time, he excluded distillers, brewers and drinksellers from his estates. In 1847 he begged the settlers on the Heronsgate estate, opened in an aura of milk-drinking and sobriety, to avoid the nearby beershop. A drunken man in Manchester was an object of envy, he said, but 'woe to him who shall be branded as a drunkard by the sober eye of the watchful and prudent here'. He knew well enough how poverty recruited the army, how drunkenness cheapened wage-labour, and how the well-to-do concealed their own sins while branding the poor as immoral; and he always took pleasure in the fact that his Chartist estates had been financed by savings filched from the beershop.[80] 'Ah! if I was monarch for twenty-four hours,' he said in 1846, 'I'd level every gin palace with the dust.... and in less than a month I'd produce a wise representation of a sober and thoughtful national mind'. Was O'Connor, then, 'the only leading Chartist who was devoid alike of idealism and of statesmanship'?[81] The verdict is surely unfair.

When challenging the idea of pledge-signing or (later) of prohibition, Chartists on either side of the 1841 divide tended to deploy libertarian rather than social-ist arguments – as illustrated by the case of J. R. Stephens, alone among Chartist leaders in frontally attacking the temperance movement. He favoured sobriety, but opposed temperance activity because he disliked its hypocrisy and its threat to working-class privacy and traditional liberties. His two extraordinary speeches at Stalybridge in 1847-8 denounced teetotal informers who had been 'entering, snake-like' into a poor widow's house 'where two or three friends were playing an innocent game of dominos'. Such intruders never presumed to interfere with the vices of the rich, and 'a more ignorant, narrow-minded, contracted, bigoted, malicious, intolerant and vindicative confederation of men, never existed'. In October 1872 he daringly accused prohibitionist officials of regularly quaffing their port and brandy in two Manchester public-houses.[82] A deeply traditional-ist and decidedly unsocialist libertarianism moulded his outlook. 'I have kept Jack company for over 40 years,' he told a beersellers' gathering in March 1872, 'and I know his principles'; Stephens was one of the few prominent Victorian defenders of the beershop, recreation-centre of the poorest working men. His libertarianism also governed his response to Sunday closing proposals. Disrupt-ing a Stalybridge Sunday-closing meeting in 1867, he contemptuously drew a parallel with Robert Lowe's recent maligning of working people. 'Englishmen in the olden time had been free,' he claimed, and amid great excitement got the meeting adjourned. At the adjourned meeting he thumped the table when de-claring Sunday closing 'opposed to every sound principle of political economy, public morals, and social order'. Emphasizing that Cobbett had recommended beer, he insisted that 'drunkenness is an evil, but drinking is not an evil'. The public-house was 'every Englishman's freehold … as old as the hills, and … one of the institutions of the country'.[83] He saw H. A. Bruce's proposal of 1871 for public-house inspectors as 'the beginning of the web of centralisation, which would ultimately spread throughout the land', an excuse for a London-based government to cover the country with spies. As in 1867, he insisted that 'by the oldest laws of the country, every Englishman has two houses – his own private house and his own public-house'.[84]

Liberal values also pervaded O'Connor's Teetotal Chartist opponents. Vin-cent did not fade out of labour history when he joined the CSU in April 1842. By championing his class in numerous reforming movements from then until he died in 1878, he prepared the ground for the middle- and working-class co-operation which bore such fruit within the Liberal Party between 1868 and 1914, and somewhat less effectively within the Labour Party after it split with the Liberals during the First World War. Vincent was hereby taking no easy road to middle-class acceptance, for Teetotal Chartists were at least as radical as any O'Connorite, but were also exposed to attack from two directions: they risked being labelled by John Watkins and his like as 'pedlaring, or prostitute,

Chartists, and pussy-cat Chartists',[85] yet could not be sure of winning new middle-class friends. A clannish loyalty to established strategies and personalities is easily presented as courageous and consistent, yet periodic pauses of thought about tactics are required, and these may generate new strategies for new or newly-perceived situations. Both before and after 1841, Lovett, Neesom and Vincent were consistently anti-aristocratic, consistently aware of the dignity of their class, but they knew that in promoting its interests, 1839-40 had changed everything.

As for the teetotal movement – popular (as was Chartism) with shopkeepers, small employers and artisans – no instant rapport with it was possible, for during 1839 middle-class Chartists had come increasingly under attack. Benevolent and genuinely radical Chartism's teetotal sympathizers might be, but their memories of 1839 died only slowly. During the Banbury election of 1841 Vincent's poster of 4 June addressed to the non-electors emphasized that the interests of middle and working class were 'one and the same', for both would gain by 'cheap, good, and responsible government'. Yet his enemies immediately harped upon Chartist violence – on 'that gang of miscreants who ... sought to excite the poorer classes against their better-situated Neighbours, and by Physical Force, the Firebrand and Bloodshed, to subvert the constituted authorities of the land'. Sceptical of Vincent's transformation, his angry denials and testimonies to his moderation, they claimed that he now curried favour 'by flattering the very traders or "shopocrats" he once denounced'. Had he not only two years before been advocating 'the doctrine of EQUAL DISTRIBUTION!' in Banbury market-place?[86]

The teetotalers had at first been embarrassed to find Teetotal Chartists on their side because teetotalers were still fighting for position within the temperance movement, still competing for respectability with the 'moderationists', or advocates of abstinence only from spirits (organized in the British and Foreign Temperance Society). Teetotal Chartism was a godsend for the latter, who leapt on the chance to identify teetotalism with infidelity and political extremism; the anti-slave trade movement in the 1790s had been crippled in rather the same way. The moderationist organ, the *Temperance Penny Magazine,* made several insinuations about teetotalism in 1839-41, and heavily emphasized the Society's Christian basis. The alleged link between teetotalism and infidelity kept the prominent evangelical Dean Close out of the teetotal movement for twenty years; it alarmed the Wesleyan conference in 1841 as well as J. R. Stephens. Teetotalers published angry rebuttals; the ex-shoemaker W. A. Pallister quite logically inquired whether such critics 'would ... rather hear of the existence of *drunken* Chartists and *drunken* Infidels than of *sober* ones?'[87] But the teetotal movement needed for the time being to keep its distance from a teetotalism whose impulse was purely political and secular.

Teetotalers were also embarrassed when some moderationist predictions were fulfilled: several working-class teetotal orators appeared on radical political platforms, including the lecturers Edmund Stallwood, James Millington, John Cluer and William S. Ellis.[88] Cluer, 'the Cumberland weaver', enraged a London temperance meeting in December 1842; claiming (with some justice) that teetotalism had begun with working men, he tried to force himself on the meeting in a colourful costume, but was eventually ejected. Teetotalers so disliked distinct working-class political activity that their periodicals scarcely mention Chartism. [89] At least five teetotal leaders – J. J. Gurney, Bishop Stanley, Canon Jenkins, Lawrence Heyworth and Rev. W. J. Shrewsbury – bitterly opposed Chartism. Chartists were expelled from several teetotal societies, and were often excluded from their premises; Chartists at Snigs End in 1847 faced opposition from Gloucester tradesmen led by Samuel Bowly, the prominent Quaker temperance reformer; and a speaker at a London teetotal meeting in 1840 was cheered for claiming that teetotalers were pledged abstainers 'not from intoxicating liquors only, but from infidelity, socialism, chartism and all manner of wickedness'.[90] At a teetotal meeting in March 1844, J. N. Osborn, a shopkeeper, attacked the idea that 'working men' were the only members of the working class: 'I fancied *I was a working man, though a shopkeeper,* – because I have worked in our good cause for upwards of seven years, to the injury of my own interest.' As late as January 1845 the *National Temperance Chronicle* failed to publish Vincent's speech at a Father Mathew fund meeting in Exeter Hall, though the *Metropolitan Temperance Intelligencer and Journal* indignantly published it in full. When there were shouts of 'Vincent' at a National Temperance Society meeting in the following May there was a pronounced flurry on the platform before he was allowed to speak.[91] Vincent after 1841, like the Whigs he had so often denounced, found himself attacked on two fronts, suspected of being all things to all men.

On the other hand, at least twelve prominent temperance reformers sympathized with Chartist objectives, or even with the movement itself. Vincent found many prominent teetotalers in the CSU – including Thomas Spencer, Henry Solly, John Bright, Joseph Sturge, John Dunlop and Thomas Beggs. The eighth of the resolutions creating the CSU recommended temperance 'in order that our movement may be peaceably and morally conducted'. In 1842 F. R. Lees, the teetotal propagandist, considered the Charter 'the only remedy for national poverty and national impending ruin', and at Bradford, Clitheroe, Leeds and Rochdale, Chartists and teetotalers shared meeting-places and equipment.[92] Chartist and teetotal concepts of respectability were not irreconcilable. A classless radical crusade against privilege and power could readily accommodate class-conscious Chartists non-violent in tactics, and it could yoke them without undue strain to a teetotal movement whose tone was dissenting, independent, principled, resolute, and (in its radical and prohibitionist wing) militantly anti-aristocratic. Both Chartists and teetotalers championed the thrifty, industrious and self-reliant urban virtues against a traditionalist and subservient rural dependence; the rural areas were, in Vincent's words, 'steeped in ignorance, beer, and superstition'. Both movements hoped to tackle poverty by reducing taxation and state interference, and by extending individual initiative. Their ideal was a locally self-governing society which would need little policing, fighting or governing on its behalf, and whose citizens' Christian self-discipline would minimize the need for paternalistic public largesse. Both before and after 1839 Vincent lacked any concept of the majesty of the state, echoing Tom Paine with his claim of 1850 that government was 'but one among the many badges of lost innocence that mankind are wearing'.[93]

The teetotal leaders' moral idealism also finds an echo in the creators of the LWMA, for whom life was no May game. Chartist leaders admired the seventeenth-century puritans and covenanters: their heroes were the Whig heroes Russell, Sidney and Hampden. Lovett's writings and Vincent's speeches all reflect a single-minded pursuit of self-cultivation amidst a world of snares and temptations. Lovett and Collins's *Chartism* defended the respectable working man whose children were beset by a corrupting environment, with their ears 'assailed by brutal and disgusting language in the midst of his dwelling, their eyes meet with corruption and evil in every street, and seductions and temptations await them in every corner'.[94] Chartist leaders in old age, like the teetotalers, often deplored the increased interest in recreation, drinking and sport displayed by the working men whom they had struggled to enfranchise. As for religious obstacles to reunion, a secularist tone had been assumed by only a minority within the Chartist movement; its working-class constituency never broke completely with organized religion, and its religious links were likely to strengthen as mid-Victorian religion became less sectarian.

We now know that Vincent and Lovett were not pursuing an impossible political alliance. It has been claimed that 'it was not possible to contain both traditional nineteenth-century Liberalism and a dynamic policy of social reform within the same party',[95] yet this is to read back into the 1840s a much later definition of 'social reform' which the Chartist mainstream never favoured. Both Chartism and mid-Victorian Liberalism flourished on moralistic crusades against Authority – crusades stuffed with implications for social reform as early-Victorian working men understood it. Once the preliminary dispute between free traders and regulationists (that is, between the beersellers, whom the Chartists sometimes supported, and the publican advocates of licensing restriction) had been resolved, the way was open for all the excitements of a sustained attack, through the prohibitionist United Kingdom Alliance, on all the compromises and corruptions of privilege and power. Not surprisingly, several Chartists, including Lovett, were among the prohibitionist movement's earliest supporters. Other mid-Victorian Liberal crusades were equally attractive to working men: the Garibaldi procession, the demonstrations for the North in the American Civil War, the Reform League, the Liberation Society, the Financial Reform Association, the National Education League, Josephine Butler's campaign, the Bulgarian Atrocities agitation, the attack on newspaper taxes, Home Rule. By taking this route, former Chartists did not abandon the Chartists' 'social programme', such as it was.[96] For in the Gladstonian Liberal Party's successful approaches towards free speech, democracy, peace, education, decentralization, reduced taxation, religious liberty, moral progress and opportunity for thrift, enterprise and effort, there was a Chartist social programme and to spare.

Among the Chartist leaders, W. E. Adams, Joseph Barker and Henry Hetherington – not to mention local notabilities like James Taylor of Birmingham or Abraham Sharp of Bradford – were all influenced by temperance propaganda. Henry Vincent, Robert Dransfield, Dr. P. W. Perfitt, Benjamin Lucraft, W. H. Chadwick and Robert Lowery were all Chartists who became temperance advocates. In 1846 the LWMA itself seriously considered seeking corporate representation at the World's Temperance Convention.[97] Three teetotal leaders – Lees, R. M. Carter and Joseph Barker – were Chartist town councillors in Leeds between 1848 and 1853. Many former Chartists entered the mid-Victorian Scottish temperance movement, among them Robert Cranston – a mason's son, arrested in 1848, who later became a respectable Liberal town councillor and founded a chain of temperance hotels. This was the direction Henry Vincent himself took. By the 1850s his set-piece orations on Cromwell were famous. We get a final glimpse of him in his letters to W. L. Garrison between 1874 and 1877. He remained his ebullient, jaunty self, deeply interested in American politics, convinced of the reality of progress, 'in *hot* indignation' against the Tory government in September 1876, delighted at the retreat of 'priest-craft' throughout Europe, proud of his prison record. In his last speech, at Barrow in 1878, Vincent urged his audience to spurn Beaconsfieldism and hold to the Liberal standard.[98] In the following year the old Halifax Chartist Ben Wilson was dutifully touring Gladstone's Library at Hawarden, and in July 1885 twenty-two Halifax Chartists drank tea at Maude's Temperance Hotel and voted thanks to Gladstone for recently extending the franchise to rural working men. W. H. Chadwick, the last surviving Chartist, appeared at the general election of 1906 on a Liberal Party platform, with many years' temperance lecturing behind him.

The reforming agenda after the 1840s did not of course remain set precisely in the anti-state, cheap-government, anti-aristocratic libertarian mould where the Chartist movement had left it. Vincent in old age, with his puritanism and his continued enthusiasm for the United States, was not in touch with important late-Victorian working-class trends. He deplored working-class political apathy and industrial conflict: 'the lower strata of the working classes' enfranchised in 1867, he complained, 'is indifferent to, or ignorant of politics – and is reached easily by money, flattery, and drink'; it had 'no political past – or future'. He saw an outbreak of railway strikes in the U.S.A. in 1877 as 'the outgrowth of European ignorance and passion' which could never have erupted from native-born

Americans[99]. In the same year Lovett envisaged 'great struggling and sacrifice' between masters and men 'before this labour question is settled', whereas 'unfortunately the great bulk of our working classes are too thoughtless, and too much occupied with their beer and tobacco to probe this important subject to the bottom'.[100] Lovett's autobiography of the previous year struck a poignant note when regretting that, despite all his hard work and thrift, 'I cannot earn or live upon my own bread in old age'.[101] Such sentiments were by then drawing the next generation of reformers towards a new agenda, and socialist historians reaching back into Chartism found anticipations there of interventionist welfarism.

As early as July 1831 the *Poor Man's Guardian* had urged the anti-spirits movement to 'make the poor man's home comfortable, and he will then as GENTEELY and UNOBTRUSIVELY enjoy his glass at his own fireside, without being obliged, as at present, to fly to the gin-shop as a relief from domestic misery'. The paper blamed temperance reformers for attacking effects, not causes. This line had also been taken by the LWMA's manifesto in 1836, and by Lowery, Duncan and Brewster in their Chartist years.[102] The tory radical anti-Liberal component of late-Victorian socialism was also foreshadowed by J. R. Stephens, in his long-standing feud with Hugh Mason, the local embodiment of Gladstonian Liberal dissenting moralism. During 1871-2 Vincent and Stephens lectured in the same locality, but their views contrast strikingly. We have seen that there was a traditionalist and libertarian aspect to Stephens's vision, and the community values he favoured were defensively traditionalist, local and personal, not progressive and centralized. But whereas Vincent harped upon nonconformist grievances and eulogized the upstanding, virtuous, active citizen without recognizing any need to create him through social engineering, Stephens pointed directly to the conflicting interests of employer and employee. Whereas Vincent still crusaded for religious and political liberty, Stephens – in his speech of March 1872 – denounced the sheer tyranny of machinery; 'will you tell me that when men, women, and children are 12 hours in the mill – will you tell me that they are not liable to the temptation of wanting something to sup?' Men should be healthy and happy at their work, and should be made to feel 'limbs of the same body, members of the same community'. And whereas Vincent favoured giving ratepayers some say in licensing decisions, Stephens was conducting an all-out attack on all legislation that restricted access to drink. For Stephens the size of the wage had become more important than its deployment; and a strong, almost organic, sense of community was more urgent than any formal extension of individual liberty. Even in the 1840s he had insisted that 'if every man in Staleybridge were teetotal to-day, and were to remain so to all eternity, they would not have a halfpenny more wage'.[103]

Harney and Ernest Jones went further in their anti-Liberalism. In 1850 Harney reprimanded the *Leeds Mercury* for attacking the self-imposed taxation of the working class: 'I protest against the insolence of those who dare to lecture the working classes on their "immorality" while they themselves live by the most immoral system that ever this earth was afflicted with—a system which bases the wealth, luxuries, and pleasures of the few, upon the poverty, crime, and misery of the many.'[104] As for Jones, he announced in the same year that the Charter 'don't lie at the bottom of a glass of water'.[105] On 30 September 1854 the *People's Paper* attacked the theory of John Clay, the Preston prison chaplain, that education alone could prevent prosperity from automatically increasing the crime rate. Jones, by contrast, claimed that the working man bought drink during prosperous times because 'extreme privation breeds extreme indulgence. Had he not been cast so low yesterday he would not cast *himself* so low to-day. Had you not denied him *bread* last week, he would have denied *himself gin* in this. But those FATAL FLUCTUATIONS are ruinous to the moral character of a man. They make his very existence precarious, and endue his heart with a desperate, callous recklessness – a sort of "devil-may-care" disposition.' Men would be thrifty only if well paid, and if given a stake in the produce of their labour. In June 1855 Jones denied that an abstinent working class could acquire farms and factories: 'as though the people would not be plundered out of their savings – as though the system of competition and monopoly would not prevent those hopes – and as though the money saved would be more than a drop in the golden ocean of the competing capitalist'.[106] This was the language of the Social Democratic Federation, thirty years before its time.

Yet Jones knew that Chartism would gain by the spread of sobriety, and believed that Chartists should lead in morals as well as in politics. In 1852 he wanted temperance reformers writing in his *People's Paper,* and while opposing amalgamation he repeatedly tried to get them to co-operate with Chartists: 'he wished every Chartist to be a temperate man, and every temperate man a Chartist, and then they would obtain the rights they were striving for'. In 1855 he was even ready for prohibition: 'democracy', he said, 'must often be despotic, in order to save Liberty'.[107] When he contested Manchester as a radical candidate at the general election of 1868, he thought the prohibitionist movement's local veto progressive enough to endorse, and at his funeral in the following year two prohibitionists – Elijah Dixon and H. M. Steinthal – were among the pallbearers.[108] However much their emphasis may have diverged during their lifetimes, both Jones and Vincent knew that working people would gain ground politically at least as much from enhanced self-consciousness and dignity as from pursuing any distinctive social policy: as much from collaboration as from conflict between the classes. Socialism was but one component of a Labour Party whose Snowden, Henderson and Hardie owed much to the chapel and the temperance society, and the Party which unexpectedly supplanted the Liberals after 1918 pushed further the civil liberties and the political rights that the Liberals had pioneered. Labour speeches on the Licensing Bill of 1908, or Labour Party policy-making in the 1920s, are hardly reminiscent of Marx's view that 'temperance fanatics' were mere 'hole-and-corner reformers' who wished 'for a bourgeoisie without a proletariat'.[109] The inter-war Labour Party's classless appeal sought allies wherever it could find them, and at least as many of its adherents would have been touched by the high-toned Liberal moral idealism, internationalism, self-respect and libertarian courage of a Vincent or a Lovett as by the hard-nosed anti-Liberal anti-industrialism of a Stephens or a Jones.

Notes

[1] This level of change is discussed in B. Harrison and P. Hollis, 'Chartism, Liberalism and the Life of Robert Lowery', *English Historical Review,* July 1967, pp. 503-535.

[2] E. Yeo, 'Some Practices and Problems of Chartist Democracy' in J.Epstein and D.Thompson (eds.), *The Chartist Experience: Studies in Working-Class Radicalism and culture, 1830-60* (1982), p. 365.

[3] *Life of Thomas Cooper by himself* (1872), p. 144.

[4] W. Lovett and J. Collins, *Chartism* (1840, Leicester ed. 1969), p. 61.

[5] B[ritish]L[ibrary]. *Add. MSS.* 37775 (Working Men's Association Minutes), f.97 (29 Sept 1847). See also W.Lovett, *Life and Struggles* (1876), pp. 324-5, 329.

[6] *Scotsman,* 3 July 1841.

[7] Quoted in A. Tyrrell, 'Personality in Politics: the National Complete Suffrage Union and Pressure Group Politics in Early Victorian Britain', *Journal of Religious History,* Dec 1983, p. 382.

[8] Lovett, *Life and Struggles,* p. 91.

[9] On this pedigree see my 'A Genealogy of Reform in Modern Britain', in C.Bolt and S.Drescher (eds.), *Anti-Slavery, Religion and Reform. Essays in Memory of Roger Anstey* (1980), pp. 119-148.

[10] C. Kingsley, *Alton Locke* (Everyman ed. 1970), p. 41.

[11] On this see my *Drink and the Victorians. The Temperance Question in England 1815-1872* (2nd. ed., Keele University Press, 1994), Chs. 4-6.

[12] Lovett and Collins, *Chartism,* p. 7. For the nineteenth-century drinkseller's central role in social life, see my *Drink and the Victorians,* Ch. 2.

[13] J. Epstein 'Some Organisational and Cultural Aspects of the Chartist Movement in Nottingham', in Epstein and Thompson (eds.), *The Chartist Experience,* p. 237. D.Goodway, *London Chartism 1838-1848* (Cambridge, 1982), p. 59.

[14] W. Cobbett, *Rural Rides* (Ed. G. D. H. and M. Cole, 1930), II, p. 389.

[15] Convention, *Robert Lowery. Radical and Chartist* (Ed. B. Harrison and P. Hollis, 1979), p. 120; Manchester dinner, D. Thompson (Ed.), *The Early Chartists* (1971), p. 158.

[16] For Newport, see Mark Hovell, *The Chartist Movement* (Manchester, 1918), p. 137; for Allen, see John Salt *Chartism in South Yorkshire* (University of Sheffield Institute of Education, Local History Pamphlets No. 1, 1967), p. 18.

[17] Quotation from B.L. *Add. MSS.* 34245A (General Convention of the Industrial Classes, 1839, I), f. 413; see also Lovett and Collins, *Chartism,* p. 48.

[18] I am grateful to Dr.D.J.Rowe for the Tyneside information.

[19] *Jackson's Oxford Journal,* 6 July 1842; Raphael Samuel, then of Ruskin College, Oxford, gave me this reference.

[20] Quotation in Asa Briggs (ed.), *Chartist Studies* (1959), p. 10; see also F. G. and R. M. Black (eds.), *The Harney Papers* (Assen, 1969), p. 360; A. R. Schoyen, *Chartist Challenge* (1958), p. 124; *Red Republican,* 5 Oct 1850, p. 122.

[21] *Northern Star,* 30 April 1842, p. 6.

[22] Lovett, *Life and Struggles,* p. 441.

[23] Lovett, *Life and Struggles,* p. 58; cf. Lovett and Collins, *Chartism,* p. 7.

[24] H. N. Rickman, *British and Foreign Temperance Intelligencer*, 17 Aug 1839, p. 328.

[25] T. Trotter, *An Essay ... on Drunkenness* (2nd. ed. 1804), p. 181.

[26] H. Solly, *'These Eighty Years' or, the story of an unfinished life* (1893), I, p. 245. Lovett, *Life and Struggles*, p. 244.

[27] *Robert Lowery. Radical and Chartist*, p. 217; cf. p. 220.

[28] *New British and Foreign Temperance Intelligencer*, 26 May 1838, p. 171.

[29] Quotation from Robert Owen in *The Crisis*, 15 June 1834, p. 83; cf. R. Owen, *A New View of Society* (Everyman ed. 1927), pp. 31, 66-8; E. Yeo, 'Robert Owen and Radical Culture', in S. Pollard and J. Salt (eds.), *Robert Owen. Prophet of the Poor* (1971), p. 95.

[30] National Library of Scotland, Edinburgh, *Combe MSS.* 7302, f. 46: Lovett to Combe, 22 Nov 1849.

[31] For Lovett on temperance in the early 1830s, see *Working Man's Friend and Political Magazine*, 13 Apr 1833, p. 131; 18 May 1833, p. 176. For Buckingham, see B.L. *Add. MSS.* 27827 (Place Papers), ff. 30-1: Lovett to Place, 17 Nov 1834. Buckingham's committee is discussed in my 'Two Roads to Social Reform: Francis Place and the "Drunken Committee" of 1834', *Historical Journal*, 1968, pp. 272-300. For Lovett's disfranchisement proposal, see Birmingham City Library, *Lovett Collection*, I, p. 144: Lovett to West, 29 Nov 1837 (copy). For Lovett's position in 1842 see *Birmingham Journal*, 9 Apr 1842, p. 4.

[32] L.W.M.A. *Address and Rules* (n.d.), pp. 6, 2 (British Library shelfmark 8138 a 55); cf. Lovett, *Life and Struggles*, p. 94.

[33] L.W.M.A. *Address and Rules*, p.3.

[34] Quotations from *British Statesman*, 16 Apr 1842, p. 5; *Ashton Reporter*, 28 Oct 1871; cf. Lovett, *London Dispatch*, 30 Dec 1838; and Vincent, in *Plymouth, Devonport and Stonehouse Herald*, 18 Mar 1843.

[35] *True Scotsman*, 16 May 1840; cf. Fraser in *Northern Star*, 22 Sept 1838, p. 3.

[36] Quotations from Lovett's speech at the dinner celebrating his release from prison— *Northern Star*, 8 Aug 1840, p. 1; and from Lovett and Collins, *Chartism*, p. 44; cf. *ibid*. pp. 37, 47.

[37] *Nonconformist*, 29 Dec 1841, p. 634; *Morning Chronicle*, 22 and 23 Sept 1840.

[38] Quotations from Transport House, *Vincent MSS.* 1/1/23 (i), Vincent to Miniken, 28 Feb 1840; *Northern Star*, 3 Oct 1840 (letter to Northampton Chartists); *Vincent MSS.* 1/1/40, Vincent to Miniken, 1 Dec 1840; *Chartist Circular*, 19 Dec 1840, p. 263 (Address). For Vincent's teetotal pledge, see *National Temperance Chronicle* Feb 1845, p. 315. For his plans for an educational lecture-tour, see *Northern Star*, 19 Sept 1840, p. 7. For the moral-force Chartist welcome for his manifesto, see Cleave, *Northern Star*, 6 Mar 1841, p. 8; *True Scotsman*, 28 Nov 1840. See also my 'Henry Vincent (1813-78) Chartist and Radical Lecturer', in J. M. Bellamy and J. Saville (Eds.), *Dictionary of Labour Biography*, 1 (1972), pp. 326 and ff.

[39] Signatories listed in *English Chartist Circular*, I, No. 9 and ff. David Goodway most generously provided information on Teetotal Chartism in London.

[40] Quotation from *English Chartist Circular*, I, No. 5, p. 19; for Neesom, see *National Reformer*, 20 and 27 July 1861 and M.Chase's memoir in *Dictionary of Labour Biography*, VIII, pp. 177-181. See also B.L. *Francis Place Newspaper Collection*, Set 56 (Oct 1840-Feb 1841), Appendix [henceforth cited as *Francis Place Appendix*], p. 29; *Northern Star*, 8 May 1841, p. 6; 6 Mar 1841, p. 8; 30 Jan 1841, p. 1.

[41] Quotation from *Francis Place Appendix*, p. 29: Vincent to Place, 29 Aug 1840. For the button-maker see *Vincent MSS.* 1/1/35: Vincent to Miniken, 22 Sept 1840; for the Nottingham unemployed, see *Vincent MSS.* 1/1/49: Vincent to Miniken, 13 July 1842.

[42] For recruiting, *True Scotsman*, 30 May 1840; for police, C. Reith, *British Police and the Democratic Ideal* (1943), p. 54; cf. H. Marcuse, *Essay on Liberation* (Penguin ed. 1972), p.44.

[43] *Northern Star*, 29 July 1843, p. 8.

[44] University of Southampton Library, MS 62 Broadlands Archives MEL/BR/3: Brougham to 'L[ord Melbourne]', dated Windsor Castle, 'Monday'.

[45] Quotations from Vincent's temperance manifesto in *Chartist Circular*, 19 Dec 1840; J. S. Mill,

On Liberty (1859), in *Collected Works*, XVIII (1977), p.238.

[46] Jones, *People's Paper*, 16 June 1855; cf. N. McCord, *The Anti-Corn Law League, 1838-46* (1958), p. 110. See also W. E. Adams, *Memoirs of a Social Atom* (1903), I, pp. 158, 161.

[47] Quotations from Transport House, *Vincent MSS.* 1/1/23 (i): Vincent to Miniken, 28 Feb 1840; 1/1/40: Vincent to Miniken, 1 Dec 1840; *Francis Place Appendix*, p. 47: Vincent to Place, 31 Dec 1840 (copy); *Vincent MSS.* 1/1/41: Vincent to Miniken, 21 Dec 1840; *Northern Star*, 6 Mar 1841, p. 8. See also A. de Tocqueville, *Journeys to England and Ireland* (Ed. J. P. Mayer, 1958), p. 45.

[48] Quotation from *National Vindicator*, 8 Jan 1842, p. 4; cf. *Midland Counties Illuminator*, 3 Apr 1841, p. 30.

[49] A.O'Neill, in *Women's Suffrage Journal*, 1 Dec 1885, p. 196. See also D.Thompson, 'Women and Nineteenth-Century Radical Politics: a Lost Dimension', in J.Mitchell and A.Oakley (eds.), *The Rights and Wrongs of Women* (1976), p. 132.

[50] Quotations from Banbury Public Library, *Rusher Collection*, I, p. 146 (poster announcing meeting on 29 Nov); I, p. 161. See also *Oxford City and County Chronicle*, 26 June 1841, p. 4; 3 July 1841, p. 4.

[51] W. Godwin, *Political Justice* (2nd ed. 1796), II, p. 543.

[52] Vincent's letters of 29 Aug and 10 Nov to Place are in *Francis Place Appendix*, pp. 29, 39. Other quotations from Transport House, Vincent MSS. 1/1/36: Vincent to Miniken, 5 Oct 1840; 1/1/40: Vincent to Miniken, 1 Dec 1840. Vincent's published letter dated 9 Sept is in *Northern Star*, 3 Oct 1840.

[53] Quotation from *True Scotsman*, 30 Mar 1839. See also *Robert Lowery. Radical and Chartist*, p. 131; B.L. *Add. MSS.* 34, 245A (General Convention of the Industrial Classes, 1839, I), f. 148: Lowery to the General Convention, 22 Mar 1839; J. Rowe, *Cornwall in the Age of the Industrial Revolution* (Liverpool, 1953), p. 156. For Kennington, see *British and Foreign Temperance Intelligencer*, 25 May 1839, p. 201.

[54] Transport House, *Vincent MSS.* 1/1/40: Vincent to Miniken, 1 Dec 1840. The best study of Father Mathew is Rev. Father Augustine, *Footprints of Father Theobald Mathew* (Dublin, 1947).

[55] Quotations from *English Chartist Circular*, I, No. 11, p. 42; B.L. *Add. MSS.* 35151 (Place Papers), f. 343: Place to Vincent, 4 June 1841.

[56] Quotation from *Northern Star*, 6 Mar 1841, p. 8.

[57] *Northern Star*, 19 Dec 1840, p. 1; 16 Jan 1841, p. 5; 13 Feb 1841; 20 Feb 1841, p. 1; 27 Feb 1841, p. 8; 6 Mar 1841, p. 1; *Midland Counties Illuminator*, 27 Feb 1841, p. 9.

[58] Quotation from *Nottingham Review*, 9 Apr 1841; see also my *Drink and the Victorians*, pp. 120, 126, 132-3.

[59] Quotation from Cooper *Life*, p. 165. See also *Oxford City and County Chronicle*, 13 Mar 1841, p. 4; *Cooper's Journal*, 19 Oct 1850, p. 453; *Weekly Record of the Temperance Movement*, 16 Feb 1861, p. 58.

[60] Quotations from *Nottingham Review*, 9 Apr 1841; *English Chartist Circular*, I, No. 17, p. 68. See also *Leicestershire Mercury*, 27 Mar, 3 Apr 1841.

[61] For Harney, see Schoyen, *Chartist Challenge*, p. 124; for Lowery, see *Robert Lowery. Radical and Chartist*, pp.179-80. See also Harrison and Hollis, 'Chartism, Liberalism and the Life of Robert Lowery', pp. 519-20.

[62] Quotations from *Northern Star*, 13 Mar 1841, p. 7; 3 Apr 1841, p. 4; cf. O'Connor's remarks in the convention, *ibid.*, 14 May 1842, p. 7.

[63] Quotations from *Northern Star*, 1 May 1841 (Bradford); 3 Apr 1841 (Hill). For Warrington, *ibid.*, 20 Mar 1841, p. 1; for Leeds, *ibid.*, 29 May 1841, p. 1; for Bradford, *ibid.*, 10 Apr 1841.

[64] *Midland Counties Illumintor*, 17 Apr 1841, p. 39; 24 Apr 1841, p. 43.

[65] Neesom quotations from *National Reformer*, 27 July 1861, p. 6; G. D. H. Cole, *Chartist Portraits* (1941), p. 54.

[66] For Lovett's later temperance attitudes, see my *Drink and the Victorians*, p. 205.

[67] Quotations from *Northern Star*, 1 May 1841, pp. 5, 7; 15 May 1841, p. 1; 26 June 1841, p. 4.

[68] Quotation from *Vincent MSS.* 1/1/47: Vincent to Miniken, 25 July 1841. See also *English Chartist*

Circular, I, No. 21, p. 82; *Northern Star,* 2 Oct 1841, p. 8; *National Association Gazette,* 26 Feb 1841, p. 69; *National Vindicator,* 17 July 1841, p. 3.

[69] O'Connor, *Northern Star* 14 May 1842, p. 7; see also *ibid.,* 23 Apr 1842, p. 6 (Ridley); 30 Apr 1842, p. 6 (Philp).

[70] *Vincent MSS.* 1/1/10: Vincent to Miniken, 26 Aug 1838.

[71] *Northern Star,* 3 Oct 1846. For Cooper, *ibid.,* 30 July 1842, p. 1; R. G. Gammage, *History of the Chartist Movement* (1854), p. 447; cf. *Vincent MSS. 1/1/51:* Vincent to Miniken, 30 July 1842.

[72] *Northern Star,* 13 Mar 1841, p. 7; *Midland Counties Illuminator,* 10 Apr 1841, p. 34. For Leicester, see Bairstow, *Northern Star,* 30 Apr 1842, p. 6.

[73] Quotations from *Northern Star,* 23 Sept 1848, p. 1; *Francis Place Appendix,* p. 57: Vincent to Place, 20 Jan 1841.

[74] Quotation from *London Teetotal Magazine,* Sept 1840, p. 286. For late-Victorian socialist attacks on the temperance movement, see my *Drink and the Victorians,* pp. 372-83.

[75] Quotations from M. Hovell, *op. cit.,* p.202; H. T-N. Gaitskell, *Chartism* (1929), p. 32. See also Cole, *Chartist Portraits,* p. 61.

[76] Quotation from *Northern Star,* 3 Apr 1841, p. 4.

[77] *Northern Star,* 2 Oct 1841, p. 8; 17 Apr 1847, p. 1; *People's Paper,* 6 Oct 1855, p. 1.

[78] Quotations from *Northern Star,* 29 Dec 1838, p. 8; 31 Aug 1839, p. 6.

[79] *Northern Star,* 28 May 1842, p. 1; cf. *ibid.,* 9 Oct 1841, p. 4; 16 Sept 1843, p. 1; 16 Nov 1844. For O'Connor's attacks on drunken lecturers, *ibid.,* 18 July 1840; 30 Apr 1842, p. 6; 16 Sept 1843, p. 1.

[80] Quotations from *ibid.,* 16 May 1840, p. 6; 8 May 1847, p. 1. For the exclusion of drinksellers, see *ibid.,* 29 Apr 1843, 7 Dec 1844. For the army see *English Chartist Circular,* II, No. 62, p. 34. For upper-class hypocrisy on the drink issue see *Northern Star,* 21 Apr 1838, p. 6; cf. *ibid.,* 24 Feb 1838; 31 Aug 1839; 30 Nov 1839.

[81] Quotations from *Northern Star,* 10 Oct 1846, p. 5; M. Hovell, *Chartist Movement,* p. 194.

[82] For the 1847-8 attacks see *National Temperance Advocate,* IV (1848), pp. 29, 38, 39-42; the late Professor T. S. Ashton owned an interesting letter from Stephens to the secretary of Ashton Temperance Society, dated 22 March 1848, relating to this controversy, and kindly allowed me to consult it. See also *Ashton Reporter,* 9 Mar 1872, 26 Oct 1872.

[83] *Ashton Reporter,* 9 Mar 1872, p. 3; the Sunday closing meetings are reported *ibid.,* 30 Mar, 13 Apr 1867.

[84] *Licensed Victuallers' Guardian,* 29 Apr 1871, p. 172; *Ashton Reporter,* 29 Apr 1871, p. 7.

[85] Y. V. Kovalev, *An Anthology of Chartist Literature* (Moscow, 1956), p. 341.

[86] Quotations from Banbury Public Library, *Rusher Collection,* I, p. 159; *Poster Collection,* Case C. 7 ('Beauties of Chartism No. 2'); Case C. 4 (dated 18 June 1841); *Rusher Collection,* I, p. 171.

[87] W. A. Pallister, *Essays, Chiefly on the Temperance Question* (1849), p. 64; the book deals with such critics in two articles, on pp. 47-58, 58-65.

[88] *Northern Star,* 7 May 1842, p. 2 (Millington); *Journal of the New British and Foreign Temperance Society,* 20 July 1839, p. 249 (Cluer, whose later American career is discussed in R. Boston, *British Chartists in America 1839-1900,* Manchester, 1971, p. 90); *English Chartist Circular,* II, No. 145, p. 371 (W. S. Ellis, whose sad subsequent decline is chronicled by R. Fyson in 'The Transported Chartist: The Case of William Ellis', in O. Ashton *et al.* (eds.), *The Chartist Legacy,* 1999, pp. 80-101). Stallwood, agent to the United Temperance Association, signed Vincent's temperance manifesto – *ibid.,* I, No. 9; for a biographical note on him see I. Prothero, 'Chartism in London', *Past and Present,* Aug 1969, p. 87.

[89] *British and Foreign Temperance Intelligencer,* 3 Dec 1842, p. 490 (Cluer).

[90] Quotation from *Times,* 18 Apr 1840, p.5. For Bowly, see A. M. Hadfield, *The Chartist Land Company* (Newton Abbot, 1970) p. 141; the incident is ignored by Marion Taylor, *Memorials of Samuel Bowly* (Gloucester, 1884).

[91] *Metropolitan Temperance Intelligencer and Journal,* 16 Mar 1844, p. 85 (Osborn). See also *ibid.,* 11 Jan 1845, p. 12; 24 May 1845, pp. 165-6.

[92] Quotations from *Birmingham Journal*, 9 Apr 1842, p. 4; *Northern Star*, 23 Apr 1842, p. 1. For Bradford, see Peggy Rastrick, 'The Bradford Temperance Movement'(unpublished essay, Margaret Macmillan Training College, 1970), p. 16; I am most grateful to Miss Rastrick for allowing me to read her essay. See also *Northern Star*, 24 Sept 1842, p. 1 (Clitheroe); Leeds Temperance Society, *MS. Minute Book, II,* several entries (Leeds Central Library); Rochdale Temperance Society, *MS. Minute Book 1842-53* (in Rochdale Public Library), minutes for 19 Dec 1844.

[93] Quotations from *English Chartist Circular*, I, No. 17, p. 68; *Preston Guardian*, 20 Apr 1850.

[94] Lovett and Collins, *Chartism*, p. 70. See also Lovett, *Life and Struggles*, p. 374, and my 'Pubs', in H. J. Dyos and M. Wolff, (Eds.), *The Victorian City* (1973), I, pp. 161-190.

[95] D. Thompson, *Early Chartists*, p. 15.

[96] D. Thompson, *Early Chartists*, p. 15.

[97] B.L. *Add. MSS.* 37775 (Working Men's Association Minutes), f. 50 (14 July 1846).

[8] For Vincent's last speeches, see *Barrow Times*, 7 Dec 1878; *Barrow Herald*, 7 Dec 1878, p. 5.

[99] Boston Public Library, U.S.A., *Vincent-Garrison Correspondence* (photostat copies): Vincent to Garrison, 30 September 1876, 11 July 1876, 23 Aug 1877; cf. *Derbyshire Times*, 2 June 1877, p. 5; *Burnley Gazette*, 30 Sept 1876, p. 5.

[100] Lovett to his nephew Hugh Carne (in U.S.A.), 25 Mar 1877, letter in the care of Carne's great-granddaughter Mrs. Barbara Avery.

[101] *Life and Struggles*, p.400; cf. Cooper, *Life*, p.390.

[102] *Poor Man's Guardian,* 16 July 1831, p. 13; 13 Aug 1831, p. 44; cf. *The Charter,* 10 Nov 1839, p. 667; P. Brewster, *Seven Chartist and Military Discourses* (Paisley, 1843), p. 88.

[103] Quotations from *Ashton Reporter*, 9 Mar 1872, p. 3; and see fn. 84 above. Vincent's speeches are *ibid.*, 18 Mar 1871, p. 3; 28 Oct 1871; 12 October 1872.

[104] *Red Republican*, 5 October 1850, p. 122.

[105] Kovalev, *Anthology of Chartist Literature*, p. 361.

[106] Quotations from *People's Paper,* 16 July 1853, p. 2; 6 June 1855; cf. *ibid.*, 23 May 1857, p. 1; J. Saville, *Ernest Jones, Chartist* (1952), p. 160.

[107] Quotation from *People's Paper*, 16 June 1855. See also *Notes to the People*, I, pp. 88-9; II, pp. 624-5, 890, 893; *Northern Star*, 17 Oct 1846, p. 5; *Leicester Chronicle*, 16 July 1853, p. 2; J. Saville, *Ernest Jones*, p. 123.

[108] *Manchester Examiner and Times,* 24 Aug 1868, p. 3; B.Wilson, *Struggles of an Old Chartist* (Halifax, 1887), p. 35; and my 'The British Prohibitionists 1853-1872. A Biographical Analysis', *International Review of Social History,* XV (1970), pp. 391, 434, 438.

[109] K. Marx, *Communist Manifesto* (Ed. Laski, 1948), p. 154.

CHRISTIANITY IN CHARTIST STRUGGLE 1838-1842

Eileen Yeo

The prisoners were assembled in the chapel of the gaol for prayers, after the reading of which the officiating clergyman was giving a short lecture on the virtues and excellence of Jesus Christ, when one of the prisoners … named Laing, or who is better known by the name "Radical Jack", of Stockton, stood up and with a loud voice exclaimed: "Sir, Jesus Christ was the first Chartist. He was the best man that ever came into the world. He taught the doctrines of humility and equality, and even instructed men to sell their garments and buy a sword". "Poor Jack" received, for his part of the morning service, three days' solitary confinement.[1]

"Radical Jack" was jailed in 1839 for his activity in Chartism, a political movement agitating for the Six Points of the Charter which demanded universal manhood suffrage and parliamentary reform. But Chartists were also engaged in a wider struggle which extended into religion, as Jack's outburst shows, and into many other areas of social life. Direct confrontations were not the only way of living out the conflict: like people in other working-class movements between 1830 and 1850, the Chartists also came to produce their own versions of educational, recreational and religious activities in their local groups or branches.[2] Historians of labour movements and historians of nineteenth-century religion have taken too little account of Christianity, not as the possession of any one social group, but as contested territory.[3] This essay will examine the religious conflict that was part of the Chartist struggle between 1838 and 1842, with a special focus on the culminating episode of Chartist demonstrations in more than thirty-one parish churches in the late summer of 1839. It will also explore the Christian elements of Chartist culture over the same period, when, through their experience of struggle, Chartists were making critical changes in the shape of their branch life.

I

The public rhetoric of Chartism was mainly constitutionalist. However, from the earliest days of the movement, a body of radical Christian beliefs was clearly in evidence and already well authenticated by struggle. These beliefs need to be related to the history of popular Christianity and compared at least to the ideas of the plebeian radicals of the 1640s: but, given the constraint of space, all that can be noted here is that earlier nineteenth-century experience, and particularly the Peter-loo massacre of 1819, had ensured that Christianity would remain a battleground in the social war. Two Anglican clerics were prominent among the magistrates who ordered the cavalry charge on a peaceful demonstration and then used the courts to punish the victims. With equal zeal, Anglican and Wesleyan officials in south Lancashire hounded radicals out of their worship and Sunday schools.[4] This experience certainly pushed many working people into the infidel camp, but it also provoked many radical Christians to spell out a counter-Christianity, in an effort "to deliver the religion of Jesus Christ from the disgrace brought upon it" and to retain credibility with the working class.[5] Their formulations of belief, developing further as need arose, were carried by working-class chapels and movements over the next twenty years.[6]

A radical Christian sensibility was conspicuous in the embryonic phase of Chartism when the *Northern Star* newspaper started publication in late 1837 and early 1838. The fight against the 1834 Poor Law Amendment Act, which was being implemented in the north for the first time, occupied a central place on the agita-tional stage. This campaign was being conducted in religious terms by a group of preachers and ministers, including the Rev. Joseph Rayner Stephens, Anglican Parson Bull, and the Swedenborgian editor of the *Northern Star,* the Rev. William Hill, who denounced the Act as contrary to the will of God. By treating poverty as a crime, the act denied the distressed poor their God-given right to a dignified support on their native soil ("dwell in the land, and verily thou shalt be fed" was a popular banner text):[7] by insisting on age and sex separation in the workhouse, the Act dissolved the sacred bonds of marriage and violated God's injunction to "be fruitful, and multiply, and replenish the earth, and subdue it, for all is yours, (very loud cheers)".[8] These ideas had deep resonance in a large area of working-class sensibility and were expressed repeatedly in proletarian banners, speeches and in less premeditated ways. At a Burnley meeting, which adopted a petition against the New Poor Law, a woman shouted, "'if eawr pearson winna sign it, we winna goo yer him preach'. 'Now nor goe t'be marrit nother'," said another.[9]

It is important to stress how compatible, indeed mutually reinforcing, the radical Christian and constitutional outlooks were within Chartism. Both put great emphasis on the rights of labour and the poor, and both made a powerful critique of social oppression. In radical Christianity, the dignity of labour was underlined not only by the fact that Christ had come to earth as a working man, but also by a labour-value theology which posited a special relationship between God and the working classes. God had created the earth as potential abundance but it was labour which actually turned the potential into fruits, wealth and prop-erty: as Chartist preacher Abraham Hanson put it, "their labour was the source of all property, they performed that labour by the physical power of their bodies, they derived that power from none but God".[10] Labour had the first claim to the fruits (usually to a fair share rather than, as the socialists insisted, to the whole produce). The people, in the popular banner motto "The Voice of the People is the Voice of God",[11] was increasingly coming to mean the working classes (whether employed or in poverty through no fault of their own). The truly Christian society was one that not only honoured the divine rights of labour and the poor but also embodied Christ's teaching about equality and mutuality ("Do unto others as ye would they do unto you" was a favourite text for Chartist sermons).[12]

In the Chartist constitutional view, "the people" which was "the legitimate source of all power" was also coming to mean the working classes. During the agitation for the 1832 Reform Bill, radicals had included the middle class as part of "the people" and as part of the industrious or the productive classes. Since then, those of the middle class who had allied with the Whigs, who had supported the New Poor Law and endorsed the persecution of trade unionists, had disqualified themselves, leaving the working classes as the overwhelming body of the people to whom power legitimately belonged.[13] To radical constitutionalists, oppression was the result of rich and powerful "factions" repudiating the rights of the people, while for Christian Chartists, social oppression was a repudiation of God: "He who oppresseth the poor", ran a popular banner text, "reproacheth his maker".[14] The cast of oppressors in the constitutional and biblical views coincided nicely. The Old Testament prophets and then Christ and his apostles had pointed to princes, rulers, unjust employers and Jewish state priests as usurpers of the rights of labour and the poor: the constitutional roll-call added the "base, brutal and bloody Whigs" and grasping capitalists to the Old Corruption of aristocracy, sinecurists and bishops. It was the people or the working classes and their friends who would have to be the instruments of their own salvation. And they could legitimately prepare for a situation where their enemies might compel them to use force, for the free-born Englishman had a constitutional right to arm, and even Christ had instructed his disciples, when injustice was rampant in the land, "he that hath no sword, let him sell his garment and buy one".[15]

Although a Christian consciousness was evident, nascent Chartist culture contained few religious forms or observances.[16] From mid-1838 to mid-1839 the movement was busy with demanding tasks. Local activity was harnessed to the strategy chosen to win the Charter, a strategy which was partly a huge prefigurative drama, partly an acting out of universal suffrage in the process of agitating for it. There was a General Convention of the Industrious Classes to be elected and financially supported.[17] The Convention would plan and co-ordinate the strategy of the movement and pilot the National Petition through the House of Commons; it would decide on contingency plans or, in the contemporary jargon, ulterior measures, to be implemented if the Petition were rejected and, although this was a contentious point, some felt it would sit as an embryonic, alternative, people's parliament, the shape of things to come if the Charter were granted. Besides the fairly standard practice of setting up a reading room and devoting one day a week to reading the radical press aloud and another to a lecture/discussion on a political subject, there was now the business of organizing the collection of signatures for the Petition, of organizing the great county hustings which would elect the people's delegates to the Convention and of collecting the National Rent to pay the expenses of the delegates. As the Convention started to deliberate, there was a constant dialogue between the delegates and their constituents which further occupied the time of local groups. The delegate was supposed to be a mouthpiece of the will of the people and his accountability to his constituents was considered very important (and was the basis for the Charter demand for annual parliaments).

Winning the Charter was the primary task. But an important event at the close of 1838 stepped up the battle on the religious front. In late December, in the wake of a ban on torchlight meetings, the Rev. J. R. Stephens was arrested on a charge of seditious conspiracy for a speech delivered to a meeting at Leigh. The movement was outraged by this act, which seemed like the opening shot in a campaign of government repression, aimed both at constitutional rights and at true religion: in some places Chartist committees of public safety were formed to contain any premature outbreak of Chartist violence. Later, in August, Stephens was to disown any commitment to the Charter (as distinct from the Bible) and earn the disapprobation of many Chartists, but at the time of his arrest he was the exemplary minister of religion. Not only did he preach that the Christian minister must be humble in personal ambition but fearless in prophecy ("to stand for ever as a moral breakwater against the swelling surge of pride and oppression"), he lived the part.[18]

Stephens jeopardized his professional chances and his personal safety by changing sides in the religious class war. As the son of the Rev. John Stephens, pillar of the Wesleyan establishment, friend of Jabez Bunting, president of the Conference in 1827, chairman of the Manchester district at Peterloo time and arch-persecutor of radicals and dissidents, the Rev. Joseph Rayner Stephens could have had a brilliant Wesleyan career. But in 1834 he resigned from the Connexion rather than obey Conference orders to stop his disestablishment activity in Ashton and took with him several Wesleyan congregations in south Lancashire and elsewhere. From 1836 he became active in the Ten Hours movement and was so outspoken in condemning factory exploitation that he provoked open war with the mill-owners and overseers in his congregations. They nailed a placard to the Staleybridge Chapel which read: "STEPHENS'S EVANGELICAL COTTON MANUFACTORY AND LUNATIC ASYLUM FOR TURNED-OFF PARSONS, ADMITTANCE GRATIS"; he responded by preaching only sermons in which he called mill-owners murderers and swindlers and denounced the existing factory system as contrary to the word of God. The bourgeois membership deserted but the Stephensite Methodists grew quickly as a working-class denomination and by 1839 could boast ten preaching stations and thirty-one preachers in the Ashton circuit alone.[19]

Stephens constantly raged at religious oppressors. In a powerful sermon preached outdoors in March 1839 he insisted that most churches and chapels had lost all claim to spiritual authority: ministers not only shirked their prophetic duty but the poor were "shut out" by humiliating free seating arrangements, by never-ending money collections, by incomprehensible sermons and by the sight of oppressors sitting there unchallenged. He urged working people to meet in any surroundings for worship, select one of their body to minister and replace him if he stopped preaching the truth. "What right have I to stand before you this afternoon", Stephens asked, "unless I be speaking the truth? I have none". The minister was the religious delegate of a congregation of the people who were the medium and arbiter of divine truth.[20] Stephens had model relations with his own flock: when in 1838 over one hundred workers were sacked from local factories for supporting him, he shared his stipend with them. Despite his charisma on a platform, he restrained his power in matters of organization: he refused to become sole trustee of chapels which had been financed from working-class pennies, insisting that the subscribers should have the control.

After the arrest of Stephens, local groups throughout the country started contributing to a Defence Fund (alongside and necessarily in competition with the National Rent). From early March through May, a common way of raising money was to borrow a friendly chapel, often of some Methodist persuasion, or a Sunday school room (which was often under working-class control),[21] where a Chartist preacher would deliver a Sunday sermon with the collection going to the Stephens Defence Fund. The Chartist preachers were working men and active radicals, who had sometimes already done battle for their religious views. One of the Lancashire preachers was Isaac Barrow, a Bolton factory spinner, and member of a radical congregation which had left the Wesleyans at Peterloo time and later joined a loose federation of Independent Methodists.[22]

The West Riding preachers also shared the lives of their congregations: Benjamin Rushton was a working handloom weaver, William Thornton a woolcomber, while John Arran plied a number of callings, blacksmith, teacher and later dealer in coffee and tea and Chartist missionary, getting his livelihood from the movement. They were often veteran radicals: Rushton had stopped paying church rates after Peterloo and had actively campaigned for the weavers and against the New Poor Law during the 1830s. They sometimes paid a heavy penalty for their commitment: Rushton was gaoled in 1842 for leading a group of plug strikers, while Thornton reputedly fled to America in 1839 to escape arrest. They preached to a network of radical congregations not confined to any one denomination: thus while Thornton often visited Primitive Methodist chapels, he also preached in the Skircoat Green Wesleyan Sunday school (which joined the Reform schism in

1850), the Mt. Carmel chapel of Gospel Pilgrims in Little Horton and the Clayton Baptist schoolroom.[23] The local authority of these men could rest on an impressive range of accomplishments: Abraham Hanson of Elland had a versatility reminiscent of the mechanic-preachers of the 1640s. Not only was he a shoemaker and active Chartist, and possibly the Wesleyan preacher expelled in 1839 for a Chartist speech, but he was also the local cunning man, his medical skill learned "in the college of nature", and a keen thespian, whose career culminated with the part of Last, the political cobbler in William Cobbett's play, *Surplus Population*. He supposedly decided to preach while thinking about Cromwell and the Ironsides: he rushed to his wife asking her to find a white neckerchief (preaching garb) for Sunday, exclaiming "I've just fun aght that t'Charter is to be gotten by preaching and praying".[24]

The upsurge of religious support for Stephens ran into opposition; there were clear cases of conflict between the Sunday school and chapel and between local chapel and denomination over the use of premises. In the New Connexion, the president of the Conference for 1839, the Rev. Simon Woodhouse, chastised the Sutton-in-Ashfield chapel in his midlands circuit, while the Halifax circuit quarterly meeting publicly reprimanded the already troublesome Amblerthorne chapel for playing host to a sermon for Stephens. Amblerthorne responded by proudly shouldering the responsibility themselves:

we desire to exculpate the Connexion and place the stigma on ourselves and though the Society be poor (and whether our poverty derives from the just and merciful decrees of the Supreme Governor of the universe, or from the free agency of wicked men, very few attempt to instruct us) yet we are jealous of the honour we have in this instance and we will not give it to any other.[25]

The Primitives seem to have been the most tolerant. When the Queenshead Baptists refused their chapel and even withdrew their schoolroom, the usual place for Chartist meetings, despite "a unanimous vote of its managers and teachers", the Primitive Methodists rescued the situation by offering their chapel instead. In Lancashire and Cheshire, Primitive chapels rallied behind the Stephensites and Independent Methodists. Yet in Huddersfield, no chapel would lend itself, so three lay preachers gave sermons for Stephens in the New Court House and Mr. Kay's room.[26] There is also some evidence of a quiet schism from the Primitives to Chartism around this time: not a shift from religion to politics, the Keighley Primitive Methodist chapel and the Round Hill chapel in Northowram severed their Methodist connection and carried on as religious and political centres more comfortably within the Chartist movement.[27]

As could be expected, most hostility came from and went towards the Wesleyans. The Rev. W. V. Jackson of Leigh lost no opportunity to point out that two of the main prosecution witnesses against Stephens were active Wesleyans – Dale, a class-leader, and Boardman a preacher. Clearly the episode at Leigh was being used by both sides to settle old scores. Jackson, once a shoemaker, had seceded from the Wesleyans and was now pastor of a radical congregation called the Christian Society which devotedly continued to see to his needs during a later period of imprisonment for his Chartist activity. After asserting that "all sects of Methodists universally deviated from the truth of God, and condemned Mr. Stephens for preaching it", Jackson exhorted Wesleyans not to contribute to the Centenary Fund but to give their money to the Stephens Defence Fund instead.[28] Another radical, the Rev. William Essler of Stockport, an Aitkenite who was probably once a Wesleyan, enjoyed pointing out the inconsistency of contributions to the Centenary Fund of a Christian group which condoned oppression. In the West Riding of Yorkshire, it was the Wesleyans who expelled their local preachers for Chartist activity: J. A. Sloane of Dalston who took the chair at a pro-Stephens meeting was discharged. The Wesleyans of Leeds threatened to expel any preacher who attended the Peep Green meeting on 21st May and the Huddersfield circuit carried out the threat against Benjamin Haigh, the Halifax circuit against Abraham Hanson.[29]

II

From May, as the Chartist agitation moved towards a climax, there was a quickening of religious activity – both more use of religious forms in the movement and also more collective confrontation with Christian denominations. The summer of 1839 was widely expected to have pivotal historic and cosmic importance. Until May there was still hope that the House of Commons, under massive pressure from the people, might grant the National Petition and thereby suddenly act as the instrument of God's will or as the purifier of the Constitution in Britain. But in early May ominous clouds began to gather. On 3rd May a royal proclamation appeared which empowered local magistrates to outlaw Chartist meetings virtually at will and this was supplemented by an offer from the Home Secretary, Lord John Russell, to help arm a local force for the protection of life and property. These powers were invoked at varying times in different localities and with varying severity, but wherever local magistrates adopted them, a crisis in social relations ensued. The constitutional nerve was a particularly sensitive one. Chartists felt that the final shred of restraint on power had been torn away by this licence to use force both to suppress their constitutional right of public assembly and to close down their access to customary meeting places, especially those "public" buildings where the constitution was administered like the court-house or the town hall.

Stockport magistrates acted swiftly to ban a meeting scheduled for 9th May. To Chartists this was a stab in the back from the Liberals, whom they had helped to win a resounding victory in the local elections of 1838. Although the magistrates pulled back, by permitting daylight meetings, they would not allow Chartists to meet in the court room and so the radicals determined to break up every meeting there until access was granted. One such meeting was the anniversary of the Bible Society. The Chartists were embarrassed about the occasion: it was not the Bible they had meant to attack, although the episode was interpreted in that way by the outraged local bourgeoisie. Indeed the first demonstration in an Anglican church was partly conceived to redeem the Chartists from the charge of being "infidels, and therefore not fit to be trusted with the suffrage".[30]

An atmosphere of high tension surrounded the Whit-tide meetings, scheduled to take place simultaneously across the country on 21st May and intended as an awesome show of strength just before the National Petition was presented to parliament. The Chartists tried to be impeccably constitutional in their procedure. In the West Riding of Yorkshire, for example, a large number of householders requisitioned the lord lieutenant of the county to call the Peep Green meeting.[31] Here (as elsewhere) not only did the lord lieutenant refuse, but twenty-four county magistrates declared the meeting illegal and swore in a special constabulary. The stage seemed set for another Peterloo (although in the event, the day passed off without incident). The Chartists responded by putting themselves forward as the arbiters of constitutionality and summoned the demonstration themselves. In west Yorkshire they seemed intent upon demonstrating that they were the true Christians as well, no doubt having very much in mind the way that some Nonconformist officialdom was obstructing the campaign for Stephens and trying to intimidate preachers from taking part in Chartist meetings. The massive Peep Green demonstration was one of the first to take on some of the features of a Primitive Methodist camp meeting: it opened with a prayer led by Thornton and then with a hymn whose words had been published the previous week in the *Northern Star*. Chartist preachers Arran, Rushton and Hanson all raised the themes of true and false Christianity while speaking to the final resolution which urged a boycott of hostile churches:

> it is the opinion of this meeting that civil liberty is in perfect agreement with the precepts held forth by the founder of the Christian religion, Jesus Christ; and that all ministers who are faithful and true to their calling will uphold the same. We are therefore resolved not to attend any place of worship where the administration of the services are inimical to civil liberty, or where the ministers refuse to declare the whole truth unto the people, as contained in the Word of God, and will therefore meet in such way and manner in our separate localities in future, as the trying circumstances of the case requires, until the ministers of all denominations come forward to aid us in our most holy struggle in the establishment of the whole of our institutions upon that golden rule which says – "Do unto others as ye would they should do unto you".[32]

Seeking a safer venue, in mid-May the Convention had moved from London to Birmingham and declared: "the mask of CONSTITUTIONAL LIBERTY is thrown for ever aside, and the face of Despotism stands hideously before us". Birmingham was chosen because several of its middle-class political leaders and magistrates had been Chartist supporters and even Convention delegates.[33] But 4th July revealed that no place was safe. To help put down Chartist meetings in the Bull Ring, the authorities imported a body of London police who attacked the crowd and provoked a riot. Arrests were indiscriminate and treatment harsh, culminating in death sentences on three prisoners at the August assizes. Then, on 12th July, by an overwhelming majority, the House of Commons rejected the National Petition with its 1,280,000 signatures. Now began an awesome time, when a decisive confrontation became imminent and inevitable. "These are the times that try men's souls", warned the Bristol Female Patriotic Association, "our country is on the verge of the mightiest revolution that ever occurred in the annals of history; ancient or modern".[34] The Chartists now had to implement their ulterior measures and decide about the gravest step of all, a month-long general strike called the sacred month: after canvassing the country and deciding it was unprepared for such action, the Convention commuted the sacred month to a solemn two- or three-day national holiday, to begin on Monday, 12th August.

Christians on both sides used their most apocalyptic language to articulate the sense of impending revolution, as the national holiday drew near. A collect "appointed to be used in times of war and tumult" was read in several churches in Birmingham on Sunday, 11th August. Before going to trial at the Chester assizes, on 3rd August, the Rev. J. R. Stephens preached an apocalyptic sermon, in which he warned that God's destruction of unrighteous civilizations was a perpetual truth not restricted to biblical times and in which he insisted that a millennial moment was imminent (although he thought the general strike was a design of false prophets):

> We are now arrived at the period when God is saying to us for the last time, "How often – how often would I have gathered you as a nation, taken you under my especial protection, as a hen gathers her brood under her wings, but ye would not!" God, in my judgment, is now giving England her last opportunity – (hear, hear); we are now at the eleventh hour of the day of our salvation – (hear, hear); – we are now favoured with an opportunity of lighting our lamps, of following the bridegroom, of entering in to the marriage supper … All men are agreed in believing that we are on the eve of a change, and a very great change, a very awful change, and perhaps a very sudden change.[35]

The radical Christian idea of the millennium was of an epochal historical change brought about by human agency; in this civilization the agency was to be the awakened people, or the working classes organized into a movement creating, again in the Rev. Stephens's words, "that unity of thought and simultaneousness of action, without which it would seem God, through any people could not act". The Manchester bourgeoisie was reportedly panic-struck by a placard urging

Chartists to "Reserve themselves for the Eleventh Hour".

It was only natural that Chartists with a Christian commitment should seek communion with their God in such grave and climactic times, even before, but especially after the National Petition was rejected. They prayed God "to protect and assist their glorious cause" and, through the devices of worship, ratified the righteousness of their cause.[36] At Peep Green in May, 200,000 had sung:

> God is our Guide! From field, from wave From plough, from anvil and from loom We come, our country's rights to save. And speak a tyrant faction's doom! And hark! We raise from sea to sea The sacred watchword, Liberty .... We will, we will, we will be free.

After Peep Green there were attempts to absorb worship into branch life: indoor services were held in Whitby, Keighley and Leeds. From late July, as ulterior measures were being implemented and the national holiday drew near, as local magistrates became more nervous and swore large numbers of special constables, there was a marked increase of outdoor preaching in the movement on Sundays, with collections sometimes going to the General Defence Fund.[37] Perhaps Chartists felt that a religious form of meeting offered some protection from the authorities: but the outdoor sermons did not take place only in places where meetings had been outlawed, nor were they only cover. Religious forms could serve several purposes at once. From June the Chartist grass roots were increasingly being organized into Methodist-type class groups, which formed a tight and invisible organizational network which could generate simultaneous action in the way that public meetings had before. The idea of classes was formally adopted by a five-county delegate meeting in Rochdale on 25th June (which also urged the holding of camp meetings) and classes visibly multiplied as the situation became more climactic and repressive. Hymns, prayers and religious addresses were also part of some of these class meetings according to spy reports.[38]

Choosing religious forms was not simply an act of political expediency; these came organically out of Chartists' experience and served very real and important additional functions. Revolutionary confrontation is never a light-hearted game. Christian Chartists must have gathered strength and felt their fears and tensions somewhat eased by assurances that they were truly the agents of God's work. Peter Foden told his Chartist audience that "their cause was of God, and whatever the hand of man might attempt to do, God was still on the side of the poor, and they were sure to prosper". Their confidence must have been bolstered by a sense of analogy with biblical characters which might even have allowed them to transcend themselves by imaginatively becoming those characters in a drama with divine reverberations. Not only did biblical calls to battle, like "to your tents, oh Israel", have a special resonance now, but there was a clear identification of the working man with Christ. Just after the queen's proclamation, a Mr. North asked a Bradford meeting:

What did Christ say to the rulers? He said that they did not do justice between man and man, and the rulers then went about to kill him (as our rulers now do to us); and yet for all that, he went to as large a meeting as this is. Christ tried moral force, and when he found that failed, what did he say? Why he said, "if t'hesn't gotten a sword, go an sell the' coit and by one": an I'll give ye t'same advice. Some said this meant the sword of the spirit, but it was a sword that cut a man's ear off. They were told to increase and multiply, and Christ said that no man was to part man and wife; but our laws say that they are to be parted. If he died fighting in their cause he should die fighting for the laws of God and Christ, "and ye know he says I shall have it all made up to me after".[39]

Religion helped to gird the loins, to consecrate the battle and to face the eventuality of dying in the struggle. Between two church demonstrations John Gillespie told the Bolton Chartists that they:

> had been fasting long enough, and now they had begun to pray … They had two more Sundays to go to church before the struggle commenced: and he thought, after three weeks' praying and fasting, if any of them should fall in the struggle, they would be prepared for heaven and he was *almost sure they would be received into it.*

The sense of being part of an epochal watershed of history and of "approaching a great and a holy era" mightgo a long way towards accounting for the upsurge of religious activity within the movement.[40]

III

But why should Christian Chartists (and infidels) bother to demonstrate in the Anglican church? On Sunday, 21st July, a large body of Chartists attended Stockport parish church. From then, peaking in August but continuing into September and even beyond, these demonstrations took place in at least thirty-one localities.[41] They followed a standard pattern. They were directed at the parish church. The demonstration was agreed beforehand, usually at a public meeting, and announced by placard and press advertisement. The Chartists often submitted biblical texts in advance, from which they wanted the minister to preach. On the appointed day the Chartists usually marched in a body, sometimes numbering thousands, some of the group wearing their working clothes, sometimes singing hymns on the way. They reached the church early and proceeded to fill the pews and seats, which were rented or owned, and to pack the aisles before the usual congregation arrived. To the extent that there was any commotion, it developed before the service, when pew-owners tried to eject Chartists: the few punch-ups were started by enraged gentlemen.[42] The service always took place, and if the Chartists hardly ever got the sermon they requested, nonetheless their decorum during the service was usually impressive. I can find only one instance of disruptive heckling, in St. Stephens, Norwich, when "the rev. gormandizer quoted the words of St. Paul, 'I have learned, in whatever station of life, therewith to be content'", and a number of Chartists called out "You get £200 a year – Come and weave bombazines – Put the gas out!".[43] In some places a church demonstration took place only once, but in others, like Bolton and Sheffield, it was repeated over a number of weeks.

To understand the meanings of these demonstrations, it is necessary to consider both their content and their context. Placed in the context of Chartist struggle, the church demonstrations were part of the climactic atmosphere when class relations were becoming very antagonistic, as ulterior measures were being agreed and carried out. Concerted action towards Christian denominations was frequently broached as part of ulterior measures; the earlier Peep Green meeting at Whit, which had urged a boycott of hostile churches, had also sounded West Riding opinion on some of the ulterior measures before the Convention felt able to adopt them formally and issue them as directives to local groups. The first church demonstration was proposed on Saturday, 20th July, after the House of Commons had rejected the Petition, at the same meeting where the Stockport Chartists adopted the ulterior measures so far suggested by the Convention:

> this meeting does hereby resolve to act in strict observance of the recommendation set forth to the people by the Convention: that we do individually and collectively withdraw our money from the Savings' Banks and all other Banks opposed to our interest; that we will convert all our paper money into gold; that we will cease to the utmost of our power to consume, or cause to be consumed, any articles paying taxes to the present government; that we will commence a system of exclusive dealing, and will support those only who will support the Charter; that we will avail ourselves of one of our most ancient privileges, namely, the right to possess the arms of free Englishmen.[44]

The localities were still waiting for the Convention's decision about the sacred month: the directive to take action for only a few days was given on 6th August. The church demonstrations were about equally numerous on Sunday, 4th August, and on the Sunday before the national holiday, 11th August, but they went on into September, still a period of considerable danger and mass arrests.

The Stockport authorities moved sooner. On Tuesday night, 23rd July, after the Saturday meeting and Sunday church demonstration, most of the platform speakers (who were the local leadership) were wrenched from their beds and arrested on charges which included the possession of arms. It is important to stress that the church demonstrations were not the brainchild of some pusillanimous religious rump, but were undertaken by the mainstream local leadership, who, in the case of Stockport, had experienced the whole gamut of oppressive social relations and were familiar with the many different forms, including the religious, that the class war could take. Several were factory spinners, victimized for their militancy in the Union and the Ten Hours movement. Richard Pilling, who had been at Peterloo and who now proposed the resolution on ulterior measures, forced himself to move from the handloom into the factory to save his family from the New Poor Law "bastille"; he later told how mill-owners refused food to his starving child on the grounds that he was a dangerous agitator. Charles Davies, who seconded the motion to go to church, had been unable to get mill work for two years while James Mitchell, once a spinner, was now keeping a beer shop which he claimed gave only a meagre living.

The proposer of the motion to go to church was Isaac Johnson, a smith who had tangled with the Wesleyan brand of Christian charity after Peterloo: although a chapel-goer and Sunday school scholar who had won six prizes, he was expelled for wearing a drab hat and green ribbons and "had since quitted the church". Davies was probably a dischurched Christian: he declared himself a Calvinist when later questioned in jail and in the ruckus of the Bible Society meeting in June had called the Bible "a blessed book, because it proves not only that Christ was the first man who was persecuted for the poor's sake, but it told them to 'love thy neighbour as thyself … They liked the Bible – he never denied it – but the people will not any longer have false teachers".[45] Quite a spectrum of religious belief and affiliation was represented on the platform of the Stockport meeting about ulterior measures, ranging from Mitchell, a practising Catholic, to Frederick L. P. Fogg, a practising socialist: all supported the church demonstrations.[46]

Since ulterior measures were the Chartists' strongest means (short of insurrection) of confronting and pressurizing the full range of their opponents, it was not surprising that they took on the state church in this context. The Anglican church held an established place in radical demonology as the immoral handmaiden of a corrupt political order, and a long-standing analysis of its religious bankruptcy together with decades of experience of its political role were mobilized in this moment of maximum confrontation. To constitutional radicals, the state church was at the centre of the Old Corruption and, as much as any idle aristocrat or sinecurist, was fleecing the industry of the people, particularly by means of compulsory tithes and church rates: "More Pigs and Less Parsons" was a banner which reappeared at Chartist meetings. Radical Christians bolstered the same point with biblical analogies: from Jeremiah, Thornton drew "a striking parallel between the iniquities practised by the priests, rulers and governors of the Jewish people … and modern priests, and rulers, who, like their prototypes of old, rob God and the poor, and say 'wherein have we robbed thee'". To compound the felony, the clergy preyed on the most vulnerable of the poor, who were their special responsibility to protect. "Who devour widows' houses and make long prayers?", asked a Chartist banner, which replied with a portrait of a bishop and the words "wolves in sheep's clothing": the *Star* made much of funeral incidents where the clergy quibbled about burying working people because fees were not forthcoming. Many other elements entered into the critique: the clergy grew rich while the flock grew poor; the clergy preached false doctrine and submission to corrupt power; the clergy in their Evangelical zeal foreclosed the rare moments of working-class pleasure and rest.[47]

The corrupted church was juxtaposed to the true church, which was the property of the people. The claim to possession rested not only on the grounds that working people in the aggregate actually financed the parish church but also on a historical argument that the Church of England had come out of the theft of the property of the people at the Reformation. Following William Cobbett's line of argument, the Rev. J. R. Stephens insisted that tithes were originally established to provide the poor with:

> all that they wanted to make themselves comfortable and happy: and the clergy were to have all that was necessary to maintain them, not in pride, pomp and luxury, but as became their sacred calling, humbly and meekly, as did their master Jesus Christ. Thus this question existed until the Reformation, when the property of the people was plundered to give to the ancestors of my Lord John Russell [the Home Secretary] and others ... by Henry VIII.[48]

The only way to redeem the Anglican church was to restore it to the people. Disestablishment had long been part of radical programmes but, in the period around the sacred days, repossession could be imminent and the church demonstration a symbolic taste of things to come. The idea most commonly expressed, on the few occasions when Chartists can be heard talking before church demonstrations, was that "the parish church is our own" (as Davies put it at Stockport) "and we will for the last time go to hear the parson, before the people take possession of their own public property".[49]

The state church was a notorious symbol of enclosure but enclosure at present by a particular establishment. The church was embedded in the structure of Tory-Anglican power (mainly landed but industrial too) which was always present and sometimes in control of the towns, where the Chartists were active. The Chartist church demonstrations must also be placed in the context of the challenge to the political role of the church and this establishment, an attack which had been gathering local momentum for a decade. The bishops' resistance to the Reform Bill in 1831 provoked local campaigns against compulsory church rates which became increasingly militant over the 1830s. A coalition of working-class radicals and Nonconformist Whigs or Liberals opposed the church rates, each for their own reasons.[50] The Whigs fought compulsion, not only on conscientious grounds, but as part of their duel with the Tories for local political control. Radicals were discriminating in the way they made or unmade their alliances. While supporting the Whigs on the issue of church rates, they sometimes, as in Manchester and Bradford, opposed the bid to incorporate the borough (under the Municipal Corporations Act of 1835), the decisive step towards Whig political ascendancy.

In some places, like Bradford, radicals would line up with Anglican Tories against Nonconformist Whigs on the questions of the New Poor Law and Ten Hours legislation for factory labour. But even in Bradford (which had one trusted Anglican minister in Parson Bull), the vestry had adjourned every year since 1835 without fixing a rate and, so clamorous did proceedings become that the vicar, the Rev. Henry Heap, was seized by a fit after the 1838 meeting (and was replaced in 1839 by the more militant Dr. Scoresby). In one town at least, the church rate dispute reached a climax during the summer of 1839: in Rochdale the amount of the rate was taken to a five-day town poll in July by the vicar, none other than the Rev. W. R. Hay, "Old Peterloo" himself, who was accused of keeping the hustings open for an unwarranted extra two hours in the hope that the vote would go his way.[51]

To radicals, the Rev. Hay, who had chaired the magistrates and read the Riot Act at Peterloo, exemplified how the corrupted church and civil tyranny overlapped. The role of clergy as magistrates had been a major theme in a crescendo of anticlericalism from the late eighteenth century onwards and it was being keenly felt in Chartist lives at this time of crisis. On the county benches, the justices were still largely Anglican Tories and, among them, clergymen made a conspicuous appearance.[52] Even in the newly incorporated towns, where Chartists would appear in the first instance before the new borough benches often composed of Whigs, local vicars who were or who had been county magistrates, like the Rev. Prescott of Stockport, would still symbolize the compromised nature of the church. In the unincorporated towns, Chartists would be brought before a petty sessions of the county bench which often included clerical magistrates. By virtue of being justices of the peace the clergy were implicated in just the kinds of incidents which triggered Chartist outrage and occasioned the relatively rare episodes of Chartist violence. The local crisis which always ensued when magistrates closed down the right of public assembly and free speech has already been noted: the Peep Green motion to boycott hostile churches was also aimed at the clerical magistrates who had agreed to the order outlawing the meeting. Equally provocative was the arrest and trial of Chartist prisoners, which often occasioned rescue attempts involving violence (usually stone-throwing).

In Sheffield, where the church demonstrations were the most protracted, extending over five consecutive weeks, protest against the Anglican clergy's role in local repression certainly played a part. Here, the magistrates waited until the national holiday to put teeth into their earlier declaration that Chartist meetings were illegal. On Tuesday, 13th August, they arrested two local leaders, one of whom was Peter Foden, a baker by trade, and an "independent" Christian who had been preaching outdoor sermons for several weeks, who was now charged with attending an illegal meeting in Paradise Square, the customary place of outdoor political assembly. A crowd gathered at the town hall, where the prisoners were being held, partly of a mind to free them. The military and police arrived led by two magistrates, the Rev. G. Chandler and Mr. Charles Brownell, who read the Riot Act. A riot ensued and over seventy were arrested. On Wednesday these and other magistrates remanded Foden and Fox in custody outside Sheffield without bail to await the assizes. On Sunday the 18th, the Chartists convened in Paradise Square, and then paraded to the cathedral singing hymns, in a body so numerous that an overspill meeting was necessary in the churchyard.[53]

The context in which the demonstrations took place was explosive, yet their content was strikingly restrained. Even though pew rents and sales were hated, there was no destruction of property, and no violence which resulted in anything worse than a few bruises. Such restraint did not operate elsewhere in the culture: the Rev. John Mason Neale expressed his opposition by taking an axe and hacking up the pews in his church in Crawley, Sussex.[54] Chartist demonstrations were not the most clamorous meetings to take place in the parish church. At some of the huge open vestry meetings, especially in the early 1830s, not only did the "unwashed" commandeer the pews, but they participated with great vocal gusto throughout the proceedings, presenting to hostile eyes "all the features of a beer garden".[55] Nor were church visits the most rowdy demonstrations in the Chartist repertoire at the time. Take-overs of Anti-Corn Law meetings or of meetings sponsored by religious groups on issues like national education or the sabbath, involved packing the hall, putting a radical into the chair and passing resolutions favourable to the radical cause – all this accompanied by continual uproar.[56] The Chartists did not try to capture the pulpit of the parish church. To the extent that they wished to spell out a different kind of service or sermon, they held additional afternoon or evening meetings, churchyard overspill meetings, or visited friendly churches like St. James', Bradford, with a trusted cleric, like Parson Bull, in charge.[57]

Chartist decorum during the service was, on the whole, impressive, a fact admitted even by the most hostile observers. The Bolton "gentleman" who reported how "one man was actually smoking in the gallery, and others had the impudence to *** and a great number of them in front of the gallery were seen asleep", conceded that the Chartists "generally behaved themselves well during divine service".[58] Chartist restraint was the more remarkable considering the provocation from the pulpit. On one of the most insulting occasions, when the junior curate of Ashton announced as his text, "my house is a house of prayer but ye have made it a den of thieves", the Chartists made perhaps their most extreme response: they immediately left the church. The next week, when the minister preached their chosen text, James v. 1-5, "there was not the slightest breach of decorum". Never did the Chartists make it impossible for the service to take place.[59]

This restraint was for a purpose. The Chartists were determined to expose the moral bankruptcy of the established church and demonstrate who had the moral authority in this time of crisis. As Davies of Stockport put it, they would "prove they were moral men, and inclined to be religious men, if they know where true religion were taught. (Hear)".[60] The parish church was a splendid symbolic theatre. As part of the state and as the meeting-place for the vestry system of local government, it was a location where the Constitution as well as religion was administered and thus a good symbolic setting for dramatizing who had constitutional and Christian legitimacy. The order of the procession to church sometimes demonstrated who were the legitimate people in the Constitution. In Nottingham, where General Napier, the commander of the army for the north, was stationed, the Chartists placed themselves at the head of the parade of troops to the parish church. In Brad-ford, the Chartist parade was headed by the Member of Convention, Peter Bussey, who established himself in a pew close to the altar, while the parlia-mentary member and active local magistrate, E. C. Lister, had to retire, finding his pew occupied by some collier lads. In Newcastle, when only the "Gentry, Clergy and Freeholders of the County" had been invited to meet the judges of assize on Saturday, the Chartists "out of respect" invited themselves to meet the same judges at church on Sunday, in a placard ending with the words "God save the People!".[61]

The demonstrations were rich in double-edged tones of voice and double meanings, all the more so because the contest was going on within and for possession of the same cultural vocabulary. While the Chartists were trying to display their own moral authority, they were also, in a satirical and even aggressive way, showing their contempt for Anglican usurpation of Christi-anity and Constitution. Their rhetoric was an assertion of true belief, recall-ing the church to her duties, but their action was a calculated insult to key features of Anglican-style church-going, which the congregations felt to be vital and reverent but the Chartists considered unchristian and designed to keep the workers out. The experiences of 1839 intensified a kind of schizo-phrenia in class perception, where different social groups gave antagonistic definitions to the same thing. Just as the Chartists' public meeting was the magistrates' illegal meeting and the Chartists' people was the middle class's mob, so the issue of the pews and of dress exposed incompatible attitudes. The Anglicans bitterly complained about the deliberate mockery of some Chartists appearing in working aprons and clogs, sometimes uncombed, unwashed and unshaven.[62] No doubt Chartists did mean to show disrespect to Anglican-style church-going; but, at the same time, wearing a militant badge of class in this capi-talist setting asserted the value of their labour in the sight of God and the inanity of exclusion (and self-exclusion) because of dress.[63] If dress and church segregation were part of the sustaining theatricality of the eighteenth-century ruling class, then the Chartists were clearly out to demystify and discard the props.[64] Wearing working clothes in the other class's auditorium was not incompatible with wearing your best attire in your own proletarian chapels, although there were accounts of worship with preachers (like Rushton) and congregations wearing working clothes as the best they could afford.[65]

The occupation of the pews was more contentious. It involved at once a gesture of menace to private property and the disruption of a carefully contrived display of social hierarchy.[66] The Chartists were dramatizing the equality of all men before God and particularly their "equality with their proud oppressors which is denied them elsewhere". They were also protesting against the establishment of private property in the parish church leaving the poor only the humiliating free seats: "by what authority has this been done?", asked a Bolton correspondent, "who has made this into private property, which was once part and portion of the state, and still maintained by church rate?"[67] To the Chartists, this enclosure of church space had nothing to do with real religion. It was in the course of commandeering the often-locked pews that the most undignified acrobatics, yelling and rough-housing took place. Such fist fights as broke out seemed to involve powerful local "gentlemen", who were sometimes notorious for hounding radicals and who would have been provoked beyond endurance by such seizure of their property. In Ashton the "enraged gentleman" who struck a Chartist was John Howard, the Hyde magistrate and factory owner who had fired workers for supporting the Rev. J. R. Stephens.[68] In Sheffield the Mr. Sorby who sat on a Chartist's lap and whose friend started a punch-up was probably the local Tory kingmaker. His pew became the locus for the collision of two antagonistic views of property: "Mr. Sorby said that the pew was his, and he wished to have it. A man said, 'we pay Easter Dues, and have as much right to it as you have'. Mr. Sorby said 'I pay Easter Dues, and £6 a year for the pew beside'".

The texts submitted by the Chartists not only conveyed the content of the Christianity they wanted to hear, but also their ideal of the clergy as enemies, not allies, of oppression. Usually the texts dealt either with the claims of the poor, or the value of the workers compared with the idle rich, or the duties of the rich to the poor, or the divine judgement and punishment which would fall upon the powerful who abused their power. A choice of four texts was offered by the Stockport Chartists: "Six days shalt thou labour"; "he that will not work, neither shall he eat"; "thou shalt not worship any graven image"; "As Jesus said to the young man who professed to be perfect, 'If thou wilt be perfect, go and sell that thou hast and give it to the poor'".[69] But the most requested text was James v. 1-6:

> Go to now, ye rich men, weep and howl for your miseries that shall come upon you.
> Your riches are corrupted, and your garments motheaten.
> Your gold and silver is cankered; and the rust of them shall be a witness against you, and shall eat your flesh as it were fire. Ye have reaped treasure together for the last days.
> Behold, the hire of the labourers who have reaped down your fields, which is of you

kept back by fraud, crieth: and the cries of them which have reaped are entered into the ears of the Lord of Sabbaoth.

Ye have lived in pleasure on the earth, and been wanton; ye have nourished your hearts as in a day of slaughter.

Ye have condemned and killed the just; and he doth not resist you.[70]

The clergy were in no mood to be told their business by a Chartist mob.They entered into the battle of the Bible with gusto, determined to put the Chartists firmly in their place. The sermons played on themes like: submission to the powers that be, quietness as godliness, contentment with your present station and attention to the afterlife where all due rewards will be meted out. The texts submitted by the Stockport Chartists were ignored: the Rev. Prescott instead preached on "What must I do to be saved?" and urged his hearers "not to struggle for temporal things, but for eternal salvation". The Blackburn Chartists got their James v, but from a Dr. Whittaker who insisted that while the Roman rich might have been culpable, to castigate the modern rich would be "the grossest injustice". He exhorted the Chartists to "patience and endurance" and obedience to the existing authorities.[71] The clergy could not have played their parts better had they set out to prove the Chartist case that they were wolves in sheep's clothing who legitimized oppression while pretending to speak the word of God. The setting of public confrontation was not one in which the clergy could be expected to extend an olive branch: but they went extravagantly to the opposite extreme, heaping fulsome praise on the existing social order, allowing the Chartists no shred of dignity or vestige of a case.

The vicar of Preston, the Rev. R. Carus Wilson, was asked to preach on James ii. 15-16: "If a brother or sister be naked, and destitute of daily food, and one of you say unto them, depart in peace, by ye warmed and filled; notwithstanding ye give them not those things which are needful to the body; what does it profit?" Instead he preached two weeks running on Job xxxiv. 29 starting: "When he giveth quietness, who then can make trouble?". He asked: "was there anything in the state of the country to justify a discontented spirit and to call for turbulence and trouble?". His answer was a resounding NO. Social inequality was inevitable but "in happy England every man was protected in the possession of his earnings, Đ every man was sure to reap the benefits of his energy and prudence". As for religion, "we possessed the most enlightened, the most pious, the most industrious clergy, and the most tolerant church in the Christian world". If God had partly "hidden his face" from the nation recently, this was because Chartists did not ascribe "the evils of their condition to their own misconduct, they were too apt to lay them at the door of the virtuous and the Godly". Also there was a want of "Christian tone" in government, exampled not by the Poor Law but by "the injury done to the holy sacrament of baptism by the registration act". Finally he gave comfort to those wishing "to promote a Godly quietness", assuring them that ultimately they would have "run a good race" and would find repose "on the bosom of . . . God".[72] Carus Wilson's sermon was only a local event. But the Religious Tract Society printed, and widely distributed, a number of the other anti-Chartist sermons, including one by a Rev. Evan Jenkins who argued relentlessly to the conclusion that "the Church of England and Chartism totally oppose each other".[73]

The church demonstrations further inflamed what the bourgeoisie and gentry also saw as a revolutionary situation in which they had everything to lose. Assaults on private property (the pews), the loosening of religious restraint and even, in the case of Cheltenham, women Chartists so perverted as to stage the church visit themselves, raised up (even in the Nonconformist imagination) the recurrent ruling-class nightmare of the French Revolution. The Rev. Close accused the Cheltenham women of becoming like their French sisters, who "glutted themselves with blood; and danced like maniacs amidst the most fearful scenes of the Reign of Terror!"[74] There was a time in the eighteenth century when an anonymous note posted on the parish church recalling the rich to their duties to the poor was one recognized signal to the gentry that it was time to give a bit of ground in order to preserve a power equilibrium that was basically in their favour.[75] In the 1839 crisis there was no question of accommodation to Chartist demands. The Chartists seemed out to seize power altogether: they were met only with increased displays of ruling-class power. Faced with the threat of imminent revolution, the Anglican and Nonconformist factions in the ruling class could (however petulantly) close ranks. Even where, as in Bolton, a Whig mayor was reluctant to produce a show of force at the three church demonstrations (and was pilloried by the Tory press for his inactivity), there was no hesitation about pouncing on Chartists during the national holiday.[76] In other localities armed force was paraded in church, but nowhere did the crescendo of conflict reach such a pitch as in Sheffield.

Two weeks of well-behaved but enormous church visits were enough for the Sheffield churchwardens, who got leave from the magistrates to declare that meetings in the churchyard constituted trespassing. On Sunday, 1st September, police occupied Paradise Square, where the Chartists usually formed up, and also cleared the churchyard. On the 8th, police actually entered the church and, perhaps fortified by their presence, pew-holders now tried to eject Chartists and scuffles broke out: Thomas Mason, a tailor occupying Sorby's pew, was arrested. This, along with another arrest in mid-week, triggered a large silent protest meeting, which turned into a riot when confronted by the magistrates the Rev. Chandler and Mr. Brownell with troops and police: some thirty-six more were arrested. On Saturday, the bench, which sat to hear the Chartist cases and included the Rev. W. Alderson and the Venerable Archdeacon Corbett, was determined to make examples. Mason, for arguing that there was nothing in the prayer-book to justify turning Chartists out of the pews, not even for striking a blow, was sent to quarter sessions and allowed bail only on production of two enormous sureties, each of £50 (compared with a fine of 2s. 6d. levied on a drunk for a violent disturbance in a pub). The next Sunday, the 15th, Chartists witnessed the extraordinary spectacle of the "Poor Man's Church" totally barred against him:

> "To the poor the Gospel is preached". "Whatsoever ye do unto one of the least of these, my brethren, ye do it unto me", said the holy Jesus during his sojourn upon earth, and the Church *professes* to follow his maxims up by dubbing itself the "Poor Man's Church". Yet no "straight gate or narrow way", but a band of armed policemen, and a host of special constables, backed by a troop of dragoons, in readiness if wanted, shut up the entrance to the Church, and the garb of poverty was a sufficient reason for exclusion. It was an extraordinary exhibition, in England, to see a dozen policemen armed with cutlasses surrounding the Church-yard gates on the outside, a posse of constables inside, stationed about five or six yards apart around the inside of the railings, admitting only those who had good coats on their backs, and whose *respectable* external appearance would warrant the conclusion that they were not Chartists. The "Poor Man's Church" now calls in the aid of the civil power and the military to prevent the poor from contaminating with their presence the cushioned pews and velvet hassocks of her more wealthy and aristocratic sons.[77]

The church demonstrations had reached the end of their logic. Faced with a challenge and an alternative, the Anglican church simply overacted the role that had caused the offence in the first place. The church even became an armed battleground in the class war.

IV

After 1839, Chartists staged fewer church demonstrations.[78] The tactic, however, passed into the radical repertoire and was used more disruptively by the Owenite socialists and then later in the century by the Social Democratic Federation as part of their agitation for the unemployed.[79] The decline of Chartist church visits did not mean an end to confrontation with the Anglican church. The Chartists became more militant in local fights over church rates: they spoke powerfully at vestry meetings (even when they had no vote), contested and actually won churchwarden elections and resisted payment where rates had been levied (one Norwich Chartist paid his church rates to the Vincent Defence Fund).[80] Within the movement, abuse was continually hurled at the state church in Chartist lectures and religious services.

During the experiences of 1839, Chartists had become more determined to apply to ruling-class religion the principle of boycott which underlay the other ulterior measures (withdrawal of money from savings banks, boycott of excisable articles, boycott of hostile shopkeepers, exclusive dealing only with supporters). In May at Peep Green, Chartists had been instructed to boycott hostile churches and chapels, while in August, Durham Chartists advised "the people to keep away from the desecrated chapels, desecrated by wolves in sheep's clothing, till the priesthood advocates the Christian doctrines of equality".[81] When the national holiday failed to deliver a quick Charter, the ulterior measures were installed as a longer-term strategy, which involved not only boycotts, but developing the practice of collective self-provision through Chartist branch life. From mid-August onwards, abstention from taxable articles, especially alcoholic drink, often turned into Chartist teetotalism and led to the adoption of a new kind of festivity from the socialists, the tea-party, soiree and ball, which catered for the whole family and served as an invaluable fund-raising function. Exclusive dealing developed, in many places, into Chartist co-operative stores, with profits often going to families of imprisoned comrades.[82] The appropriation of religious worship, which began in the summer during the height of the agitation, continued into the autumn and eventually became an integral feature of Chartist branch life in many places through, and beyond, the next phase of "political" excitement in 1842.[83]

The new developments in Chartist strategy gained momentum in England in the spring of 1840 as part of the revival which culminated in the founding of the National Charter Association in July. During the preceding autumn and winter months, many local Chartists had faded temporarily from view as insurrectionary attempts at Newport, Dewsbury, Bradford and Sheffield provoked even heavier repression. If the strategy of the first eight months of 1839 had been to mount a massive democratic constitutional drama, the accent was now also on grass-roots organization, to cultivate a vigorous branch life which would develop a staunch Chartist following, capable of sustaining a long-term struggle and making the best social use of the Charter once it was won. Prefigurative strategy, or enabling people to experience the shape of things to come while agitating, was still a major concern but this time the democratic principle was also applied to the government of local groups, to education, to recreation and to religion. An NCA missionary lectured the Stockport Chartists on:

> the question of total abstinence, as a powerful lever in gaining their liberties, on forming day schools for training their own offspring; on adopting their own forms of faith; getting their own places of worship; their debating societies; a growing interest in each other's welfare; and, by a steady devotion to the cause of democracy, they would be triumphant.[84]

In Scotland, where repression was less severe, branch life elaborated more quickly: by October 1839 regular religious services were held in at least eight localities, spreading to thirty places during 1840, with twenty taking the further step of formally setting up a Christian Chartist Church.[85] In England few local groups organized into Chartist churches but, by 1841, many NCA branches were holding services on Sundays in the same rooms where they had weekday meetings, including socialist halls and pubs: Chartist hymn-books were compiled to meet the growing demand.[86] From prison, the leader Feargus O'Connor made a fierce attack on Church Chartism, aimed particularly at the Birmingham Chartist Church, for standing outside the NCA and dividing the movement. Nevertheless, as the editor of the *Star*, the Rev. William Hill, insisted, most other Christian Chartists "were the most consistent advocates of the Charter and of the National Charter Association, to which they serve as the most powerful right hands; and of which the proof is, that nearly all the most able and talented of the Chartist lecturers and missionaries have found it necessary to become preachers". It is fitting to leave the last word to Hill, not only because he understood the importance of religion in the Chartist agitation but because he so clearly grasped the religious lessons that Chartists had learned in their struggle:

> they find that in almost all churches and chapels, appertaining to whatever sect, the principles of social benevolence and justice, of civil equality and of political right, though recognised by the Bible, are denounced by the priesthood; and hence their determination to erect their own temples, and offer their own worship, to the God of Justice, whom they serve.[87]

Notes

[1] *Northern Liberator*, 7 Sept. 1839.

[2] Many historians, starting with R. G. Gammage, *History of the Chartist Movement, 1837-1854* (London, 1854), 2nd edn. (London, 1894), have studied Chartism as a national movement seen from its centre, while the local studies approach pioneered in A. Briggs (ed.), *Chartist Studies* (London, 1959), has stimulated much work which focuses more on the socio-economic roots of Chartist action than on the forms of that action. However, for activity in the round, see A. Wilson, *The Chartist Movement in Scotland* (Manchester, 1970); D. Jones, *Chartism and the Chartists* (London, 1975); and my study of socialist branch life, "Robert Owen and Radical Culture", in S. Pollard and J. Salt (eds.), *Robert Owen: Prophet of the Poor* (London, 1971). Also see in J. Epstein and D. Thompson, eds. *The Chartist Experience* (London, 1982) pp. 345-80.

[3] The prevailing view, shared both by Marxist and non-Marxist historians, with Halevy the most influential of the latter, is that nineteenth-century Christianity was mainly ruling-class territory or serviceable to the continuance of capitalism. For a useful review of the Halevy thesis and the debate it has provoked, cf. R. Moore, "The Political Effects of Village Methodism", in M. Hill (ed.), *A Sociological Yearbook of Religion in Britain*, vi (London, 1973). The predominant view is strong in Chartist studies, e.g., J. K. Edwards, "Chartism in Norwich", *Yorks. Bull. of Econ. and Social Research*, no. 19 (1967), p.100, despite the early work of H. U. Faulkner, *Chartism and the Churches: A Study in Democracy* (New York, 1916), pointing to the active conflict over true religion. Coming from a different concern, seeking a form of Christianity relevant to modern social conditions, a group of historians of religion, starting with E. T. Wickham, *Church and People in an Industrial City* (London, 1957), have also argued that Christianity was enclosed by the affluent classes, while the urban poor, receiving little accommodation or prophecy, remained indifferent. More recently, the amount of conflict and schism has been stressed in R. Currie, *Methodism Divided* (London, 1968) and by W. R. Ward, *Religion and Society in England* (London, 1972), who gives a detailed picture of the social struggle over religion at Peterloo time but (pp. 201-2) only a cursory sketch

of the Chartist period.

[4] The clerical magistrates were Rev. W. R. Hay, chairman of Salford quarter sessions, absentee vicar of Ackworth, Yorks., and nephew of an earl, who was rewarded for his role at Peterloo with the rich living of Rochdale, and Rev. C. W. Ethelston, a pluralist with livings in Manchester and Flintshire: D. Read, *Peterloo: The "Massacre" and its Background* (Manchester, 1958), pp. 75-7, 201-5; Ward, *Religion and Society in England*, pp. 88-95; E. P. Thompson, *The Making of the English Working Class* (London, 1963), pp. 684-7. Peterloo really was a massacre: the relief committee tally was 11 dead, more than 421 wounded, with 160 more cases still to investigate.

[5] G. A. Williams, *Rowland Detrosier, a Working-Class Infidel, 1800-1834* (Borthwick Papers, no. 28, York, 1965), gives a lively picture of Lancashire infidelism, which had many features of a replacement faith. E. Royle feels that Owenite socialism then absorbed much of the infidel tradition and argues that "few Chartists went as far as many Owenites, or Harney and O'Brien, in rejecting Christianity": *The Infidel Tradition from Paine to Bradlaugh* (London, 1976) and *Chartism* (London, 1980), pp. 80-1. For the experience of persecution and the reassertion of true Christianity, *Manchester Observer*, Sept. 1819 ff., especially the texts cited by "A Lover of Justice and of Souls", *ibid.*, 6 Nov. 1819, including Proverbs xiv. 31 and James v. 1-6, which were also much used in Chartism. A wedge must not be driven too far between radical Christians and infidels, who shared common religious enemies, treated them with equal sarcasm and aggression and sometimes worked amicably together, even if Christians, unlike infidels, gave a special authority to the Bible and Christ: e.g. Stephensite Methodists lent their pulpits to socialist infidels who conversely raised funds for Rev. Stephens's defence: *New Moral World*, 2 Sept. 1837; *Northern Star*, 16 Mar. 1839. After Peterloo, radical Wesleyans in Lancashire remained dischurched, joined friendlier denominations or, as on Tyneside, whole chapels became autonomous and sometimes joined a loose federation of Independent Methodists: Read, *Peterloo*, pp. 203-4 for movement to the New Connexion and Primitive Methodists; Peter Lineham, "The English Swedenborgians, 1770-1840: A Study in the Social Dimensions of Religious Sectarianism" (Univ. of Sussex Ph.D. thesis, 1978), p. 316; Ward, *Religion and Society in England*, pp. 92-3 for Independent chapels. In west Yorkshire radicals seemed able to stay in the Wesleyan orbit until the Chartist period, when lay preachers were expelled and large-scale secession of radical congregations took place in the Reform movement of 1849 onwards (and during the Barkerite breakaway from the New Connexion in 1841): E. V. Chapman, *John Wesley and Co.* (Halifax, 1952), chs. 6-7, for the impact of schisms in the Halifax area; Currie, *Methodism Divided*, pp. 65 ff., and Faulkner, *Chartism and the Churches*, pp. 82-3, 91-3 for the Reform controversy. More research is needed to clarify the picture.

[6] Banners with favoured religious texts were carried in the Ten Hours and Anti-Poor Law movements (*Times*, 18 May 1837 for examples) and banners (sometimes bloodstained) which had been at Peterloo or were made to mark the tragic events were carried into Chartist times: *Northern Star*, 29 Sept., 16 Oct., 3 Nov. 1838. For Methodist trade unionists in Belper using the Bible to defend themselves against threat of expulsion and then setting up a schismatic chapel, *Herald of the Rights of Industry* [Manchester], 15 Feb. 1834. For later use of popular Chartist texts, Nigel Scotland, "The Role of Methodism in the Origin and Development of the Revolt of the Field in Lincolnshire, Norfolk and Suffolk, 1872-1926" (Univ. of Aberdeen Ph.D. thesis, 1975), pp. 185-8.

[7] For this banner text or similar variants, cf. *Northern Star*, 6 Jan., 29 Sept., 16, 20 Oct. 1838, 9 Feb. 1839.

[8] Rev. J. R. Stephens reported in *ibid.*, 27 Oct. 1838. For Stephens, see pp. 114 ff. below; for Rev. Bull, J. C. Gill, *Parson Bull of Byerley* (London, 1953). Once a hand-loom weaver and also active in the factory movement, Rev. Hill remained the minister of Bethel Chapel, Hull, during his period of editorship: cf. J. A. Epstein, "Feargus O'Connor and the Northern Star", *Internat. Rev. Social Hist.*, xxi (1976), p. 81.

[9] *Northern Star*, 20 Jan. 1838, 30 Mar. 1839, for Amblerthorne New Connexion Methodists walking out before a sermon by Rev. G. Beaumont, the circuit minister and a Poor Law guardian, to

dramatize "the incongruity of the accursed New Poor Law and that Gospel which enjoins that those 'whom God has joined together no man shall put asunder' ".

[10] Ibid., 16 Oct. 1838; also J. R. Stephens, ibid., 6 Jan., 16 Oct. 1838.

[11] This text and variants were carried by Rochdale, Hyde, and at Newcastle: ibid., 29 Sept., 17 Nov. 1838, 25 May 1839.

[12] Cf. sermons by Stephens and Hill, ibid., 16 Mar., 14 Sept. 1839 for tests of a righteous civilization; ibid., 16 Jan. 1841 for Worcester's use of "Do unto others", the text also requested by Bradford Chartists in their parish church demonstration, *Bradford Observer*, 8 Aug. 1839.

[13] For a useful discussion of early nineteenth-century changes in the concept of the people, Iorwerth Prothero, "William Benbow and the Concept of the 'General Strike' ", *Past and Present*, no. 63 (May 1974), pp. 143-5. Bronterre O'Brien in the *Destructive*, 9 Mar. 1833, exemplifies the working-class radical understanding after 1832: "The people the legitimate source of all power" was usually the opening Chartist toast, whereas the first toast at orthodox political dinners was "the Queen".

[14] Proverbs xiv. 31 carried at Dewsbury and by Almondbury, *Northern Star*, 14 Apr., 16 Oct. 1838; Isaiah iii. 15 carried at Newcastle and Nottingham, *ibid.*, 6 Jan., 10 Nov. 1838; Isaiah x. 1-2, "Woe unto them that decree unrighteous decrees, to turn aside my people from judgment and to take away the rights of my people" on a banner at Derby and in a Barnsley sermon, ibid., 9 Feb. 1839, 3 Apr. 1841. For the biblical roll-call of oppressors, Micah iii. 9-11 and James v. 1-5.

[15] Luke xxii. 36, quoted here, was much used on banners and often coupled with Lamentations iv. 9, "Better to die by the sword than to perish with hunger", ibid., 20 Oct., 17 Nov. 1838. Stephens, ibid., 23 Feb. 1839, for the people as the instruments of salvation.

[16] There was little politico-religious preaching in branch life. In a few places like Middleton, so many meetings took place in the Reformer's or Ebenezer chapel that it is hard to separate what was Chartist from what was religious life. But elsewhere, while chapels had been used for larger meetings against the New Poor Law, groups organizing behind the Charter tended to take rooms in pubs or in halls owned by other working-class organizations: Padiham radicals, e.g., switched from the Unitarian chapel to the Socialist Institution, ibid., 12 Jan. 1839. Rev. Stephens thundered regularly from his pulpits and got coverage in the *Star* but it was not until about June 1839 that these very sermons were read aloud in Chartist gatherings: J. T. Ward, "Revolutionary Tory: The Life of Joseph Rayner Stephens of Ashton-under-Lyne, 1805-79", *Trans. Lancs. and Cheshire Antiq. Soc.*, lxviii (1958), p. 106; *Northern Star*, 22 June 1839.

[17] For the Convention and activity surrounding it, see Gammage, *History of the Chartist Movement*, 2nd edn., chs. 3-7; T. M. Parssinen, "Association, Convention and Anti-Parliament in British Radical Politics, 1771-1848", *Eng. Hist. Rev.*, lxxxviii (1973), pp. 521-30, and esp. J. A. Epstein, "Feargus O'Connor and the English Working-Class Radical Movement, 1832-41" (Univ. of Birmingham Ph.D. thesis, 1977), chs. 3-4, for the best discussion of the constitutionalist strategy. Also K. Judge, "Early Chartist Organization and the Convention of 1839", Internat. *Rev. Social Hist.*,xx (1975); T. Kemnitz, "Approaches to the Chartist Movement: Feargus O'Connor and Chartist Strategy", *Albion*, v (1973).

[18] J. R. Stephens, *The Political Preacher: An Appeal from the Pulpit on Behalf of the Poor* (London, 1839), p. 29. M. S. Edwards, *Joseph Rayner Stephens, 1805-1879* (Wesley Hist. Soc., Lancs, and Cheshire Branch, Occas. Pubn., no. 3, 1968); an admiring biography was written by G. J. Holyoake, the militant secularist, *Life of Joseph Rayner Stephens, Preacher and Political Orator (London*, nd.). For an unconvincing treatment of his views, D. A. Johnson, "Between Evangelicalism and a Social Gospel: The Case of Joseph Rayner Stephens", *Church Hist.*, xlii (1973), pp. 229-42; for his relations with Chartism, T. Kemnitz and J. Fleurange, "J. R. Stephens and the Chartist Movement", *Internal. Rev. Social Hist.*, xix (1974).

[19] Edwards, *J. R. Stephens*, p. 9; "Preachers' Plan for the Ashton Circuit, 1839" of the Stephensite Methodists, in the Tameside Borough Library.

[20] *Northern Star*, 9 Mar. 1839: Stephens's conduct as a minister was described in sketches introducing him to areas where he was not well known, ibid., 5, 12 Jan. 1839; for victimization of Stephen-

sites, ibid., 18 Aug. 1838.

[21] T. Laqueur, *Religion and Respectability: Sunday Schools and Working-Class Culture, 1780-1850* (New Haven, 1976), ch. 3.

[22] S. Rothwell, *Memorials of the Independent Methodist Chapel, Folds Road, Bolton* (Bolton, 1887), pp. 91, 101; *Northern Star,* 22 June 1839, for Stephens's defence sermon at Daisy Hill Methodist schoolroom.

[23] Thompson, *Making of the English Working Class,* pp. 398-400, for Rushton. For Thornton, B. Wilson, *Struggles of an Old Chartist* (Halifax, n.d.), p. 3; for his earlier sermons and itinerary for Stephens, *Northern Star,* 9 June, 14 July 1838, 2 Mar.-6 Apr. 1839. My thanks to John Sanders for finding Thornton's occupation. For Arran, ibid., 8 May 1841; *Leeds Times,* 17 Aug. 1839.

[24] Cutting from the *Boot and Shoemaker,* n.d., in a file compiled by J. Horsfall Turner, Halifax Central Library; C. Hill, *The World Turned Upside Down* (London, 1972), ch. 14, esp. p. 240.

[25] *Northern Star,* 20 Apr, 1839, *Halifax Express,* 13 Apr. 1839, for Amblerthorne which went Barkerite in 1841. For Sutton, *Northern Star,* 13 Apr. 1839, which also reported that Newcastle Dissenting ministers had ostracized a Rev. Wyper for preaching for Stephens.

[26] Ibid., 6 Apr., 30 Mar. 1839. Primitive chapels were lent in Glossop, Dukinfield, Delph in Saddleworth and Heywood (which also condemned Rev. Woodhouse), ibid., 8, 16Mar., 4 May 1839.

[27] Ibid., 23 Feb., 27 Apr., 6 July 1839 for Keighley. Ibid., 9 June 1838, 30 Mar. 1839, *Halifax Express,* 13 Apr. 1839 for Northowram.

[28] *Northern Star,* 16 Mar. 1839. For facts about Jackson's life, Public Record Office, Home Office Papers (hereafter P.R.O., H.O.), 20/10. My thanks to Dorothy Thompson for bringing to my notice this file of "Confidential Reports ... upon ... All Political Offenders in Custody on the 1st Jan. 1841," which contains invaluable biographical details. For Essler, *Northern Star,* 3 Aug. 1839.

[29] Ibid., 18,25 May, 6 July 1839. *Chapman,JohnWesley and Co.,p.* 5 8 for expulsion of Hanson. *Halifax Express,* 25 May 1839 for Bath Wesleyan circuit's decision to expel Chartists. Rev. J. Mallinson, *History of Methodism in Huddersfield, Holmfirth and Denby Dale* (London, 1898), p. 100, mentions a Wesleyan lay preacher, Joseph Newsome, probably the J. Newsome preaching for Stephens who "occasioned the reproof of ... the local preachers". Expulsions of lay preachers are not easy to trace. It was leaders and circuit meetings, rather than Conference, who disciplined lay personnel and their minutes do not always survive; expulsions of laymen were not recorded even in confidential Conference documents.

[30] *Stockport Advertiser,* 28 June, 26 July 1839.

[31] For constitutional procedure, H. U. Jephson, *The Platform: Its Rise and Progress,* 2 vols. (London, 1892), i, pp. 167-9; for its use before Peep Green, *Northern Star,* 25 May 1839. For public order in 1839 as seen from above, stressing the restraint of the authorities compared with the period before 1820, L. Radzinowicz, "New Departures in Maintaining Public Order in the Face of Chartist Disturbances", *Cambridge Law Jl.* (1960), pp. 51-80, and F. C. Mather, *Public Order in the Age of the Chartists* (Man chester, 1959). For a sense of the incompatibility of class perceptions about restraint, Dorothy Thompson, *The Early Chartists* (London, 1971), pp. 23-7.

[32] *Northern Star,* 25 May 1839.

[33] *The Charter,* 19 May 1839; T. R. Tholfsen, "The Chartist Crisis in Birmingham", *Internat. Rev. Social Hist.,* iii (1958), pp. 470-2. E.g. the magistrate P. H. Muntz had been a Convention delegate until he resigned in March 1839; Mayor W. Scholefield had addressed a Chartist rally in 1838; local M.P., T. Attwood, presented the Petition to the Commons. 34. *Northern Star,* 3 Aug. 1839.

[35] Ibid., 17 Aug. 1839. Also on bail, Rev. W. V. Jackson preached a farewell sermon on 11th August on a popular millenarian text: "it will be foul weather today; and the sky is red and lowering. Ye hypocrites, ye can discern the face of the sky but can yet not discern the signs of the times", ibid. *Northern Liberator,* 27 July 1839 for Manchester placard. For the millennium as a concept of social revolution in this period, J.F. C. Harrison, *Robert Owen and the Owenites in England and America* (London, 1969), p. 101.

[36] Part of a prayer, which, along with a patriotic hymn, opened a meeting of the Hull Female Patriotic Association: *Northern Liberator,* 13 July 1839. For Peep Green hymn, *Northern Star,* 18

May 1839.

[37] For indoor services, *ibid., 1*, 8 June, 6 July, 3 Aug. 1839 gave five instances of outdoor preaching.

[38] R.F. Wearmouth, *Methodism and the Working-Class Movements of England, 1800-1850* (London, 1937), pp. 144 ff.; *Northern Liberator*, 20 July, 17, 31 Aug., 14 Sept. 1839 for the class system. For the religious content of class meetings, see spy reports and depositions reprinted in Thompson, *Early Chartists*, pp. 241 ff., 264 ff.; A. J. Peacock, *Bradford Chartism, 1838-1840* (York, 1969), p. 29. Class groups had already been used in working-class movements: cf. W. Lovett, *Life and Struggles in Pursuit of Bread, Knowledge and Freedom* (London, 1876), p. 68 for the National Union of the Working Class and Others, formed in 1831.

[39] *Bradford Observer*, 9 May 1839; *Northern Liberator*, 27 July 1839 for Foden.

[40] *Bolton Free Press*, 3 Aug. 1839; *Northern Liberator*, 20, 27 July 1839 for comments about approaching "a great sabbath" and a "holy era".

[41] Parish church demonstrations took place in Stockport (21 July), Mansfield (21, 28 July), Wigton (21 July), Hyde (28 July), Newcastle (28 July), Bolton (28 July, 4, 11 Aug.), Blackburn (4 Aug.), Bury (4 Aug.), Chorley (4 Aug.), Preston (4, 11 Aug.), Leigh (4 Aug.), Manchester (4 Aug. – see *Manchester and Salford Advertiser*, 10 Aug. 1839 for an account of a visit which the *Manchester Guardian* said did not take place), Rochdale (4 Aug.), Nottingham (4, n Aug.), Bradford (4, 11 Aug.), Ashton (11, 18 Aug.), Barnsley (11 Aug.), Dewsbury (11 Aug.), Chester (11 Aug.), Hull (11 Aug.), London, St. Paul's (11 Aug.), Loughborough (11 Aug.), Norwich (11, 18, 25 Aug. – in a different church each evening and in the cathedral on two of the mornings), Sheffield (18, 25 Aug., I, 8, 15 Sept.), Halifax (18, 25 Aug.), Cheltenham (18, 25 Aug.), London, Spitalfields (25 Aug.), Merthyr (25 Aug.), Bristol (1 Sept.), Darlington (l Sept.), Pontypool (8 Sept.), Dowlais (17 Nov.). Most of these visits were reported in the Chartist press but local newspapers usually gave the fullest accounts. Secondary sources give these demonstrations only cursory mention, e.g., O. Chadwick, *The Victorian Church*, 2 vols. (London, 1966-70), i, pp. 335-6, or Jones, *Chartism*, p. 52.

[42] *Northern Star*, 3 Aug. (Hyde), 17 Aug. (Ashton), 14 Sept. (Sheffield) 1839.

[43] *Northern Liberator*, 31 Aug. 1839; *Bury and Norwich Post, 21* Aug. 1839. For hearty Bristol assents to prayers for delivery from evil councillors, *Northern Star, 14* Sept. 1839; for suppressed hissing in Bradford, *Leeds Times*, 10 Aug. 1839.

[44] *Northern Star*, 27 July 1839.

[45] For Davies, Mitchell and Johnson, *Stockport Advertiser*, 28 June, 26 July 1839, and P.R.O., H.O., 20/10. For Pilling, see also *The Trial of Feargus O'Connor and Fifty-Eight Others at Lancaster, on a Charge of Sedition, Conspiracy, Tumult and Riot* (Manchester, 1843), repr. edn. (New York, 1970), pp. 249, 251, 253.

[46] For Fogg, *New Moral World*, 18 Apr., 2, 9 May 1840. Rev. Stephens was elected as Stockport's Convention delegate but, once arrested, did not take his seat; he was invited to preach in the spring by the same spectrum of Stockport leaders, *StockportAdvertiser*, 29 Mar. 1839.

[47] For earlier radical critiques, E. J. Evans, "Some Reasons for the Growth of English Rural Anti-Clericalism, *c. 1750-c. 1830*", *Past and Present*, no. 66 (Feb. 1975), pp. 84, 106-8; Royle, *Radical Politics*, pp. 6-8; Patricia Hollis, *The Pauper Press: A Study in Working-Class Radicalism in the 1830s* (London, 1970), pp. 206-7. For anticlerical banners, *Northern Star*, 16 Oct. 1838, 25 May 1839, 23 Jan. 1841. For Thornton, *ibid.*, 14 July 1838. For clergy marring funerals, *ibid.*, 6 Apr. 1839, 6 Feb. 1841. For the Evangelical attack on popular recreation, Peter Bailey, *Leisure and Class in Victorian England* (London, 1978), pp. 17-19. Faulkner, *Chartism and the Churches, pp.* 3!-3, gives a good account of the Chartist case against the clergy.

[48] *Northern Star*, 3 Feb. 1838; W. Cobbett, *A History of the Protestant "Reformation" in England and Ireland: Showing how that Event has Impoverished and Degraded theMain Body of the People in those Countries* (London, 1824-7); also O'Brien and McDouall, *Northern Star*, 19 May 1838, 13 Feb. 1841.

[49] Ibid., 27 July 1839. Hollis, *Pauper Press*, pp. 213, 252 for earlier schemes to restore church lands

to the people.

[50] For popular fury when twenty-six bishops opposed the Reform Bill, which was lost by 41 votes in the Lords in Oct. 1831, Chadwick, *Victorian Church*, i, pp. 25-38. For contests over church rates, ibid., pp. 81-9, 146-58; Ward, *Religion and Society in England*, pp. 178 ff.; G. I. T. Machin, *Politics and the Churches in Great Britain, 1832 to 1868* (Oxford, 1977), pp. 103 ff. For the clergy more openly joining local Conservative associations to defend the church from a feared Whig government attack that never came, ibid., ch. 2, p. 49; D. Foster, "The Changing Social and Political Composition of the Lancashire County Magistracy, 1821-1851" (Univ. of Lancaster Ph.D. thesis, 1971), pp. 98, 253. For a useful study of the church rate issue as part of the fight for local political control, A. Elliott, "The Establishment of Municipal Government in Bradford, 1837-1857" (Bradford Univ. Ph.D. thesis, 1976). Middle-class Dissenters were often satisfied once church rates were made voluntary, but Chartists pressed on for ownership and control of the church by the people and officially sanctioned a plan for nationalizing church property in 1851: Ward, *Religion and Society in England*, p. 178; Faulkner, *Chartism and the Churches*, p. 34.

[51] Bradford "Vestry Minutes", 1835-9, deposited in the parish church: for Rochdale, *Northern Star*, 27 July 1839, the same issue which covered the Stockport church parade.

[52] Evans, "Some Reasons for the Growth of Rural Anti-Clericalism, *c.* 1750-1830", pp. 101-8; S. and B. Webb, *English Local Government from the Revolution to the Municipal Corporations Act: The Parish and the County* (London, 1924), pp. 350-60; G. Kitson Clark, *Churchmen and the Condition of England, 1832-1855* (London, 1973), pp. 34-5. Evans says the proportion of clerical justices nearly doubled from c. 11 per cent in 1761 to c. 22 per cent in 1831. Even where there were rules about clerical exclusion, as in the Duchy of Lancaster, these could not be operated because other suitable resident candidates could not be found; rules against manufacturers sitting were similarly breached: Foster, "Lancashire County Magistracy", pp. 243-5.

[53] For the restraint of the magistrates until the sacred days, P.R.O., H.O., 40/51 and "Mr. Ellison to the Duke of Norfolk", d. 30 July 1839, Sheffield Pub. Lib., Arundel Castle MS. S478 xvii/156. For Foden, P.R.O., H.O., 20/10, and *Sheffield Iris*, 30 July, 6 Aug. 1839. Ibid. ,20 Aug. 1839 ff. for events during and after the sacred days, including the first church demonstration.

[54] Chadwick, *Victorian Church*, i, p. 521.

[55] Webb, *English Local Government: Parish and County*, pp. 99 ff.

[56] *Northern Star, j* Sept. 1839 for the take-over of an education meeting in concert with the socialists: Faulkner, *Chartism mid the Churches*, pp. 40-1, for a meeting about the sabbath in Dec. 1839. Anti-Corn Law fracas had begun in Jan. 1839.

[57] For afternoon and evening meetings in Bolton, *Bolton Free Press*, 3 (also Hyde), 10 Aug. 1839; *Manchester Guardian, 7* Aug. 1839; Nottingham, *Blackburn Gazette*, 21 Aug. 1839. For Sheffield overspill meetings, *Sheffield Iris*, 20, 27 Aug. 1839. In Norwich an outdoor, afternoon, public prayer meeting of the Primitive Christian Society made the first church visit to St. Edmunds in the evening: *Norfolk Chronicle and Norwich Gazette*, 17 Aug. 1839. For Parson Bull preaching the text requested by the Chartists, Amos viii. 4-8, *Bradford Observer*, 15 Aug. 1839. Twice Chartists also visited Catholic churches, in Bradford (18 Aug.) when Fr. Kaye agreed to preach their requested text, Isaiah xlii. 22, and in Norwich (8 Sept.) at the invitation of the priest, *Leeds Times*, 24 Aug. 1839, *Northern Liberator*, 14 Sept. 1839.

[58] *Lancaster Gazette*, 3 Aug. 1839. Other accusations levelled particularly at the minority of Bolton demonstrators included drunkenness, stealing sacred books, being Catholics or children, and using a pew drawer as a chamber pot: *Northern Star*, 27 July 1839, on the Rochdale church rate fracas, revealed that it was normal practice to reserve a pew drawer for chamber purposes – so it seems unfair to blame this especially on the Chartists!

[59] *Preston Observer*, 17 Aug. 1839, *Manchester and Salford Advertiser*, 24 Aug. 1839, for Ashton. When Chartists heckled at St. Stephens', Norwich, the vicar panicked and hastily brought his sermon to an end; but the following week in another Norwich church the "greatest order prevailed" when the Chartists got a sermon on the text they had requested, which was printed as Rev. John

Owen, *Riches and Poverty: A Sermon Preached in the Parish Church of St. Simon and Jude* ... (Norwich, 1839), *Norwich Mercury,* 24, 31 Aug. 1839.

[60] *Northern Star,* 27 July 1839.

[61] For Nottingham, W. Napier, *The Life and Opinions of General Sir Charles Napier,* 4 vols. (London, 1857), ii, p. 61; for Bradford, *Halifax Express,* 10 Aug 1839. For Newcastle, *Northern Liberator,* 20, 27 July 1839, *Preston Chronicle,* 10 Aug. 1839; here the ironic self-invitation came after a week when the Chartists' right of public assembly was closed down by the mayor, who had so fiercely defended the same right in 1832 "to serve the purposes of the middle class": Gammage, *History of the Chartist Movement,* 2nd edn., pp. 148-9.

[62] E.g., *Preston Chronicle,* 27 July, 7 Aug. 1839 for complaints about Stockport and Preston; *Bolton Chronicle,* 3 Aug. 1839 on Bolton; *Halifax Guardian,* 24, 31 Aug. 1839, about Halifax.

[63] A clear statement about self-exclusion was made by an attender at a later Chartist chapel who thought of most other churches and chapels as "no place for the poor. They had no clothing fit for such select companies, and if they ventured there in such as they had they were thrust into great pens in obscure corners called 'poor seats' and thus publicly advertised to the very respectable people present as paupers": Frank Peel, *Spen Valley Past and Present* (Heckmondwike, 1893), p. 317. *Northern Star,* 9 Mar., 13 July 1839, for Richard Carlile and J. R. Stephens urging Chartists to overcome their inhibitions and go to church wearing whatever they had.

[64] E. P. Thompson, "Patrician Society, Plebeian Culture", *Jl. Social Hist.,* viii (1973-4), p. 389.

[65] Anon., *Luddenden Dean Wesleyan Methodist Church: A Century of Methodism, 1828-1928* (Halifax, n.d.), pp. 4, 18; Thompson, *Making of the English Working Class, p.* 400; Peel, *Spen Valley,* p. 317. For a suggestive study of the different meanings of the same costume in changing contexts, Franz Fanon, "Algeria Unveiled", in *A Dying Colonialism,* trans. H. Chevalier"(Harmondsworth, 1970).

[66] A vivid picture of the extent of commercial trafficking in pews, the dependence of church finances on rentals and the sensitive questions of social status involved in assigning pews is given by M. R. Austin, "The Church of England in the Town of Derby ..., 1824-1885" (Univ. of Birmingham M.A. thesis, 1966), app. C, D. In St. Werberg's, the gentry were placed in the gallery, the lower middle class in the ground floor nave and the free seats were situated at the extreme side and back of the nave. Also Chadwick, *Victorian Church, i,* pp. 83, 521.

[67] *Northern Liberator,* 14 Sept. 1839; Bolton Free Press, 10 Aug. 1839.

[68] *Northern Star,* 6 Oct. 1838, 17 Aug. 1839; *Manchester Chronicle,* 10 Aug. 1839. For the Sorby episode, *Sheffield Iris,* 17 Sept. 1839.

[69] Northern Star, 27 July 1839; other requests included Matthew vii. 12 and Amos viii. 4-10: Bradford Observer, 8, 15 Aug. 1839; *Halifax Guardian,* 24 Aug. 1839.

[70] Requested Blackburn, Ashton, Sheffield and Norwich: *Preston Chronicle,* 10 Aug. 1839; Preston Observer. *17* Aug. 1839; *Sheffield Iris,* 20 Aug. 1839; *Norfolk Chronicle,*

[71] *Northern Star,* 27 July 1839; *Blackburn Standard, 7* Aug. 1839; the sermon by J. W. Whittaker, who was a county magistrate, was also printed as *The Church and the Chartists in Blackburn, 1839,* repr. edn. (Blackburn, 1972).

[72] *Preston Chronicle,* 17 Aug. 1839. Rev. Carus Wilson was a fierce church-rate warrior who condoned quite disproportionate distraints of goods for non-payment of *rates: Northern Star, 7* Apr. 1838, *Manchester Guardian,* 14 Aug. 1839, *Preston Observer,* 17 Aug. 1839. His nomination for the commission of the peace was rejected in 1840, ostensibly on the grounds of his clerical status.

[73] Rev. E. Jenkins, *Chartism Unmasked,* 19th edn. (Merthyr Tydfil, 1840), app. 3; Faulkner, *Chartism and the Churches,* pp. 60-5 for this sermon and anti-Chartist pamphlets by clergy. Rev. Jenkins, a militant Evangelical and teetotaller, was vicar of Dowlais and preached this sermon on 17th November after the Newport Rising; for a lengthy Chartist reply, *Northern Star,* 30 May 1840. Other printed sermons included Rev. F. Close, *The Chartists' Visit to the Parish Church ... Sunday, Aug. 18th 1839,* another edn. (Edinburgh, 1840), and his *A Sermon Addressed to the Female Chartists of Cheltenham, Sunday, Aug. 25, 1839* (London, 1839), and the Bishop of Norwich, *A Sermon Preached in Norwich Cathedral ... before an Assemblage of a Body of Mechanics Termed Chartists*

(London, n.d); these were countered in *Chartist Circular, 22* Aug., 12 Sept., 7 Nov. 1840.

[74] Close, *Sermon Addressed to the Female Chartists*, p. 14; Faulkner, *Chartism and the Churches*, pp. 60-2. The powerful Evangelical Close was a fierce opponent of the theatre and racing and was a key instigator of G. J. Holyoake's blasphemy trial in 1842.

[75] E. P. Thompson, "The Crime of Anonymity", in D. Hay, P. Linebaugh et al, *Albion's Fatal Tree: Crime and Society in Eighteenth-Century England* (London, 1975), pp. 278-9, 301-2.

[76] A complicated situation existed in Bolton, where the Tories refused to recognize the legitimacy of the charter of incorporation granted the previous year, so that two rival local government authorities seemed to be operating side by side. Although the Whig mayor, C. J. Darbishire (who had defended the Chartist right of public meeting the previous year) refused to call out the new police during the church demonstrations, the borough reeve and the old constables turned out. Darbishire wrote to the Home Secretary underplaying any danger while the borough reeve's letters were more alarmist and became more furious as the Home Office soft-pedalled by refusing to give advice on how to act. Nonetheless, Tories turned out to be sworn as special constables, accompanied by a solicitor to ensure that this was not construed as a "recognition of the Charter (of Incorporation)", and concerted police action during the sacred days provoked riots. *Bolton Chronicle*, 10 Aug. 1839; P.R.O., H.O., 40/44; *Manchester Guardian*, 14 Aug. 1839.

[77] *Sheffield Iris*, 17 Sept. 1839; also 27 Aug., 3, 10 Sept. for the Sheffield events. Mason was finally sentenced to two months imprisonment in Jan. 1840.

[78] Two types of occasion for further church visits were the dedication of new churches or again a moment of climactic class confrontation. In November 1841 a group of Chartists with banners and a band attended when the bishop was to dedicate Catton new church (Norwich): prevented by police from entering the church, they stayed outside playing "rough music", including God Save the Queen and the Old Hundreth, during the consecration exercises. Interestingly this action was censured by the Chartists of Ryde. *Northern Star,* 4 Dec. 1841, 8 Jan. 1842; Faulkner, *Chartism and theChurches, p.*39. During the period of the plug strike, Chartists of Ratcliffe Bridge visited the parish church, a la 1839, requesting the vicar to preach James v. 1-6:*Northern Star,* 10 Sept. 1842.

[79] *New Moral World,* 21 Dec. 1844, 5 Apr. 1845 for examples of Owenite visits when Emma Martin tried to deliver a rival sermon in church; for S.D.F. church parades,which often involved submitting suitable texts for the minister to preach, cf. *Justice,* particularly during the first three months of 1887. My thanks to Barbara Taylor and Victor Rabinovitch for these references.

[80] For Chartist interventions in Birmingham and Newcastle, *Northern Star, I,* 8 May 1841. For Chartist election success in Cheltenham, Leeds (1842) and Rochdale (disputed until 1843), *Cheltenham Free Press*, 25 Apr. 1840, 5 Oct. 1844 (my thanks to Owen Ashton for these references); J. F. C. Harrison, "Chartism in Leeds", in Briggs (ed.), *Chartist Studies*, p. 87; Ward, *Religion and Society in England, p.* 186; also *Northern Star,* 18 Apr. 1840 for other Rochdale vestry wins. For rates to the Defence Fund, ibid., 4 Apr. 1840.

[81] Ibid., 25 May 1839; *Halifax Guardian*, 25 May 1839; *Northern Liberator,* 31 Aug. 1839.

[82] Brian Harrison, "Teetotal Chartism", *History*, lviii (1973); the development of Chartist co-operation can be traced through the *Northern Star* and *Northern Liberator* from the end of August 1839.

[83] *Sheffield Iris,* 24 Sept., 8 Oct. 1839 for the series of Sheffield Chartist camp meetings which began the Sunday following the armed expulsion from church. *Northern Star,* 31 Aug., 14 Sept. 1839 for religious/political centres in Bradford and Leeds.

[84] Ibid., 16 Jan. 1841. For Chartist schools, B. Simon, *Studies in the History of Education, 1780-1870* (London, 1960), pts. 4-5; for theatre, C. Barker, "The Chartists, Theatre, Reform and Research", *Theatre Quart.,* i (1971).

[85] Wilson, *Chartist Movement in Scotland*, pp. 142 ff.

[86] *Northern Star,* 9 Jan., 10 Apr. 1841 for pubs in Newport and Redruth; ibid., 10 Apr. 1841, 3 Sept. 1842 for hymn-books. Faulkner, *Chartism and the Churches,* pp. 42ff., deals with Christian Chartist churches.

[87] *Northern Star,* 3 Apr. 1841 for Hill and O'Connor.

Speech and Writing in the *Northern Star*

Cris Yelland

This paper will discuss aspects of the language of the *Northern Star*, using technical concepts drawn from linguistics and literary criticism and especially concerned with details. In particular, my discussion will be concerned with exploring ways in which the *Northern Star* addressed its audience, and how that audience used the paper. The *Northern Star was* the most important of the many Chartist newspapers, and for an individual member of its audience, the paper and the ways in which it was used were an important element in the experience of being a Chartist. This importance was essentially dual: the *Northern Star*, in Epstein's words, was 'part of a larger Chartist cultural experience' and also 'central to local Chartist activity'.[1] In Epstein's discussion of the *Northern Star*, the paper had a crucial role in negotiating the relationship between the local and the national. 'It brought national perspective to the localities and gave local radicalism national coverage.'[2] Writing in and of his paper. O'Connor could stress either the local or the national identity of the *Northern Star*, as he saw fit:

> The *Northern Star* is not, nor was it ever intended to be, a mere Leeds paper. Tis a national organ; devoted to the interests of Democracy in the fullest and most definite sense of the word: and it is, consequently, supported by every true Democrat in every place where it became known.[3]

Here, O'Connor asserts the national power of the paper, and its connection with the abstract term 'Democracy', but at other times he expressed pride in the provincial, particularising qualities of the *Star*, the fact that its contents, and its large circulation, were alike rooted in provincial experience: 'Did the men of Glasgow know that such a place as Barnsley existed? No, but now they are acquainted even with the names of its inhabitants,'[4] and most often, he asserted the local and national dimensions of Chartist activity simultaneously, in language which defined local activities as the numerous expressions of the same guiding, nationwide consciousness:

> In our present number will be found reports of 'gatherings' in Staley Bridge, Leeds, and Bradford; in all which places the Giant Spirit of Democracy upreared its awful form in proper attitude ... In our present number will be found reports of public meetings at ... Barnsley, Dewsbury and Hull, at all of which the

people speak out boldly.[5]

Similarly, the *Star's* report on the second giant meeting at Peep Green ap-plauds 'a British People', and then follows this with a detailed listing of the ban-ners and slogans of localities, Leeds, Gomersal, East Bierley, Heckmondwike and Wakefield.[6]

In the course of my discussion of the *Northern Star*, I shall try to explore ways in which the language of the paper negotiated this relationship between the local and the general.[7] In particular, 1 shall consider the practice of reading the paper aloud, which was a common, though not the only, mode of consumption of it, especially in its early years. Reading aloud, which was a traditional part of radical political activity, involved the *Star* in language which implied an engaged and participatory sense of audienceship, in which the paper related closely to its readers on a local level. As Roberts puts it, in the early years especially, '...Readers closely identified with the *Star*. They felt it spoke for them.'[8] By contrast, at the end of the 1840s, when the level of Chartist activity in the localities had declined (apart from a brief revival in 1848), a different sense of audienceship was in play. Epstein points out that '... It is obvious from the highly rhetorical style of the *Star's* lead articles that the paper was designed to be read aloud.'[9] This is undoubtedly true, but the point can be developed. I shall argue later that not only the lead articles but the *Star's* reports of meetings were written in language which would reward being read aloud. Further, reading aloud can cover a va-riety of situations and relationships between a speaker/reader and an audience. Especially, a distinction can be drawn between proclamation or declamation to a large audience, and the more intimate reading which took place in small weekly meetings or discussion-groups. Both of these situations were parts of the concrete experience of being a Chartist, part of an individual's sense of belong-ing to a movement which was both local and national. Further, the language of the *Northern Star* is capable both of proclamation and of a more intimate mode. It sometimes addresses its audience as a 'mass', and sometimes in a more dia-logic and dramatic way, in which there is not one speaker but several. The paper persistently evoked both a local and a national aspect to being a Chartist, in language (more precisely in different varieties of language) which rewarded and reinforced either aspect alternately. In this respect, the *Northern Star* was more complex stylistically than, say, the *Leeds Intelligencer*. The *Intelligencer* was, from time to time, capable of language which was every bit as rhetorical as the *Star's*. The following, for example, comes from the *Intelligencer's* report on the trial of the Glasgow spinners:

> Crimes like this make the blood run cold ... they stain our national annals ... they outrage the Majesty of Heaven ... they are plague-spots upon the boasted morality of Scotland ... they would bring odium on a tribe of savages.[10]

The extravagantly heightened lexis, the repetition of the same syntactical structure, and the loose punctuation by dashes, all suggest a mode of oratory, and in this respect the *Intelligencer* and the *Star* are similar, and both similar to a great deal of early Victorian written prose, notably Carlyle's. I shall argue that the *Northern Star* differed from this fairly common feature in two ways: firstly because it would in reality have been commonly read aloud, which was not the case with the *Intelligencer,* and secondly because the highly rhetorical, declamatory style was only one of the ways in which it suggested speech and rewarded being read aloud.

In the course of my discussion, I shall concentrate particularly on the *Northern Star's* treatment of speech in its columns, and the ways in which the paper, like most early-Victorian (and modern) newspapers, sought to imitate or to suggest speech. 1 shall draw especially on work done on orality in the modern press, by Short[11] and by Fowler.[12] Both of these discuss the relation between spoken and written language in newspapers and identify it as a close but very problematic one. For one thing, a modern newspaper is typically bought by an individual and read in a solitary and silent fashion, yet many features of newspaper language are designed to suggest a mode of face-to-face conversation. Fowler has identified a number of features of newspaper language which have this function: they include colloquial lexis, contractions like 'won't' or 'can't', a high incidence of personal pronouns, especially 'we', minor 'sentences' which do not conform to usual written norms, and variety in typography, different type-sizes and fonts, italics, white-on-black, and so on, which suggest variations in volume and emphasis. Fowler also offers a theory which I find hugely productive – that there are many varieties of language which are intermediate between speech and writing, and in which different styles of writing suggest different kinds of speech. Short's work on modern newspaper language shows that newspapers are keen to define and report events in terms of quoted speech, even when such speech is invented – thus (this is Short's example) a meeting likely to lead to a vote of confidence in a football manager is given as a few terse words of speech, '"Your job is safe," soccer boss told.' This device, of expressing complex processes of decision and discussion as if they were brief and emphatic conversational events, is typical of modern press language. As a preliminary, it can be said that spoken language, or the idea of it, is important to modern newspapers, although speaking and reading a newspaper are now quite different activities.

Speech and the idea of it were centrally important to the *Northern Star* too, but in different ways. The paper was strikingly without the energy and variety of typography with which a modern tabloid suggests and simulates speech. To look at, the *Star* presents the forbidding aspect which is typical of an early Victorian newspaper ... six columns a page of unbroken nonpareil (roughly equivalent to 6-point) type, sparsely paragraphed and wholly without crossheads, the subheadings which break up a story into small units (first used in 1827 in the *Weekly Dispatch*, but slow to catch on more generally).[13] In newspaper history there may indeed be a roughly inverse correlation between real speech and the typographical faking of speech, as the practice of reading newspapers aloud declined between the nineteenth and twentieth centuries, as individual purchase of newspapers increased hugely, and as tabloids in particular devoted more and more energy to layout and variety of typography.

However, real speech was a major part of the *Northern Star's* business. The reporting of speech of one kind or another took between a quarter and a half of an average issue in the early 1840s. The issue for 18 March 1840, for instance, has extensive reports of the trials of prominent Chartists, a report of a Commons debate about the petition for mercy to be shown to Chartists convicted after the Newport rising, and smaller items reporting meetings, dinners with speeches and debates in various parts of the country as Chartists carried on their routine activities, in particular as they pursued the tactic of disrupting and hijacking meetings of the Anti-Corn Law League. It is also the case that, unlike a modern newspaper, the *Northern Star* would characteristically be read aloud to an audience, usually in a meeting or discussion group: it thus functioned in a significant real relationship between spoken and written language. The practice of reading aloud was a fundamentally important part of the *Star's* role as the leading Chartist paper.

For one thing, the reading aloud of the *Star* was the mechanism by which its influence spread to a much greater number of people than the 48,000 to 50,000 who bought it at its peak of sales in the spring of 1839. Hollis suggests that to estimate the *Star's*, total audience, the sales figures should be multiplied by 20,[14] which gives a peak figure of one million. Seaton and Curran [15] suggest a more modest multiplication by 10, but even the lower figure is hugely impressive. As well as being a mechanism for wide distribution, however, reading aloud was a traditional part of radical political activity. It was part of the usual sequence of events at meetings of the London Corresponding Society; the Political Protestants societies adopted the practice, and it is not surprising that Chartist groups adopted it too, mixing it with other social and educational activities. As well as being a means of communicating content to an audience who could not all afford the money to buy a book or the leisure to read it, or perhaps could not read at all, reading followed by discussion had powerful educative and social effects, fostering critical attitudes and a sense of group identity. Simon describes it as a method for encouraging 'self-confidence, clear thinking, and the capacity for self-expression'.[16] There are numerous references to the reading and discussion sessions in Chartist autobiography. Merrick's *The Warp of Life* has: 'After tea a short article would be read from *The Northern Star*, and this would form the subject matter for consideration and chat during the remainder of the day'.[17] Similarly, Adams' *Memoirs of a Social Atom* describes the practice in a moving and famous passage. Adams' grandmother was a veteran radical, and around 1840 used her kitchen as a meeting place for reading and discussion:

> The most constant of our visitors was a crippled shoemaker ... we called him Larry ... [who] made his appearance every Sunday morning as regular as clock-work, with a copy of the *Northern Star,* damp from the press, for the purpose of hearing some member of our household read out to him and others Feargus's letter'. The paper had first to be dried before the fire, and then carefully and evenly cut, so as not to damage a single line of the almost sacred production.[18]

Even a moral-force Chartist like Lovett, who was thoroughly antagonistic towards O'Connor and the *Northern Star,* saw great value in reading aloud. In *Chartism: a New Organisation of the People* he goes into detail about what he considers to be 'one of the best modes' of organising it. In Lovett's model, there is a strict rotation of readers, each reading from a selected list of verse or prose texts. Each reading is to be followed by constructive criticism from the others present, on matters of 'manner, pronunciation, emphasis, &c.'. As well as the moral and aesthetic benefits which Lovett finds in elocution, there are to be political and social benefits:

> In every country, it becomes the duty of every man to cultivate the abilities God has given him, so that by speaking and writing he may preserve its liberties, by exposing private peculations and public wrong.[19]

Lovett was far from the only Chartist to make connections between elocution and political rectitude. O'Connor's account of his father's heroic 1795 speech on Catholic Emancipation draws attention to its aesthetic qualities as much as to its politics, in a report which is itself melodramatic and elaborately rhetorical:

> O'Connor [senior], in a speech seldom equalled and never surpassed, either for eloquence, delivery, diction, or patriotism, paralyzed the House, astonished the nation, and disappointed the servile expectations of his profligate uncle.[20]

The profligate uncle is particularly fine. Like O'Connor, Gammage attached a lot of importance to questions of oratory. His *History of the Chartist Movement*[21] evaluates the speaking style of each Chartist leader in turn, so that Dr Taylor had 'the happiest combination of natural gifts and artistic power', O'Connor was 'racy and rambling', O'Brien could speak for four or five hours while 'rivetting his audience', Vincent used 'grand and beautiful language', Harney's delivery was 'imperfect', Jones's 'voice was stentorian, his delivery good', and so on.

To sum up my argument so far, technical and aesthetic questions about speech as performance were clearly important elements of Chartism. The *Northern Star* was much concerned to report speech, and it was often used by its audience in a spoken mode. Vernon has described the radical press as 'particularly adept' at working on the frontier between speech and writing: 'Print had first to use the dynamics of orality before it could supersede them'.[22] The next stage is to analyse in detail how the 'dynamics of orality' worked: how the language of the *Northern Star* represented speech, and how that language, in use, rewarded and reinforced its audience's sense of Chartist identity.

EARLY CONVENTIONS FOR THE REPRESENTATION OF SPEECH

Throughout my discussion, I shall treat the written representation of speech as a conventional, highly mediated, matter, not as a question of whether or not a written report is a true version. There are several reasons why this is appropriate: the first set of reasons is to do with industry practices and intentions. From the beginning of reporting political speeches, newspapers were explicit about their mediating role. The first issue of the *Daily Universal Register* conceded that there was a 'rage' for the reporting of Parliamentary speeches, but announced that it would 'abridge' speeches, and edit them so that '... the substance shall be faithfully preserved; but all the uninteresting parts will be omitted'.[23] When Macaulay prepared a volume of his Commons speeches for print, he was equally explicit about mediation and reconstruction:

> I have almost invariably found that in *The Times* newspaper, my speech has been correctly reported, though often in words different from those which I had used ... Nor have I, in this part of my task, derived much assistance from any report. My delivery is, 1 believe, too rapid. Very able shorthand writers have complained that they could not follow me, and have contented themselves with setting down the substance of what I said. As 1 am unable to recall the precise words which I used, I have done my best to put my meaning into words which 1 might have used.[24]

Pickering[25] has discussed the weaknesses of reporters' shorthand in the Chartist period, and the various difficulties of audibility and intelligibility in the way of a written report of a speech being anything other than a reconstruction. And there are fundamental linguistic reasons why a written speech is different from a spoken one: speech and writing are simply very different from each other. Speech involves resources of sound, pitch, volume, duration, etc., and other paralinguistic factors which have no written equivalents, and spoken language does not work according to the same structural principles as does written language. Writing works in sentences, speech in tone-groups. These differences, and their implications for written versions of spoken language, are discussed by Halliday[26] and by Fowler.[27] In the context of oral history, Portelli[28] and Thompson[29] have discussed writing as reconstructing speech.

   To sum up, press reports of spoken language are not replications, partly because newspapers did not set out to replicate, partly because practical circumstances made replication impossible, and partly because even if circumstances had been perfect, writing can suggest speech, but cannot replicate it. In asserting this, I do not mean to diminish the importance of the *Northern Star's* reporting of speech, nor to regard it as fictional. What I want to do is to reposition it, so that discussion does not focus primarily on the relation between the original speech and the written version, but on the ways that written speech was produced in the *Northern Star*, and the ways it was used by the people who were the audience for it.

To look first at the conventions in use for representing speech, writers in the press and elsewhere developed a very rich and vivid repertoire of devices. The two major ones in the early nineteenth century were:

(i) in Parliamentary reports such as *Hansard* and Reports of Commissions, Direct Speech, that is, the words which purport to be those actually used by a speaker (as far as possible), introduced not by inverted commas, but by the speaker's name and a dash;

(ii) in newspapers, mainly Indirect Speech, in which the reporting voice of the newspaper takes over the original words and grammatically alters them in line with the newspaper's position: thus in the *Star's* report of a Leeds meeting of the Anti-Corn Law League, the opening remark by Mr Rider is given in Indirect form, 'Mr Rider, who stated that he would not detain them two minutes,'[30] in which pronouns are changed so that the original 'I' and 'you' become 'he' and 'them', and the verb tenses are backshifted, Rider's original 'will not detain' becoming 'would not detain'. This was the most often used device in the early nineteenth-century press, and it was standard across most newspapers.

The above two were the major devices, but there was very striking variety and resourcefulness in reporting speech, and frequent shifting from one device to another. *The Times*, for instance, usually used IS, but also used DS with quotation marks for various purposes, for scare-quotes, when the quoter wishes to dissociate him/herself from the quoted, for quoting a written source, for toasts, motions, or other solemn or ceremonial utterances, or within a speech, when a speaker quotes someone else. Within the *Northern Star's* report cited above, one Chartist speaker, George White, is given in DS for the first few lines of his speech, then this switches to IS. In general, almost any conceivable variation is visible in the nineteenth-century press, including variations which are theoretically contradictory, like the *Leeds Mercury's*, odd combination of Indirect grammar with the quotation marks typical of Direct Speech:

Of course, he [Macaulay] declared himself in favour of an entire abolition of the Corn Laws ... was opposed to Universal Suffrage, upon which he observed - 'that the end of all government was the good of the people, and he did not think that at present the people would be governed for their happiness under a system of universal suffrage'.[31]

The inventiveness of journalists is remarkable here: it is worth remarking, too, that devices in written speech which are often cited as effective or expressive in fiction have their counterparts and precursors in the press. To give one example from very many possible ones, in Dickens' *Bleak House*, the crossing-sweeper Jo, made to give evidence at an inquest, is shifty and ill-at-ease under questioning, and this is rendered by the abbreviation of his speech, in particular the omission of I in his succession of unwilling answers: 'Name, Jo. Nothing else that he knows on. Don't know that everybody has two names. Never heerd of sich a think.'[32] Guilt and shiftiness are done by the same device in *the Northern Star's* reports of prosecution witnesses in the trial of the Glasgow spinners: '... Could not say he ever saw William McLean there. Knows Patrick McGowan. Has seen him there,'[33] and for prosecution witnesses in the trial of the Newport Chartists: '... I am no relation to the prisoner. I am a labourer, living in Newport. Was there on Monday the 4th of November. Saw part of the mob arrive there.'[34]

In all these cases, the writers have satirically adopted a mode of speech presentation which was used in the reports of Royal Commissions, where the responses of working-class speakers are truncated, and the eliciting questions also omitted. The effect is to present the speaker as a dull automaton.[35]

Most significantly, the device of Free Indirect Speech is common in press reports of Parliamentary and other speeches. FIS is a hybrid form ... grammatically it resembles IS, but it lacks reporting clauses, and keeps elements of DS, close deixis, colloquiality, question and exclamation structures. Its effect, broadly speaking, is to merge the reporting voice and the original speaking voice into one. It has been much studied in narratology, and is usually regarded as a sophisticated device associated with nineteenth-century realist fiction, especially Austen and Eliot in English, and Flaubert in French. It is clear from the evidence of press reports of speech that a narrow literary view of FIS ... for instance the view that it was largely developed by Austen, with only the occasional scattering of examples earlier than hers,[36] is mistaken. FIS was a familiar feature of newspaper writing at least from the late eighteenth century on. Before going on to examine an extract from the *Northern Star* in detail, it will be helpful to set out the broad outlines of the devices available for representing speech, the basic repertoire which writers use and produce variations on. Many books on narratology in fiction contain tables or diagrams of this kind. The following has been discussed and defended in the context of discussion of newspapers by Short.[37]

Cline of narrator interference in reported-character speech

	Character alone	Increasing narrator control		Narrator alone
FDS	DS	FIS	IS	NRSA

FDS = Free Direct Speech. I really like it here!

DS = Direct Speech. 'I really like it here!' he said.

FIS = Free Indirect Speech. He really liked it here!

IS Ñ Indirect Speech. He said that he really liked it there.

NRSA = Narrative Report of Speech Acts. He expressed enthusiasm for the place.

For our purposes, we might want to use the term 'reporter' for 'narrator', to stress the non-fictional nature of the material, but otherwise, this diagram will serve. One very important feature of it to stress is the idea of a cline, a scale of possibilities rather than very distinct alternatives. Further, it is possible that a given passage of speech may move some distance across the cline and back, as the reporting voice varies the degree of interference or control it has. To illustrate this, and some of the mechanisms which increase or lessen interference, here is one speech from a member of the Anti-Corn Law League:

> Mr Hamer Stansfield (a Magistrate) came forward to propose the first resolution. He said that if any subject was an important one it was the subject of the Corn Laws. These laws were worse in their operation than the arrow that flyeth by night, or the pestilence that walketh at noon-day. They were overt acts of aggression against the people of this country, and a violation alike of the laws of God and the rights of man. Was it not the height of impiety, when thousands of ministers of the Gospel, who taught the people to pray, 'Give us this day our daily bread!' virtually refused the repeal of those laws which hindered the people from obtaining their daily bread by their labour? Mr Stansfield then alluded to the case of the Shetland Islanders ... He then proceeded to contrast the condition of the people of the United States with that of the people of this country; attributing the happy condition of the former to cheap bread ... Mr Stansfield then, after a few other observations, moved the first resolution, which, as well as the following ones, will be found in our advertising columns.[38]

The movement here is clearly marked. The report opens in complete control, at the right-hand end of the cline. From sentence three on, the report moves leftwards, into the area of FIS, in which the reporter's grammar combines with what sounds as if they are Stansfield's actual words. The report moves furthest left with the question in sentence five, which is retained as a question, not reported as 'He asked whether ...'. At this point, the two voices, of Stansfield and the reporter, are closely merged. The report then moves rightward. The two voices separate as the reporter attributes speech to Stansfield, and the report tends more and more to summary or NRSA, a state which it reaches completely by the end. The effect is of the emotional temperature of the speech being raised and then lowered, as more and then less of Stansfield's strength of feeling is allowed through to the reader. One important mechanism for moving speech across the cline is the presence or absence of attribution, the act of saying, 'Stansfield/he/the speaker said ...', which separates the two voices and asserts the power of the reporting voice. It is not the only mechanism, however ... we can say that any device which increases the sense that the original words (and strength of feeling) are being used tends to encourage a reader to imagine and experience the original speaker and situation, and that devices which assert the reporting voice between the original speaker and the reader, or that sound like a reporter's paraphrase, will tend to have the opposite effect. All this is well understood from studies of FIS, particularly, in fiction. Do reports of meetings in the *Northern Star* show significant patterns in their representation of speech?

The table below is the product of counting a number of devices which are likely to raise a reader's degree of involvement with the meeting reported, or in other words to dramatise it and present it vividly. It is one small sample of counts done on the *Star's* reports of various meetings in the early 1840s: this particular meeting took place in Leeds, in the Coloured Cloth Hall,[39] on Tuesday 31 December 1839, and was reported in three Leeds weekly papers of the time, the *Northern Star*, the *Leeds Mercury* (Whig and Anti-Corn Law) and the *Leeds Intelligencer* (Tory). The meeting had originally been organised as a public debate on the Corn Laws, with a view to sending a petition to Parliament asking for repeal. It was attended by a number of Chartists, who moved an amendment demanding universal suffrage. Although the Chartist amendment was soundly defeated, the Chartists succeeded in disrupting the meeting and diverting discussion away from the Corn Laws to the question of universal suffrage. The columns in the table are as follows:

Speaker	Lines	Alt.	Self-att.	Parentheses	Colloquialisms
Black	61	2	10	5	3
Baines	118	11	1	5	4
Connor	67	4	3	7	7

Speaker: the table deals with three speeches of substantial length in the report of the meeting. Black and Connor were both Chartists, Baines a prominent Anti-Corn Law campaigner.

Lines: this is the total number of lines in the section of the report given to each speaker. The total for the two Chartists combined is roughly the same as the total for Baines, 128 to 118.

Att: this is short for 'Attributions', and counts the number of times the reporting voice asserts its presence and control by attributing. The basic attributional clause is 'He said', but there are numerous variants, 'Mr Baines continued', and so on.

Self-attributions: speakers in a debate or any other kind of formalised speech situation make frequent use of self-attributions, references to the fact that they are speaking, in constructions like 'What I say is', 'I go so far as to say', and so on. These are grammatically similar to attributions proper: for example, when Connor responds to the Mayor's admonishment to address the question, this is, 'Well, he would come to the question'. This could be either an attribution from the reporting voice, or a Free Indirect version of 'Well, I will come to the question'. It is hardly possible to prove one alternative or the other, but the conversational 'Well' at the beginning strongly tends to the probability that this is to be read as a version of what Connor actually said, rather than a reporter's interjection.

Parentheses: interjections from the floor, (Cheers), (Groans), (No bread-stealers here!) are a common and attractive feature of nineteenth-century reports. They are vivid dramatic devices. The third one quoted above does not appear in the *Northern Star's* report: 'bread-stealers' was an Anti-Corn Law description of the Chartists, and comes from the report on this meeting in the *Leeds Mercury*.

Colloquialisms: several sentences open with conjunctions or interjections: 'why', 'well', 'but', 'and', etc. These are unusual in formal written prose and have a strong tendency to suggest speech.

Several points of interest emerge. Baines is attributed nearly twice as often as the two Chartists combined, that is, the reporting voice controls his voice more than the Chartists'. Self-attributions show a very strong opposite tendency. Things like 'Well, he would come to the question' are powerful dramatisers and are very unequally deployed. The dramatising effect of parentheses is also more than twice as strong in the Chartists' speeches as in Baines'. Lastly, Baines is only brought to life by colloquialisms four times, against the Chartists' ten. To sum up the differences represented in these counts, Baines' speech is consistently to the right of the Chartists', in narratological as well as political terms.

One simple, though correct, conclusion is that this represents a degree of bias. The more interesting question is why the report is not much more biased than it is. Baines was a formidable opponent of Chartism, one of the family which provided Liberal parliamentary representation for Leeds after Macaulay and controlled the *Leeds Mercury*. Yet he is, for long periods, represented in a dramatic and effective way. For instance, when he exposes an element of sectarianism in the Chartists' position, this is given in a leftward-leaning form of FIS:

> When he looked at the amendment, he was entirely astounded at the flat, contradiction which appeared on the face of it. It at first stated that the !' Corn Laws were both 'diabolical and infamous, and then immediately afterwards went on to say that their repeal would be a positive evil (Groans and laughter) ... Could a greater contradiction

than this be imagined by any one?[41]

We can contrast this with the reports of the same meeting in two of the *Northern Star's* rival Leeds papers. The *Leeds Mercury's* report on the meeting is done in DS, with frequent interjections from a heavily controlling reporting voice. In theory, DS is a more dramatic mode than FIS, but the extent to which it will tend to encourage empathy with the speaker is influenced by the relation of the DS to the reporting voice. Where the reporting voice is hostile, representing a speaker in DS is holding them up to ridicule. There is a literary parallel here ... in Dickens' *Hard Times,* the caricature of a trade union speaker, Slackbridge, is given in DS with frequent and substantial interjection from the narrative voice.[42] The *Leeds Mercury* does the same with the Chartist Connor, describing him thus before giving his DS:

> CHAS. CONNOR, a cobbler, came forward, and was received with mingled cheers and laughter. The speaker held in his hand a bag containing a pair of boots or shoes, which he had taken out to mend, and the inconveniences which this occasioned, combined with the interruption from the meeting, caused him to wax exceedingly warm.[43]

The *Northern Star* does not do anything as hostile as this, even when dealing with a speaker whom it strongly opposes.

To turn now to the *Leeds Intelligencer,* the striking and sharp contrast is in its treatment of Baines, who is not dramatised, but summarised, in NRSA:

> Mr Edward Baines, Jnr. then addressed the meeting at great length, both against the Corn Laws generally, and against the particular arguments urged by the opponents of the resolution. He read a long extract from the speech of Dr. Bowring at Leeds, but his observations presented no new feature.[44]

Why should the reports be so different? In particular, why should the *Northern Star* give Baines so much more generous treatment than does the *Intelligencer?* The reason is, I think, not that Chartists were necessarily more fair-minded than Whigs or Tories. It is that the entire report in the *Northern Star* is in a dramatising, representational mode, primarily FIS, with brief movements out of it. In traditional narratological terms, the meeting is 'shown', not 'told'. The mechanisms for 'bias' are thus relatively hidden (if they ceased to be hidden, it would cease to be FIS and turn into IS or NRSA), and do not damage the vividness of the report. The significance of this becomes apparent when put into the context of how the *Northern Star* was experienced and used by its audience. The dramatic nature of the *Star's* item on the Leeds meeting can be seen as functioning in the *Star's* characteristic mode of use, being read aloud. The item is essentially representing, not reporting or evaluating the meeting. The dramatising nature of the item encourages its audience to imagine the lively scene of the original meeting, and the differences between the way Baines and Connor are represented are relatively subtle variations: overall, the audience is asked for a high degree of empathy. The fundamental mode of the report, FIS, is not designed to be to be related to the audience, but to be performed to it, and to involve the audience in the experience of what had been a rousing and enjoyable part of being a Chartist. This contrasts sharply with the way in which 'non-oral' papers like the *Leeds Intelligencer* and the *Leeds Mercury* dealt with the meeting.

ADDRESSING A MASS AUDIENCE

The lively and involving reporting of meetings in different localities, the dramatising of one locality for the enjoyment of the others, is one model of the relationship between the local and the national elements of Chartism. In addition, however, O'Connor and other writers for the *Northern Star* were engaged in addressing a mass, national audience, and I shall turn now to analysis of the language which realised this, describing two different varieties of it. The first of these had a distant resemblance to conversation. A modern newspaper addresses its mass audience by the characteristic conversational mode which constructs that audience as separate individuals, imagined as taking part in dialogue with 'their' paper. O'Connor's very frequent addresses and proclamations to the entire readership of the *Star* have some conversational elements in them, particularly in their free use of personal pronouns, and elements from other oral modes. The essential exchange in the conversational mode is between 'I' and 'you', especially if the 'you' is imagined as singular. O'Connor, like Cobbett before him, was very enthusiastic about 'I', but tended to imagine his addressed 'you' as plural. He thus evoked a mode of address which resembled a highly personalised public oratory as much as conversation. Salutations used by O'Connor became more and more extravagantly plural. They routinely included 'Old Guards' and 'My Dear Children'. By the late 1840s, in fact, the relationship between the increasingly eccentric O'Connor and 'his' audience had become dysfunctional. The issues of the *Northern Star in* the early months of 1849 show this clearly.

In his column, which occupied the leftmost part of the first page of the *Star* and often spread further, O'Connor had by 1849 developed an increasingly personalised mode of address, freely confessing his preference for 'the first person singular' and discussing Chartist policies and issues in terms of his personal history. On 27 January 1849, O'Connor made an appeal for Chartists not to be 'distracted' by Socialism or Communism, and followed this up in subsequent issues with some pejorative remarks about French politics, which he described as 'Utopian' and 'moonshine', and sneered at the idea of allowing anyone 'to submit his French credentials from some French club'.[45] O'Connor's chauvinistic stance on this issue was opposed by the *Star's* editor Harney writing under the pseudonym 'L'Ami du Peuple', and also by a number of Chartist localities. O'Connor's response to his critics, which covers all of p.1 and most of p.5 of one issue, showed an embarrassing breakdown in the relationship between the national and the local. He revelled in melodramatic personal declaration:

> I have suffered more in mind, body, and estate, than any other man; let me beg of
> you ... let me pray of you ... let me implore and beseech of you, not to put another
> iron in the fire.[46]

and reached a new low when he dismissed the letter opposing him from one locality on the grounds that he had not heard of any of its signatories, so they could not possibly be 'real' Chartists. The whole is markedly self-indulgent: there are no fewer than 60 first-person pronouns in the first column alone.

O'Connor's style of address implied a mass audience, one which was united by the enthusiasms and sufferings of its charismatic leader. Other writers in the *Northern Star* addressed a mass audience too, but in less romantic and personalised terms. The third mode of address which I shall consider was one of proclamation to a nation-wide audience. This mode was present in the *Northern Star* from the earliest issues, in O'Brien's polemic against Daniel O'Connell, for example, which begins 'To The Trade Unionists of Great Britain and Ireland ... Men of the Trades ... I am inclined to address you',[47] but very soon drops its personal tone. In the early issues, the national dimension of proclamation was often mixed with local elements. The radicals of Ashton-under-Lyne published an address to 'their brother radicals of the United Kingdom', which is national in scope, but added 'particularly those Yorkshire and Lancashire lads that met on Kensal Moor and Peep Green'.[48] Here, the audience which is addressed is potentially a national one, but it is not really abstracted, but present and concrete, sharing experience with the addresser. By the late 1840s, however, when the level of activity in the localities had declined, the monologic mode of address became the dominant one. In the issue of the *Northern Star* for 15 January 1848, for example, there are several lengthy addresses to a mass audience, headed variously 'To the Old Guards of Chartism', 'To the Irish People', 'To the Factory Workers of Great Britain and Ireland' and 'To the Working Men of England, in Trade Unions Associated'. This public, monologic voice largely replaced the dramatic, dialogic representation of meetings and debate. By the late 1840s, Chartism had changed and the *Northern Star* had changed with it: it had moved from the provinces to London in 1844, dropping the *Leeds General Advertiser* from its masthead in favour of the less provincial *National Trades Journal,* and relegating reports of provincial activities to a small regular item, 'Chartist Intelligence'. In addition, it had developed admirable and extensive connections with European political organisations.[49] The following extract is from an address from one such organisation, the Fraternal Democrats, one of many 'addresses' and 'proclamations' printed in the *Star* in the late 1840s:

FELLOW LABOURERS

From the earliest ages your 'order' has been subjected to all the wrongs and miseries of slavery ... slavery sometimes disguised, as in ancient Asia, Greece and Rome, and modern Russia and America, and sometimes veiled under the forms of a nominal freedom, as in these islands and their dependencies. It is an incontestible truth that he whose labour, liberty, and life are at the disposal of another, is a slave. Such is the lot of millions of this country. You must 'beg for leave to toil', and when that leave is granted, your reward is not measured by the extent or nature of your labour, or the worth of your production, but by the avarice of the capitalists ... The legislature, elected by a minority hostile to your interests, taxes the scanty wages of your toil, and while ceaselessly passing laws for the protection of Property, leaves Labour utterly unprotected ... The rich reap the benefits, and the poor the penalties of the laws ... We know that there are thousands ... tens and hundreds of thousands of your order ready with an answer worthy of men ... He is no true Chartist who acknowledging the justice of the principles he has espoused, hesitates to perform the duties patriotism dictates ... Were they indeed desirous, as they profess to be, of promoting your welfare, they would aid you to obtain sovereign power. They well know that if you controlled the legislature, all the reforms they seek ... and reforms of much greater importance ... would be forthwith effected ... Let this great truth be impressed upon every working-man, that it is from the hut and the hovel, the garret and the cellar, must come the regenerators of his order and the social saviours of the human race ... (my ellipses).[50]

One's first reaction is that it sounds like *The Communist Manifesto:* grammatically, lexically and syntactically, there is a strong resemblance, which is true for either the 1850 Macfarlane translation, or the more famous 1888 Moore translation.[51] I shall describe the main points of similarity, as follows:

The use of the present perfect for past events, 'has been subjected' rather than the simple past, 'was subjected'. The present perfect expresses a past action continuing to the present.[52] In theory, the simple past should be the most commonly-used tense in writing of historical events and processes, but the present perfect is preferred here because it carries greater urgency and immediacy. Part 1, the historical part, of *The Communist Manifesto,* opens with a succession of present perfects: 'the history of Society has been ... oppressors and oppressed have always stood ... the battle between them has been ... which has invariably ended ...'.

The tendency to lexical expansion and reiteration. Five examples are given of states characterised by disguised slavery, for instance, and there are also 'wrongs and miseries', 'labour, liberty, and life', and 'the hut and the hovel, the garret and the cellar'. Listing things in this way produces an effect of crowdedness and activity; it is a very common effect in prose of the 1840s, for instance in Dickens and Carlyle. Part 1 of *The Communist Manifesto*, especially, shares this tendency to accumulate detail. One example among very many is its second sentence: 'All the Powers of the Past …'

Lexical and syntactical patterning, especially of parallelism and contrast. There are frequent formal arrangements of words to produce special effects, particularly effects of rather laboured contrast. Examples include 'The rich reap the benefits, and the poor the penalties of the laws' and 'all the reforms they seek – and reforms of much greater importance'.

As well as lexical repetition and contrast, there are syntactical parallels, where structures are repeated: 'acknowledging the justice of the principles he has espoused, hesitates to perform the duties patriotism dictates', where two relative clauses are arranged for effect, or the very first sentence, where two kinds of slavery are contrasted, and the contrast is pointed by the use in each case of an unusual word-order in which the adjective comes after the noun, 'slavery sometimes undisguised … sometimes veiled'.

Syntactical devices for climax and emphasis. There are two especially important effects. One is the use of variations on the 'pseudo-cleft' sentence, in which the main point is announced at the beginning but actually delayed until the end, for a strong climactic effect. 'It is an incontestible truth that …' in the second sentence is one example, and there is a variation on this later, in 'Let this great truth be impressed upon every working-man, that it is …'. The other especially marked device is 'centre-branching', the insertion of material into a clause, usually between subject and verb, so as to delay the arrival of the expected element. There are lots of examples. In the ones that follow, I have put the inserted material in square brackets: 'The legislature, [elected by a minority hostile to your interests] …', 'He is no true Chartist who [acknowledging the justice of the principles he has espoused] …', 'Were they indeed desirous, [as they profess to be] …'.

This address, like the many similar ones in the later issues of the *Northern Star*, can suggest speech, but the speech situation which correlates with it is one of proclamation to a largely passive audience. The rhetoric has a ponderous, formal quality which suggests authority on the speaker's part, and also distance. The stylistic similarities with *The Communist Manifesto* are very strong. The model of the relationship between the paper and its audience also resembles that of *The Communist Manifesto*. It is derived from the highly centralised, 'Utopian', French or German model which became influential in late Chartism, and calls for proclamation followed by an insurrection like that in Paris or Vienna.

The changes in style in the *Northern Star* imply different models of the relationship between the paper and its audience, and afford examples of the process described by Vernon, in which participatory, open, oral modes of political activity are replaced in the nineteenth century by more structured and directed modes, in which the printed word becomes monologic and dominant.[53] In one model, the early, provincial one, the paper's national status is the product of its aggregation of different provincial identities and activities. Further, there is a fairly strong similarity between the language of the paper and the way in which its audience would use it: both are dialogic and participatory, and in both the relationship between the paper and its audience is to be performed and negotiated. In the second model, O'Connor's romantic paternalist style of address in some ways resembles the hegemonic conversational mode of a modern newspaper, but his rhetoric is more melodramatic than this, and his addressed 'you' is almost invariably to be understood as plural. Like the first model, however, the second could reward being performed aloud, as Adams' reminiscence indicates.[54] In the third model, the *Northern Star* has a capital status which places it above the merely provincial. The audience is no longer present and participating, but abstracted into a 'mass'. Variations on these models of the relationship between the *Northern Star* and its audience are present in almost every issue of it, but there is a tendency for the third model to become dominant in the later 1840s. The diffuse and provincial elements of Chartism are de-emphasised in favour of the adoption of a European, centralised model of proclamation followed by insurrection.

Notes

[1] J. Epstein. *The Lion of Freedom,* London. 1982, p. 72.

[2] Ibid., p. 60.

[3] *Northern Star (NS),* 26 March 1838, quoted in Epstein. *Lion of Freedom,* p. 65

[4] NS, 20 April 1840.

[5] NS. 13 January 1838 and 27 January 1838.

"NS, 16 October 1838.

[7] This duality between the local and the national was not confined to the *Northern Star* but was a feature of other Chartist papers too, in fact of Chartism itself. See, for instance, Joan Hugman's study of the Newcastle *Northern Liberator,* A Small Drop of Ink', in O. Ashton et al., *The Chartist Legacy,* London, 1999.

[8] S. Roberts. 'Who Wrote to the *Northern Star?',* O. Ashton, et al., *The Duty of Discontent,* London, 1995. p. 64

[9] Epstein. *Lion of Freedom,* p. 6810.

[10] *Leeds Intelligencer,* 20 January 1838

[11] M. Short, 'Speech Presentation, the Novel and the Press', in W. van Peer (ed.). *Taming the Text, London,* 1988.

[12] R. Fowler. *Language in the News,* London, 1990, and 'Oral Models in the Press', in M. McLure, T. Phillips and A. Wilinson (eds), *Oracy Matters,* London, 1988.

[13] S. Morison. *The English Newspaper 1622-1932,* London, 1932, p. 279.

[14] P. Hollis, *The Pauper Press,* Oxford, 1970, p. 119.

[15] J. Seaton and J. Curran, *Power Without Responsibility,* London. 1988, p. 14.

[16] B. Simon, The Two Nations and the Educational Structure 1780-1870, London. 1974, p.

181.

[17] D. Merrick. *The Warp of Life*, Leicester, 1876. quoted in Epstein, op. cit., p. 71.

[18] W. Adams. *Memoirs of a Social Atom*, London, 1903, quoted in 0. Ashton, *W.E. Adams: Chartist Radical and Journalist*, Whitley Bay, 1991, p. 31.

[19] W. Lovett and J. Collins, *Chartism: a New Organisation of the People* [1840]. Leicester. 1969, repr, pp. 5-12.

[20] *NS*, 24 February 1838.

[21] R.C. Gammage, *History of the Chartist Movement* [1894], London, 1969, passim.

[22] J. Vernon, *Politics and the People*, Cambridge, 1993.p. 145.

[23] *Daily Universal Register*. 1 January 1785.

[24] T.B. Macaulay, Preface to *Collected Speeches* [1865]. London, 1909, p. xx.

[25] P. Pickering. 'Class Without Words: Symbolic Communication in the Chartist Movement', *Past and Present*, vol. 112.

[26] M. Halliday. Preface to *Introduction to Functional Grammar*, London. 1985, p. xx, and 'Spoken and Written Modes of Meaning', in D. Graddol and O. Boyd-Barrett (eds), *Media Texts: Authors and Readers*, Milton Keynes, 1994.

[27] Fowler, *Language* (1988).

[28] A. Portelli, The Peculiarities of Oral History', *History Workshop Journal*, Autumn 1981.

[29] P. Thompson, *The Voice of the Past: Oral History*, London, 1988, pp. 228-31.

[30] *NS*, 4 January 1840.

[31] *Leeds Mercury*. 8 June 1839.

[32] C. Dickens, *Bleak House*, 1852-3, Ch. 11.

[33] *NS*, 3 February 1838.

[34] *NS*, 11 January 1840.

[35] I am grateful to Dr Tony Nicholson for pointing this out to me.

[36] See, for example, R. Pascal, *The Dual Voice*, Manchester, 1976. There is a much better account of the history of Free Indirect Speech in more recent work by M. Fludernik. *Fictions of Language*, London, 1993.

[37] Short, 'Speech Presentation'.

[38] *NS*, 4 January 1840.

[39] The Coloured Cloth Hall no longer exists: it was a large, centrally placed building. adjoining what is now City Square.

[40] The *Leeds Intelligencer*, which was a 'non-oral' paper, used parentheses very sparingly, and sneered at the practice in an editorial (27 January 1838).

[41] NS, 4 January 1840.

[42] Dickens. *Hard Times*, 1854, Book 2, Ch. 4.

[43] *Leeds Mercury*, 4 January 1 840.

[44] *Leeds Intelligencer*, 4 January 1840.

[45] *NS*, 3 March 1849.

[46] *NS*, 17 March 1849.

[47] *NS*, 10 February 1838.

[48] *NS*, 27 October 1838.

[49] H.Weisser,'ChartistInternationalism 1845-1848', *The Historical Journal*, xiv, 1, 1971.

[50] *NS*, 8 January 1848

[51] Quotations from *The Communist Manifesto* are from the first English translation, which appeared in the *Red Republican* in November 1850. What I say about its style holds good for the more familiar 1888 translation. See C. Yelland, '*The Communist Manifesto*: a Linguistic Approach', *Studies in Marxism*, 4, 1998.

[52] My account of the difference between the present perfect and the simple past is based on G. Leech, *Meaning and the English Verb*, London, 1970, pp. 30-6, Adams, *Memoirs of a Social Atom*.

[53] Vernon, *Politics of the People*, passim.
[54] Adams, *Memoirs of a Social Atom.*

'Diffusing the light of liberty': the Geography of Political Lecturing in the Chartist Movement

Philip Howell

Lecturing activity was central to the ambitions of the Chartist movement for universal suffrage in early Victorian Britain, not merely because it was an effective means of political proselytism, but also because it was emblematic of Chartist political aims. Political lecturing followed a long radical tradition, but Chartism was able to systematize and to professionalize it on an unprecedented scale, binding together local and regional initiatives within a genuinely national politics. This essay describes this organizational geography. An awareness of the symbolic and organizational commitment within Chartism to a national system of communication also prompts a reassessment of the significance of political media, however. It is argued here that the formal geography of political lecturing should be taken to be consistent and complementary, rather than merely instrumental, to Chartism's broader political culture.

> "Go on, glorious spirit of intelligence! In a little time every village will have its galaxy of lecturers who will mutually visit their adjacent localities, pleasing their hearers by variety, improving themselves by emulation, and diffusing the light of liberty around them."[1]

As the most important manifestation of popular politics in early-Victorian Britain, Chartism has received a considerable amount of attention from historians and historical geographers. There has been some concern for instance from the latter about the degree to which Chartism's "complex topography" was marked by regional rather than national contours, and the extent to which the movement was politically fragmented as well as geographically differentiated.[2] Moreover, historical geographers are able to draw upon studies of the dynamics of political communication in the radical protests to which Chartism was indebted.[3] As a result, the geography of Chartism is demonstrably important to our understanding of the movement.[4] However, where historians have increasingly asserted the need to understand Chartism in terms of its wider "cultural experience" rather than in its "straightforward political organisation", historical geography – on the whole largely concerned with the latter rather than the former – has had little to add.[5] This essay therefore attempts to focus on one form of activity within

Chartism's political culture – political lecturing – in both an organizational and a cultural sense The geography of Chartist lecturing, it is argued here, was more than a matter of organizational coherence, mappable by static geographical distributions; nor can it be described by diffusion models. Its fullest significance stems from the fact that it was a part of a political culture that was itself suffused with geographical considerations. That geography was neither incidental nor instrumental to the broader cultural experience of Chartist politics.

Chartist political lecturing

When Chartism's first chronicler wrote that "a new group of Chartist orators" had taken the field after the initial excitements of the movement, he was well aware that the role of lecturer or political missionary was not a new one.[6] There had been prominent lecturers in the early-Chartist years, in the diverse agitation that acted as the crucible for Chartism, and in the long and unbroken tradition of radical politics itself. From the pioneering "missionary tours" made by agitators in the 1790s, through their revival by Major Cartwright in the Luddite years, down to the prominence of speakers like Henry Vincent in the emergence of Chartism, lecturing was clearly central to the ambitions of political radicals.[7] There was nothing unprecedented about the techniques of organization, proselytism and agitation developed in the Chartist movement. Indeed, to trace the lineage even further back, Chartist "missionaries" can be said to have carried on the vocation of the non-conformist preachers who have played such a large role in the radical tradition. The leading Chartists of Birmingham, when they recommended to their members a plan of local lecturing in 1842 that was designed to ensure "a constant supply of varied talent, so that there be no lack of the 'word of life'" could almost be said to be honouring such an inheritance.[8] Political lecturing should therefore rightly be seen as inseparable from the broad and encompassing cultural experience that has been recognized as central to the development of radical politics in Britain.[9] It is equally true, furthermore, that the role of the Chartist lecturer or missionary is not an easy one to define. The continuity of political lecturing is matched by its diversity. Chartist lectures might consist of political education and commentary, or much more nebulously a whole range of topics considered to be relevant, instructive or simply amusing to a Chartist audience. The influential Leicester Chartist, Thomas Cooper, recalled for example that he would lecture, in the absence of any "stirring local or political topic" on Milton, Shakespeare or Burns, on the history of England, on geology, or even phrenology.[10] We should be rightly wary of assigning the Chartist lecturing commitment a single meaning or significance.

Yet we can argue just as correctly that Chartist lecturing took on an unprecedented importance to the movement in the 1840s, and moreover one that was thoroughly consistent with Chartism's political culture. The Chartist historian

Robert Gammage pointed this out, and so too did the engraver and poet W. E. Adams, contrasting the earliest leaders of the movement with its later representatives. "The usual notion of an agitator", Adams wrote, "is that he is a man with 'the gift of the gab' – what the Americans would call a spellbinder." But five of the six representatives of the Working Men's Association who assisted in framing the People's Charter were not platform people at all. None of the five – John Cleave, Henry Hetherington, William Lovett. James Watson, Richard Moore – made any pretence to oratory, and seldom appeared before the public in person.[11] By the peak of the National Charter Association's activity. however, the situation was transformed, and in 1842 the Chartist National Executive was wholly composed of regular public speakers. Indeed, as David Jones has pointed out, the association was often remembered, long after its demise, as primarily, even exclusively, a lecturing organization.[12] Further, the travelling orator and the itinerant agitator became the archetypal Chartist figures in these years, in the minds of the authorities, in novelists' melodramas, and not least in the eyes of the Chartists themselves.[13] The great Chartist newspaper the *Northern Star* declared that "We know not a more decidedly useful and patriotic body of men at the present time as this. The proud position of the people as to intelligence on matters of moral and political right is owing in a great measure to their labours and exertions."[14] Even more clearly the paper later noted that

> the spirit of Chartism is essentially one of expansion and diffusion; like the small seeds borne upon the winds of Heaven, our principles bear with them the seed of fructification, and wherever they fall, they cannot fail to take root, and bring forth fruit. This is shown by the reception our agents, and lecturers, have met with, in whatever part of the country, as yet to which our missionaries have penetrated, they have invariably been received by their especial clients, the poor, with open arms, and the truths they have preached have been eagerly imbibed by thousands in every part of the kingdom.[15]

The centrality of lecturing to Chartist political ambitions in the early 1840s can best be demonstrated in two ways. Firstly, it can be shown that the lecturers were increasingly part of a *professionalised* lecturing system in these years, contributing to a national geography of political lecturing and a national public.[16] Secondly, and more importantly, the geography of lecturing shared and symbolised the Chartists' consistent but increasingly important cultural commitment to democratic *communication* and public discussion.[17] The lecturers therefore both contributed to the formation of a national political community, and embodied the principles that underwrote the movement's political culture.

The professionalisation of Chartist lecturing

Virtually all of the schemes proposed for the revitalisation of Chartism in the early 1840s agreed that a redoubled agitational effort should complement the new organizational architecture, and the eventual formation of the National Charter Association (NCA) in July 1840 was no exception to this.[18] The revival of Chartist fortunes was to be based on a systematic extension of its principles based around missionary activity. The fact that so many of its early leaders and agitators had been gaoled in the preceding months did nothing to dampen the Chartists' enthusiasm. James Sweet of Nottingham, for instance, reflecting on the impending release of his incarcerated colleagues, could look forward to a flurry of missionary activity in the crucial months ahead, thanking the authorities for their considerate contribution to the spread of Chartist principles:

> BROTHER DEMOCRATS, – In a short time, nearly the whole of our brethren, who have been confined in the dungeons of the *Liberty-loving Whigs,* will be again at large, and I am happy to observe that while at *College* the greater portion of them have pursued their *studies* very assiduously: – in fact they have become, what their enemies never intended nor ever contemplated, by incarcerating them, that they should become. *viz. – Lecturers. Advocates,* and *Missionaries,* to preach the glad tidings contained in the People's Charter.[19]

Lecturers had to be paid for and organized, however, and the local and relatively unsystematic organization of missionary activity which had marked the early Chartist years had to be thoroughly overhauled. Gammage noted that even when the Convention of 1839 had made use of travelling orators, "the error was committed of sending them nearly all to those districts that were already in the agitation, instead of opening up new ground in the more unenlightened parts, where the masses were still as ignorant of their rights as if those rights had never existed.[20] The Chartist lawyer and delegate, W.P. Roberts, in much the same vein pointed out the need for a map showing "the particular shades of opinion in each district", for whilst in some places lecturers were needed "who would lay down the first broad principles", in others "men of a more philosophic cast" were desired.[21] It fell to the Chartist Convention of 1842 to tackle these difficulties head on, to establish the framework of a national system of lecturing. There, William Beesley of North Lancashire argued not only that more lecturers were needed, but also that the plan of the organisation should be changed in order to sustain the lecturing work, proposing that instead of one-fourth of the subscriptions of the NCA's members being earmarked for the agitation, a scale of 6d for every 50 members, and 3d for every 25 above that, should be paid, to be gathered in quarterly collections. Speaking in support, and recommending the formation of a committee to organize national lecturing activity, George White of Birmingham emphasized "the necessity of appointing lecturers to those country districts in which so great a necessity existed for them". "At present", he noted, "where they had a large number of members, and funds, they had plenty of speakers and lecturers, but he wanted to see the other districts organized. If the Convention did not do this they would disappoint the expectations of the country and of his constituents"[22] The Chartist leader Feargus O'Connor also enthusiastically expressed his approval, noting that:

> They were not to suppose that because they were now enjoying the sunny side of Toryism that it would long remain so; no sooner would Sir Robert Peel have finished his finance plans, and firmly seated himself and his coadjutors in office, than he would take steps to control public opinion, which now, as ever had been, the grand aim of a Tory government; it was therefore pre-eminently necessary that they should have a well organised body of lecturers. The present body of lecturers had exercised every nerve in producing a good public opinion; there had never existed a body of men more calculated to produce good, and he thought that this plan of extending their operations was one of the best resolutions yet made in the Convention.[23]

From this recognition of the need for a more systematic approach to political lecturing, the Chartists managed to create, in the face of numerous difficulties, a genuinely national framework of agitation that perfectly complemented the new national organization. Indeed, in many ways the lecture circuits became the most visible and material expression of that organization, establishing co-operative practices, binding localities together, and securing them within the national geography of the NCA. Characteristically, furthermore, this lecturing commitment followed a hierarchical geography in which local and regional activity could be co-ordinated within an emergent national system.

The use of local lecturers

At the level of the localities, the National Executive preferred not to interfere. Some areas were able to establish from their local resources an effective number of lecturers to serve the needs of their various localities. Such a situation was regarded as highly satisfactory, as it circumvented both undue national interference and additional expense. Executive member Peter McDouall readily declared to the 1842 Convention for instance that lecturers should only be assigned to those districts where Chartism was dormant as "he did not want any power over those places which could appoint their own lecturers". "The Executive", he was quick to point out, "had never interfered in local business – they had looked only to the general business of the Association."[24] The Executive's valedictory address made this point even clearer. Recommending the appointment of district lecturers, a point of principle was made out of local authority and autonomy:

PLACES	Time of Meeting	January.					February.				March.			
		3	10	17	24	31	7	14	21	28	7	14	21	28
Tib-street, Manchester, Sunday	6	8	2	5	13	14	3	6	5	4	2	12	3	9
Brown-street, Do.	6	6	3	9	8	11	17	2	7	5	6	10	14	4
Salford, Do.	6½	2	7	17	10	6	8	3	9	2	4	5	6	11
Oldham, Do.	2	13	11	2	14	3	13	14	11	6	5	2	13	14
Do. Do.	6	12	14	2	11	3	12	11	13	6	5	2	12	15
Middleton, Do.	6	9	17	3	6	4	8	5	4	7	3	9	8	10
Ashton, Do.	2½	3	8	10	7	6	10	4	13	8	9	4	7	3
Newton Heath Do.	2½		1				6				8			
Do. Saturday	7				4			7				6		
Bolton, Monday Evening	8	16	15	16	2	15	16	11	15	16	15	16	2	16
Mottram, Thursday Evening	8				3			2				11		
Droylsden, Tuesday	8	3	5	2	6	7	3	8	10	11	4	9	3	2
Failsworth, Sunday	6		1		9		17		14		10		5	
Rochdale, Do.	2	14	5	11	3	2	12	11	17	9	14	3	16	6
Do. Do.	6	14	5	11	3	2	12	11	17	9	14	3	16	6

LECTURERS		
	6. James Cartledge, Do.	12. John Greaves, Shaw
1. James Leech, Manchester	7. William Shearer, Do.	13. Francis Lowes, Oldham
2. William Tillman, Do.	8. John Campbell, Salford	14. Henry Smethurst, Do.
3. Charles Conner, Do.	9. William Bell, Do.	15. Richard Marsden, Bolton
4. Joseph Linney, Do.	10. Richard Littler, Do.	16. John Gardiner, Do.
5. Edward Curran, Do.	11. James Greaves, Austerlands	17. Edward Clark, Manchester

Figure I. Chartist plan of lecturers for South Lancashire, 1841. *Source:* Public Record Office, HO 45/46, in D. Jones, *Chartism and the Chartists* (New York, 1975), 105.

We ... desire to point out to the people the principle upon which the agitation of the various districts should be conducted. We are of the opinion that the perfection of freedom consists in local government being unchecked in each of its workings; and therefore we recommend that each district capable of supporting a lecturer, to empower the General Council to elect an eligible person, and pay a salary sufficient for his maintenance and the remuneration for his labours. We do not desire to have undue power placed in our hands; and therefore disapprove of the proposed plan of giving the Executive the power of appointing a corps of lecturers on the principle that the directing power is quite enough for us to possess, and that the agitating power should be held and controlled by the General Council. We likewise disapprove of the plan of electing a limited number of lecturers, on the principle that it would be a restriction on the genius which we observe springing up in the ranks of our association, which talent should have a fair chance of being matured, a wide field to exercise itself in, and therefore to afford the young an honourable opening for a wise and just competition, we would leave the choice of the lecturers to the General Council in the districts, the whole association being the class from which the lecturers should be chosen. We have no objection to offer to the principle of allowing the Executive the temporary power of sending qualified persons to parts of the country where the Association has not yet been established, but that power should not be retained after the districts were organized and capable of directing their own movements. Each locality knows its own wants best, and should endeavour to supply them whilst the Executive should overlook, direct, and devise plans of organization for the whole. The efforts of the General Council should be local, the duties of the Executive National, and if we always made that honest and Chartist distinction we would fulfil our separate duties without the chance of dispute, and with every prospect of success to our glorious principles.[25]

Table 1

Major Lecture Circuits, 1842

District/title	Lecturer	Months
Yorkshire	William Jones	Jan., Feb., Mar.
'East and North Riding	John West	Mar., Apr.
Lecturer'	W. Dean Taylor	Jul., Aug., Sep.
	Jonathan Bairstow	Oct., Nov., Dec.
North Lancashire	William Beesley	Jan., Mar., May, Jun., Jul., Nov., Dec.
South Lancashire 'Missionary'	William Bell	May, Jun., Jul., Aug.
Nottinghamshire	W. Dean Taylor	Jan., Feb., Mar., Aug.
'County Missionary'	E. P. Mead	Jun., Jul., Aug.
Birmingham 'District Lecturer'	John Mason	Jan., Feb., May, Jun.
Northamptonshire	John Mason	Mar.
	Jonathan Bairstow	May, Jun.
	William Jones	Jul., Aug.
	R.K. Philp	Nov.

Now only a very few regions could claim to be in such a favourable position, as the Executive were also keenly aware. One of these was undoubtedly South Lancashire which was able to draw up a plan of regular lectures as early as 1841 (Figure 1). Organized by James Cartledge, the plan demonstrated the degree of security and self-sufficiency that this leading Chartist region could command. In 1842, Cartledge could declare that the system was able to bring on young and untrained individuals and prepare them for a public career:

> There are now in Manchester and district, twenty-one good lecturers, which is an emphatic illustration of the progress of the cause, as many of the persons whose names appear on the plan, could not for twelve months, speak with any degree of confidence before an audience more than a quarter of an hour or so without notes, but now they can deliver lectures which occupy two hours with perfect composure, and highly interesting to the listeners.[26]

Perhaps only London could claim a greater degree of self-sufficiency. The nature of the capital both encouraged and demanded greater co-operation amongst Chartist localities than was to be found in other towns, and it was uniquely served by a central committee meeting at the Dispatch public house in Bride Lane, responsible for supplying the city with lecturers. This committee took pleasure in announcing early in 1842 arrangements guaranteeing a regular supply of lecturers for every locality in London.[27] The sheer number of associations in London, and again the geography of the capital itself, ensured that for every locality a rapid turnover of lecturers was possible.

County and regional lecturers

The alternative to local self-sufficiency was to engage a paid lecturer for a fixed period of time. This necessitated a considerable financial commitment on behalf of the localities involved, and a number of regions accordingly established county lecturer's funds, collecting money from their various localities at regular intervals. Some lecturers thus engaged were appointed for strictly temporary tours, some were swapped between regions and districts, whilst others were retained for longer periods, usually months but sometimes over a year.[28] The major county circuits for 1842 and the lecturers who filled the county missionary posts at different times in that year, are listed in Table 1. These lecturers were famous figures whose reputation within the movement was derived from their prowess as public speakers; and they embodied the new importance that Chartist lecturers could command within the ranks of the NCA.[29] The East and North Riding circuit was particularly well-established and organized, followed closely by the example of the Nottinghamshire and North Lancashire Chartists. The Yorkshire Chartists supported the post of lecturer for virtually the whole year, North Lancashire kept Beesley for most of the year, and Nottinghamshire hung on to Dean Taylor through much of 1841 and 1842. Some of these districts in fact could become very attached to the lecturer appointed, so that the latter's fortunes were often intimately linked to particular regions. In Nottinghamshire, for example, Dean Taylor's imminent departure was lamented and prevented by the local Chartists:

> A majority of the Chartists of this town and neighbourhood were extremely sorry on account of the decision lately come by the decision of the delegate meeting to discontinue the services of Mr W. D. Taylor, as his conduct since he has been amongst us has created the greatest respect towards him. Mr Taylor is a stern, unflinching Chartist, and his labours have been productive of the greatest good to the cause of Chartism. Many persons wishing that Mr Taylor could be retained during the summer in this neighbourhood, and to give such persons an opportunity of proving their attachment to him, the Council, meeting at the King George on Horseback, have engaged him as lecturer, for one month longer.[30]

Lecture tours

Finally, if the use of county lecturers demonstrates the extent to which cooperation between localities could produce, at a district and regional level, a systematic
approach to the lecturing needs of the Chartist body, much the same can be said
of the NCA's approach to extending the bases of Chartist support. Proselytism
of Chartist principles was also by and large a regional affair. John Campbell, for

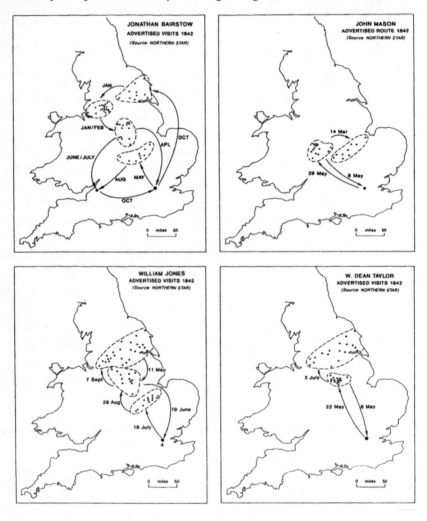

Figure 2. Selected advertised Chartist lecture tours, 1842.

the Chartist Executive, celebrated the sterling work of the regional missionaries
in his Secretary's Report of July, 1842 accordingly:

Doyle, West, Jones and the local agitators, have spread our principles far and wide in Yorkshire; Cockburn in the Newcastle district; Williams in Durham and Sunderland; in Lancashire, Bell, Leach, Cartlidge Duffy, Brophy, Dixon, Littler, Roberts, Clark, and a host of others, meet the enemy in any direction he may choose to appear; baffle and destroy him. Harney, Bairstow, Cooper, Harrison, Taylor, Sweet, and others, have worked wonders in the Midlands. Richards, and the good men of the Potteries, have earned Chartism into almost every hamlet in their district. Linney is doing his share of the work in Bilston. Mason and White in the Birmingham district. Mogg and Child are extending it into the remotest parts of Shropshire. Ridley, Wheeler, Parker, Maynard, Stallwood, and a host of others, too numerous to mention, have made greater progress in forwarding Chartism in the Metropolis, than was ever done before. Williams and Simeon in Wales. whilst Beesley has carried it into the hills of Cumberland.[31]

If the major speaking tours and engagements for Chartist lecturers were arranged through the established regional circuits, however, this did not preclude a national and systematic approach to political lecturing. Lecture tours were typically regional itineraries but lecturers moved on a national scale: "their horizons were national, not local, because this was the arena within which their lives were played out."[32] Jonathan Bairstow, for example, started his speaking engagements in Lancashire and Cheshire in January and February, before transferring to the East Midlands in April to Northamptonshire in May and June, towards the end of the year taking up the East and North Riding lecturer's appointment, and other lecturers followed the same pattern (Figure 2).

What this hierarchical structure meant was that the operation of the lecturing system was both regionally differentiated and at the same time systematically organized at a national level. Any given region would inevitably be favoured with a mixture of lecturing from the home-grown talent encouraged to take up public speaking, visiting lecturers from neighbouring Chartist localities, paid missionaries treading well-worn circuits, all the way up to the demonstrations and celebrations surrounding the visit of a great Chartist leader. We might illustrate this by looking at the experience of Nottinghamshire in 1842 (Figure 3).

The county's local lecturers, such as James Simmons from Sutton-in-Ashfield, or Henry Dorman, who kept a Chartist temperance hotel in Nottingham. spoke at localities within the county. In addition, localities in the district were occasionally or regularly visited by Chartist orators from neighbouring counties and associations; North Leicestershire in particular provided a number of lecturers, such as the Loughborough leader John Skevington. Then there were the lecture tours of P. M. Brophy, Thomas Clark, E. P. Mead and Dean Taylor, operating out of Nottingham, which were more systematic and organized, as one would expect. And at the top of the lecturing hierarchy the celebrated visits of O'Connor to the county in the summer months were accompanied by processions and presentations, tea parties and soirees. Chartist lecturing was therefore a characteristically layered but systematically organized activity.

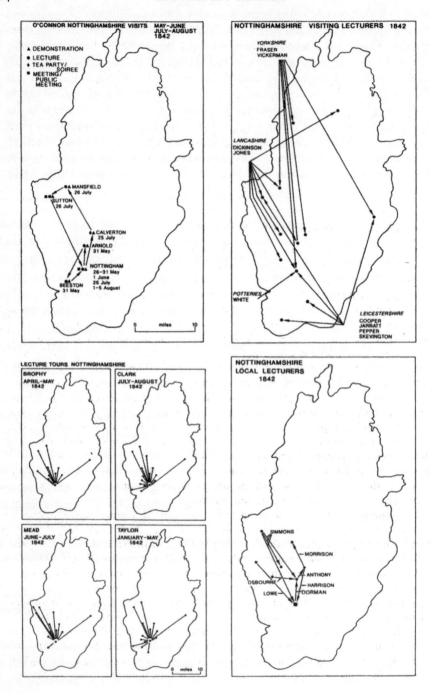

Figure 3. Lecturing activity in Nottinghamshire, 1842.

The cultural significance of Chartist lecturing

The geography of Chartist lecturing was just as important, though, in its cultural significance. The priority that the Chartists accorded to the principle and power of public *communication* is the most striking element in the lecturing commitment, over and above the instrumental efficacy of such activity. Chartism encouraged and revelled in the free flow of ideas and information, and the movement's desire for knowledge was thus up to a point indiscriminate. This however was wholly consistent with their political ideals. The *Northern Star* could welcome the introduction of the penny post, recognizing that whilst it would not help to remedy national wrongs, nevertheless it represented a victory of principle: "We desire to see communication and information spread in every direction on the easiest terms"[33] Put in its essence, communication between fellow Chartists, and – beyond that – to the popular constituency to which they appealed, was inseparable from their democratic ambitions. Lecturing meant far more than political proselytism in its pragmatic sense. It was not simply a matter of transmitting the message of Chartist politics to its widest audience, but of encouraging debate, political pedagogy and intellectual independence amongst the disenfranchised. Knowledge, as they continually reminded themselves, was power, and it followed from this that the diffusion of knowledge depended on the most open and democratic communication between Chartists and between Chartist localities.[34]

For instance, as the experience of lecturing involved a great deal of stamina and sacrifice, in the service of democratic political communication, it carried with it a signal rhetorical and political value that went beyond organizational matters. The experience of lecturers, covering the country in exhausting tours and regular circuits, was reported to the Chartist membership within a rhetorical mode that emphasized the principle of democratic communication – a discourse of hard-won communication and enlightenment in the service of a political public.[35] At one level, this is a common enough rhetorical ploy; at another, though, it can be taken as an analogue of the political struggle itself.[36] At best, therefore, the lecturing experience was routinely arduous, Jonathan Bairstow petulantly reminding his audiences in the East Midlands, for instance. that "Derbyshire ... is *not* flat as a pancake. Its jagged and towering mountains rather resemble the Alps or Appennines. The country is thus none the easier for Missionary exertion, though certainly healthier"[37] Police attention might be equally frustrating – as Peter McDouall reported from his tour of the Midlands in 1842:

I next marched, escorted as usual, through the snow to Pitchford, and was greeted by a joyful peal of bells rung for the occasion. I lectured in a barn where there were two pigs outside and two policemen inside. The pigs grunted, the police grumbled, and the people were gratified. The police were sent for by an old lady, who either imagined we were going to storm her house, or steal the pigs. The pigs remained unmolested to digest the first Chartist lecture addressed to the swinish multitude, and the police, like all watchful guardians on a frosty night, repaired to the nearest public house, for the purpose of drinking the old lady's health, at her especial expense .[38]

In the same county, furthermore, it was reported that the opposition Jonathan Bairstow had met with "was not of the most pleasant description. Dead cats, brick-bats, &c., were plentifully showered upon him – even fire arms were brought into requisition to intimidate him."[39] More seriously, therefore, lecturers risked their freedom and their health. John Mason's arrest in Sedgley in July of 1842, where the authorities were reported to have boasted of charging the first Chartist ever to have arrived in the place, was an ever-present possibility.[40] Cooper, Bairstow, West, Jones, and other lecturers, all followed Mason to the courts in the clampdown during the Plug Riots, for at times of crisis the lecturers were inevitably the first to feel the authorities' displeasure. These dangers and hardships endured by the missionaries were taken as necessary sacrifices, however, made in order to establish and keep open the lines of political communication. Indeed, their significance is so great that it is no wonder that the lecturing life took on religious connotations. Jonathan Bairstow could appeal to his fellow Chartists in just this manner:

> To you, the members of the body which called me into my present capacity, I am amenable, and to you only: beneath no other earthly God will I worship; nor will I prostrate myself beneath any other shine than that which is resplendent with the lustre of our common and immortal principles. In their advocacy I have given upwards of 560 lectures, speeches, and addresses; travelled upwards of 5,000 miles; and literally worn out a splendid constitution of body to a mere shade of what it was; and am ready, at any hour, sooner than recant, to lose my life on their behalf.[41]

The geography of political lecturing was freighted therefore with a significance for the Chartists' political culture that the need simply for organizational coherence does not capture. The lecturers could feel, and did, that they bore a special responsibility to the Chartist body, for to them was the critical burden of political communication largely assigned. In this sense we can speak of the lecturers having a calling or a vocation, for they had a common devotion to the principles of unfettered communication.

Something of the link that Humphrey Southall has posited between geographical mobility and political radicalism is evident here. On the one hand the lecturers were perhaps the dominant agents acting as an integrative force, breaking down local chauvinism and isolation, building an "artisan sense of community that was national rather than local", but at the same time geographical mobility carried a political significance that was not lost on the Chartists.[42] The movement's lecturers themselves embodied and emblematized democratic political ambitions. Perhaps this is brought out most clearly with reference to the experience of Robert Lowery, whose autobiographical reflections painstakingly trace his entry into public life, from his initiation into a political discussion group to his career as a Chartist and later as a temperance lecturer.[43] What is strikingly evident in Lowery's memoirs is an abiding interest in the art of communication, and the link made between this fascination with popular oratory and a truly democratic politics. Having, as he notes, "mixed with the working people privately and publicly, at their firesides, in their workshops, and in committee;

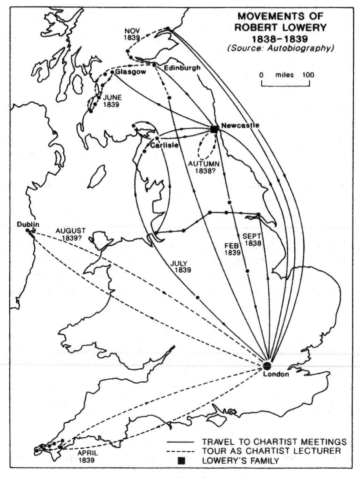

Figure 4. Movements of Robert Lowery, 1838-9

and ... publicly addressed them in cities, towns and villages, from the Lands-end to the Orkney Islands", Lowery's declared intention is to share the lessons of his public career with the rest of his class. We note that that public life, even just in its Chartist phase, was one of constant movement, speaking for the Charter on lecture tours to Cornwall, Dublin, Scotland. Durham. Westmoreland, Cumberland, travelling to, from, and through his home in Newcastle to delegate meeting and National Convention (Figure 4). More importantly, though. Lowery's developing political consciousness is paralleled to his growing abilities as a public speaker. Of his participation in a political discussion group, for instance, Lowery notes that:

> I derived much advantage from these discussions: they set us a-thinking and reading on the topics, and accustomed me to try to arrange in consecutive order all the arguments I could think of. This developed constructiveness, and helped to give me a readiness of thought and a greater facility of expression. I remember I was so diffident and deficient in language before that I could not speak a few consecutive sentences extempore: but I gradually got quicker in arranging my ideas, so that, when listening to an adverse argument, I could dot down the answers as the argument went on. I could rise thus to repeat them with more clearness and force … Of the twenty who composed the society one half became public speakers or writers.[44]

The leap from debating society to the platform and to a lecturing role was a daunting one, and Lowery recounts his experiences of political communication with great attention to preparation and detail. Of his first public speech, for instance, Lowery writes:

> I remember this maiden effort; it was a new position to occupy, and produced a new class of fears. Instead of twenty people, as in our debating society, above one hundred had taken tickets, and instead of being able to sit down if one liked after a sentence or two, or five minutes time, it would have to be twenty minutes, speaking, or a failure, and hit on the following mode of preparation, which although not quite as sublime as that of Demosthenes speaking to the roaring waves on the sea shore, was perhaps equally applicable to my purpose. I took a walk into the neighbouring fields in the afternoon until I got to an elevated part of one, where I could see all round, and thus know if any person was approaching within the sound of my voice. I tried to conceive the full tone and manner of speech which I thought it necessary I should deliver, and see how long I could sustain myself without faltering for matter or expression. This I did, and I remember well there was a flock of sheep grazing close by, and they were on the whole perhaps a superior audience to many, for if they did not reflect on what I said, they were quiet and orderly; they did not run away, but remained to the end, and there were some old ewes and rams which occasionally turned up their countenances and observed me with serious gravity. I was satisfied that I could "talk awhile"[45]

Such skills, Lowery avers, were essential ones for a public career. In this sense the steps taken on the road to becoming a Chartist lecturer paralleled the democratic demands of the disenfranchised. Lowery's reflections and reminiscences are instructive for the reason that they are entirely characteristic of the fascination within the Chartist movement with the process of communication. This is entirely evident furthermore in the characterization of Chartist lecturers according to their oratorical styles. One of the most striking things about how the Chartists saw themselves is this emphasis they placed on the appearance and performance of individual Chartist orators when lecturing their audiences.[46] The important point is, however, that the experience of lecturing was bound up with the business and the art of communication, and that this in itself was heavy with democratic significance.

Conclusions

The connections between geographical mobility and political consciousness, and the Chartist concern for oratory and public communication, suggest strongly that we treat lecturing as a key component of Chartism's political culture. Whilst I have been concerned here to demonstrate the level of national integration achieved through the professionalization of political lecturing, it has been emphasized too that the formal geography of Chartist lecturing cannot be divorced from the political substance of the movement. That is, the geography of political lecturing was inescapably charged with a profound cultural and political significance. Indeed, we might go further than this and argue that if political communication, rather than social structure, is taken to be pre-eminent in the creation of political identities, as much attention should then be devoted to the media of politics as to its specific political messages or ideologies.[47] Regarded in this light, the movement's political geography was not marginal but central to the construction of Chartism's very identity.

We might be tempted to call this construction a Chartist "public sphere". given the privileging of the principles and the institutions of public communication.[48] The cultural significance of Chartist lecturing has been celebrated here in just this way. It is realized that the message of politics can he subtly and repressively changed in ways that work *against* democratic participation. of course. Though there is not the space here to discuss the gendered nature of this public geography and the wider Chartist political culture of which it is a part, nor indeed the role lecturing played in the replacement of an older, rougher and more confrontational style of politics by a more restricted and conventional form, these conclusions follow from a concentration on the media of political communication.[49] Nevertheless, an awareness of the cultural and the political significance of Chartist lecturing does serve to highlight at the very least the construction of a cultural form of politics that contrasted sharply with the established polity. The geography of political lecturing was inseparable from this popular democratic culture, and from the priority it assigned to constructing a national political community underwritten by geographical mobility and unrestricted political communication.

Indeed, just as Raymond Williams has reminded us that communication has among its unresolved meanings a root in the notion of the common or mutual process of sharing, we should understand the geography of political lecturing in terms of this "culture of mutuality".[50] The link between the lecturing platform and the new democratic age was glaringly obvious both to the latter's supporters and to its detractors.[51] The Chartist lecturers or missionaries bore the weight of this expanded and inclusive notion of communication, bringing together many of the preoccupations that run through the movement as a whole: not only its educational and evangelical mission, but also its concern for free and unfettered communication, knowledge as power, the construction of a community that transcended local boundaries, and the co-ordination and marshalling of popular support. The lecturer embodied all those qualities that Chartism aimed to inculcate in its constituency: the ability to speak for oneself, to debate knowledgeably and constructively with those who regarded themselves as socially and politically superior, and not least that enlarged geographical vision encouraged by the experience of travelling in the ranks of the people themselves. A lecturing career was then rightly seen to be a "new and extended sphere of observation", the experience of lecturing encouraged not merely for its utility in spreading the gospel of Chartism, but also because it was part of the political education of a Chartist.[52]

Notes

[1] William Thomson, Preface *The Chartist Circular* (Glasgow 1841) v

[2] The phrase is taken from Andrew Charlesworth, 'Labour protest, 1780-1950', in R. J. Morris and J. Langton (Eds), *Atlas of Industrialising Britain 1780-1914* (London 1986) 185-89, 189. On the historical geography of Chartism, see John Langton, 'The industrial revolution and the regional geography of England', *Transactions of the Institute of British Geographers* 9 (1984) 145-67, 152-54, and the useful comments of Derek Gregory, 'The production of regions in England's industrial revolution', *Journal of Historical Geography* 14 (1988) 50-58, and 'Contours of crisis? Sketches for a geography of class struggle in the early industrial revolution in England', in A. R. H. Baker and D. Gregory (eds), *Explorations in historical geography: interpretative essays* (Cambridge 1984) 68-117. A perceptive exception to the focus on organization is Humphrey Southall, 'Mobility, the artisan community and popular politics in early nineteenth-century England', in G. Kearns and C.W.J. Withers (eds), *Urbanising Britain: essays on class and community in the nineteenth century* (Cambridge 1991) 103-30.

[3] Thus, for instance. A. Charlesworth, *Social protest in a rural society: the spatial diffusion of the Captain Swing disturbances of 1830-1831* (Norwich, Historical Geography Research Series 1, 1979), D. Gregory, *Regional transformation and industrial revolution: a geography of the Yorkshire woollen industry* (London 1982) 139-85.

[4] This argument can be applied in a wider sense to Chartist historiography. I have tried to demonstrate in my thesis, '"A free-trade in politics": a geography of Chartism's political culture, c.1838-1848' (unpubl. Ph.D. thesis, University of Cambridge 1993), 1-25, that both implicitly and

explicitly, interpretations of the movement's geography have dominated the understanding of Chartism.

5 J. Epstein and D. Thompson (eds), *The Chartist Experience: studies in working-class radicalism and culture. 1830-1860* (London 1982) 1

6 R. G. Gammage, *The History of the Chartist Movement* (London 1969) 221-22

7 On the pre-Chartist mass platform see A. Goodwin, *The friends of liberty: the English democratic movement in the age of the French Revolution* (Cambridge MA 1979), 495, and J. Belchem, 'Orator Hunt': Henry Hunt and English working-class radicalism (Oxford 1985)

8 *Northern Star,* 5 November 1842, 1

9 See Epstein and Thompson, op. cit. The influence of E. P. Thompson, *The Making of the English Working Class* (Harmondsworth 1968) is of course profound.

10 T. Cooper, *The life of Thomas Cooper, written by himself* (Leicester 1971) 169

11 W. E. Adams, *Memoirs of a Social Atom* (London 1903) 185

12 D. Jones, *Chartism and the Chartists* (New York 1975) 103. This contains much the best account of Chartist lecturers, though see also J. Schwarzkopf, *Women in the Chartist movement* (New York 1991) 217-18 for a brief assessment of women lecturers. For a useful comparison, see Edward Royle, Propaganda, in his *Radicals, secularists and republicans: popular freethought in Britain, 1866-1915* (Manchester 1980) 149-77

13 Jones, op cit., 102-3

14 *Northern Star,* 26 February 1842, 4

15 Ibid., 28 May 1842, 4

16 Compare, for the U.S.A., Donald M. Scott, 'The popular lecture and the creation of a public in mid-nineteenth-century America', *Journal of American History* 66(1980) 791-809, and 'The profession that vanished: public lecturing in mid-nineteenth-century America', in G. L. Geison (Ed.), *Professions and professional ideologies in America* (Chapel Hill 1983) 12-28

17 See David Vincent, 'Communication, community and the state', in C. Emsley and J. Walvin (eds), *Artisans, peasants and proletarians 1760-1860: essays presented to Gwyn A. Williams* (London 1983) 166-186. Compare Richard Johnson, '"Really useful knowledge": radical education and working-class culture, 1790-1848', in J. Clarke, C. Critcher, R. Johnson (eds), *Working-class culture: studies in history and theory* (London 1979) 75-102

18 J. Epstein, *The lion of freedom: Feargus O'Connor and the Chartist movement* (London 1982) 220-36. Compare William Thomson, preface to *The Chartist Circular,* (Glasgow, 1841) iv-v

19 *Midland Counties Illuminator,* 13 March 1841, 1

20 Gammage, *op. cit.,* 107

21 *Northern Star,* 23 April 1842, 6

22 Ibid., 5

23 Ibid., 5

24 *Northern Star,* 30 April 1842, 6. Jones, *op. cit.,* 105

25 *Northern Star,* 11 June 1842, 1

26 *Northern Star,* 15 January 1842, 2

27 *Northern Star,* 2 April 1842,2. See also D. Goodwav. *London Chartism 1838-1848* (Cambridge 1982)

28 *Northern Star,* 4 June 1842, 2; 22 January 1842, 1. Jones, op. cit., 104.

29 See Gammage, op. cit., 210

30 *Northern Star,* 23 April 1842, 1. The local New Lenton Chartists praised Taylor as a public man and as a patriot, and collected £23. 2 1/2d for him, all of which he accepted as proof of the people's regard

31 *Northern Star,* 9 July 1842, 6

32 Southall. op. cit., 127

33 *Northern Star,* 27 June 1840, 3. Likewise, the paper noted with approval the cheapness of railway travel in America, Northern Star, I January 1842, 8

34 Thus, see 'On the progress of information', *Chartist Circular.* 15 May 1841. 1-2. Moral and in-

tellectual cultivation essential to the progress and final triumph of freedom. *Chartist Circular*, 25 December 1841, 1-2

[35] Jonathan Bairstow's preamble to his account of his tour as missionary in Derbyshire in early 1841 is representative: "Darkness has covered the land, and gross darkness the people!" A darkness which "steeped the sense" of the cause of our national wrongs, "in forgetfulness". Yet this darkness is being penetrated by a few beams of truth, the owls are quitting their lodgement on the ruined wrecks of humanity, and into the dismantled but magnificent receptacle, knowledge will have free ingress', *Midland Counties Illuminator*, 24 April 1841, 3

[36] See Martha Vicinus, '"To live free or die": the relationship between strategy and style in Chartist speeches, 1838-1839', *Style* 10 (1976) 481-503

[37] *Midland Counties Illuminator*, 24 April 1841, 2

[38] *Northern Star*,

22 January 1842, 4. Quoted in Jones, op. cit., 107

[39] *Northern Star*, 30 April 1842, 6

[40] *Northern Star*, 9 July 1842, 3

[41] *Northern Star*, 26 November 1842, 7

[42] Southall, *op. cit.*, 126

[43] See B. Harrison and P. Hollis, (eds), *Robert Lowery: Radical and Chartist* (London 1979); and also their 'Chartism, Liberalism and the life of Robert Lowery', *English Historical Review* 82 (1967) 503-35

[44] Harrison and Hollis, *Robert Lowery: Radical and Chartist*, 72-3

[45] Ibid., 73-4

[46] Thus, see Gammage, *op cit.* On the role of political oratory in general see G. Watson, *The English ideology: studies in the language of Victorian Politics* (London 1973), and G. S. R. Kitson Clark, *An expanding society: Britain 1830-1900* (Cambridge 1967) 121

[47] On this point, and the "linguistic turn" in general, see P. Joyce, *Visions of the people. industrial England and the question of class, 1848-1914* (Cambridge 1991), J. Vernon. *Politics and the people: a study in English political culture, c. 1815-1867* (Cambridge 1993). For a polemic entry into these debates, see John Vernon, 'Who's afraid of the "linguistic turn'? The politics of social history and its discontents', *Social History* 19 (1994) 81-97

[48] The concept comes from J. Habermas, *The structural transformation of the public sphere: an inquiry into a category of bourgeois society* (Cambridge 1989). See Philip Howell, Public space and the public sphere: political theory and the historical geography of modernity *Environment and Planning D: Society and Space* 11(1993) 303-22 for a preliminary discussion of the geography of the public sphere

[49] On the gendering of Chartism, see Anna Clark, 'The rhetoric of Chartist domesticity: gender, language and class in the 1830s and 1840s', *Journal of British Studies* 31(1992) 62-88 and J. Schwarzkopf, op. cit. On the "closure" of the public sphere, see Vernon, *Politics and the people*. For similar fears of the perversion of agitation, see P. Pickering, 'Chartism and the "trade of agitation" in early Victorian Britain', *History* 76 (1991) 221-327

[50] R. Williams, *Keywords: a vocabulary of culture and society* (London 1976) 62-3. The phrase is taken from Pickering, op. cit., 236

[51] See H. Jephson, *The platform, its rise and progress* (London 1892) and T. Carlyle, Stump orator, *Latter-day pamphlets* (London 1850)

[52] The phrase comes from an advertisement for the Social Reformer's Almanac, in which a memoir of the Socialist lecturer and missionary James Rigby was appended, eulogising his perseverance in his educational effort, *Northern Star*, 1 January 1842, 3

Thomas Cooper in Leicester, 1840-1843

Stephen Roberts

Mention the name of Thomas Cooper to a nineteenth century historian and he or she will invariably identify him as 'the Chartist'. Though Cooper was an autodidact par excellence, a poet and a novelist and, for over twenty years, an itinerant preacher, he is remembered, first and foremost, as 'General' of the Leicester Chartists. In truth this is hardly surprising. No less than one quarter of Cooper's widely read autobiography, published in 1872, is devoted to an account of the two and a half years which preceded his imprisonment.[1] These years were undeniably the most important of Cooper's life. In 1840 he was a radical local journalist. Three years later he was a state prisoner. Leicester became a Chartist stronghold in the early 1840s, and membership of the National Charter Association eclipsed other centres of support. Cooper became the fiery champion of the Chartists. Charismatic, energetic and confident, he inspired the loyalty of thousands of working men and women. In the market place on a Sunday evening he came to symbolize their defiance, and their hopes for the future.

Not surprisingly Leicester Chartism has been written about by several historians. Robert Conklin, an American scholar who published a biography of Cooper in 1935, was the first of these.[2] Though Conklin possessed a genuine affection for his subject, his account of Cooper's Leicester years, like much of the rest of his book, is long winded, disconnected and unconvincing in some of its judgements. It was in the 1950s that A. Temple Patterson and J.F.C. Harrison produced their accounts of Leicester Chartism.[3] Patterson's narrative, commendably based on an extensive use of local newspaper sources, is unfortunately marred by his conviction that Cooper, from an early stage, decided to seek control of the Chartist movement, and, eventually, intended supplanting Feargus O'Connor.[4] According to Patterson, Cooper became leader of the Chartists in Leicester, and afterwards in the county, as he strove to fulfil his ambition. Such an interpretation attempts to rationalize to too great a degree Cooper's two and a half years in Leicester. At one point Patterson almost certainly misread the evidence.[5] The standard account of Leicester Chartism is usually regarded as Harrison's. His portrayal of Cooper's activities, however, is brief, and adds only a few facts and figures, mainly derived from the *Northern Star*, to the account in the autobiography. Many years have elapsed since both Patterson and Harrison wrote about

Cooper, and new material has since emerged. For several reasons therefore a re-examination of Cooper's Leicester career seems justified.

II

Cooper was already thirty-five when he arrived in Leicester at the end of November 1840 to become a reporter for the *Leicestershire Mercury*. Behind him lay important experiences in Lincolnshire and London as an autodidact, Methodist preacher and radical journalist. Cooper's earlier life should not be ignored by those interested specifically in his Chartist years. In many ways it points to what was to happen in Leicester. Cooper spent the first thirty years of his life in Gainsborough, though it was in Leicester on 20 March 1805 that he was born. He was illegitimate and had a half sister, Ann, personal detail omitted from the autobiography.[6] Ann, who became a domestic servant in Gainsborough, remained fond of her brother, reading his Chartist journals and, when he failed to answer her letters, confessing to having 'such queer dreams about him'.[7] Cooper's astonishing feats of self education in Gainsborough are vividly re-created in the autobiography.[8] Proof of what he achieved can be found in his remarkable prison-poem, the *Purgatory of Suicides,* published in 1845. Though at times tedious and difficult to understand, the volume was an undeniable poetic and cultural achievement on Cooper's part.[9] Cooper's youthful self education should not be seen just as a quest in itself, largely unrelated to his later radical career. It in fact ensured that his radicalism bore a very special stamp. Shakespeare, Milton, Hampden and Sydney all featured prominently in his radical vocabulary. The Leicester Chartists became known as the Shakespeareans.[10] Cooper came to see himself and the Chartists as nothing less than latter day Commonwealthsmen.

The seven years before Cooper arrived in Leicester were spent in Lincoln and, for a short period, in London. In Gainsborough Cooper had become a Methodist preacher, but a quarrel with the local superintendent had ended with his departure for Lincoln in November 1833. Very energetic and utterly sincere in his religious opinions, Cooper had come to believe that the superintendent was neglecting his duties and had attempted to fill the role himself.[11] It was as a Methodist preacher that Cooper first learned to command his audiences. Before his arrival in Leicester he was already adept at delivering emotional, highly charged speeches based on passages from the Bible.

Lincoln was a different world to the young and inexperienced Cooper. He became involved in the Mechanics Institute and the Choral Society. His prodigious energy and his desire to assert his own leadership are evident in his activities in these years. At the Mechanics Institute he became a member of the committee and soon afterwards established classes in Latin and French. When the curator resigned in December 1835, Cooper put himself forward as successor. His offer, however, was not taken up, and, characteristically, he soon lost interest and eventually had to be removed from the committee for non-attendance. For a few years Cooper was the wilful secretary of the Choral Society. He ran the society singlehandedly. Inevitably there were protests, and, in January 1837, he finally resigned as secretary of what his opponents derided as 'Cooper's Society'.[12] Already, though, Cooper had new preoccupations. In summer 1836 he had become full time Lincoln correspondent for the *Lincoln, Rutland and Stamford Mercury.* The staid old business newspaper, formerly enlivened by occasional references to the weight of pigs, became for two years the scourge of the cathedral clergy and the local Tories. In his self assumed role as public defender, Cooper scrutinised the activities of the cathedral clergy.[13] At the same time, like two other men who later became Chartists, Thomas Sidaway in Gloucester and Richard Spurr in Truro, he led a successful campaign against church rates.[14]

Reading Cooper's contributions to the *Mercury,* it becomes clear that when he arrived in Leicester, far from being ignorant of politics as Harrison asserted, he was already a radical.[15] In Lincoln he enthusiastically supported the cause of the novelist-politician, Edward Bulwer, often poking fun at his Tory opponent, Colonel Sibthorp.[16] In the *Mercury* Cooper canvassed support for household suffrage, though he was not critical when C.H. Churchill, who contested Lincoln with Bulwer in 1837, subsequently announced his conversion to manhood suffrage.[17] Shorter parliaments and the ballot were also urged on the Lincoln electorate by Cooper.[18] These opinions were also put forward by Cooper in the *Kentish Mercury, Gravesend Journal and Greenwich Gazette* which he edited, after his arrival in London and unsuccessful bid for literary fame, between March and September 1840.[19] In 1840 Cooper regarded himself as a Liberal. He had written in favour of an extension of the franchise (and praised Chartist leaders, William Lovett and John Collins), the ballot, partial redistribution of the constituencies, shorter parliaments and corn law repeal.[20] He was critical of the 1834 Poor Law and the 1839 Rural Police Act.[21] Though Cooper's path to Chartism was certainly very different to that of the majority of others who subsequently also emerged as the movement's leaders, it cannot be doubted that he was a man of radical opinions when he arrived in Leicester. This said, Cooper's conversion to the Chartist cause was still a very significant break with his own past. His radical stance before 1840 was acceptable to early Victorian provincial society. In Leicester he became the full time leader of an ultra radical movement.

III

When Cooper was arrested in Leicester on 26 August 1842, just over one week after the outbreak in the Potteries, the omnibus which took him to the railway station was forced to stop on a number of occasions because of the large crowd which had gathered – many of whom thrust their hands through the open windows for a final handshake.[22] In Leicester that summer there were well over two and a half thousand Chartists. Bonds of affection between Cooper and his followers were strong. Like young Tom Goadby, many 'worshipped me mightily …'[23] Truly enough, Cooper wrote that he 'wield[ed] … a more powerful influence than any Chartist leader in England, except our chief'.[24] In 1842 he was the Feargus O'Connor of Leicester, determined to 'bear like the Turk no brother near the throne'. How did he become leader of the Leicester Chartists?

Cooper's employment as a reporter for the *Leicestershire Mercury* in fact proved to be short lived. At first the editor, H.A. Collier, himself a supporter of manhood suffrage, had raised no objections to Cooper assisting the local Chartist journal, the *Midland Counties Illuminator*, which had first appeared, under the editorship of George Bown, on 1 January 1841. Soon afterwards, however, probably early in February 1841, Collier gave Cooper notice to leave. As Patterson has indicated, Cooper was dismissed because of the hostility manifest in his articles in the *Illuminator* to the Leicester employers, whom he charged with responsibility for the sufferings of the stockingers.[25] These articles, though they only gave voice to feelings long prevalent in Leicester among working men, ran in direct contradiction to Collier's own deeply held belief in the need to seek class conciliation. Consequently on 6 March 1841, after just fifteen weeks, Cooper's employment as a reporter for the *Leicestershire Mercury* came to an end.

By this time, however, Cooper had already established himself as editor of the *Illuminator*, and was able to dismiss any thoughts of returning to London. Six issues of the journal had been produced by Bown, but these had not sold well and substantial debts had been accumulated for paper and printing. Cooper, however, was determined to make the *Illuminator* succeed. 'I don't care for myself,' he told the committee of shareholders on being appointed editor. 'I will live on a crust to make this paper answer. I have been cramped in my sentiments wherever I have been, but now I hope to have full scope'.[26] The shareholders agreed to pay him a salary of two pounds each week, and the first (enlarged) issue under Cooper's editorship appeared on 13 February 1841.[27] The precise period which elapsed between Cooper being appointed editor and assuming total control of the journal, including responsibility for its debts, after the shareholders could no longer pay his salary, cannot be established with complete certainty. Undoubtedly there are contradictions in the evidence. The recollections of both John Seal and John Markham suggest that Cooper became owner of the *Illuminator* about one month after taking over the editorship from Bown.[28] The non-insertion in the journal of a notice requesting business letters to be sent to Henry Green, secretary of the committee of shareholders, after the issue of 13 March 1841, the fifth week of Cooper's editorship, seems to confirm this. One historian, however, has suggested that it was not until a later date that Cooper took over complete control of the *Illuminator*. According to the corrective of

Robert Barnes, he did not become owner until the end of May 1841, just before the journal ceased to exist. Barnes' assertions, however, should be treated with circumspection: he offers no conclusive evidence to back up his claims, and throughout the article his dislike of Cooper is barely disguised.[29]

In truth none of this is of great consequence. What is important is that there was to be no major revival for the *Illuminator* under Cooper, either as editor or owner. The journal was advertised in the *Star* and despatched to London, Derby, Nottingham, Loughborough and Kettering, but large numbers still remained unsold. Cooper, after a discussion with Markham, wrote to Perronet Thompson, a veteran radical who contributed a weekly letter to the *Illuminator*, asking for money to continue the journal. He was rebuffed, and only received a loan of ten pounds after he invited Thompson to stand in Leicester at the next election. John Walter, the proprietor of *The Times*, who contested Nottingham in a by election in April 1841, gave another five pounds after Cooper printed his election address in the *Illuminator*.[30] This Cooper used to help pay off some of the journal's long standing debt to its printer, Albert Cockshaw.

The *Illuminator* was a fine Chartist journal. Written for the most part by Cooper, it also contained interesting contributions from James Sweet and Henry Vincent.[31] Its four pages each week were devoted largely to Chartist politics. 'It would be easy to throw into our pages an infusion of nonsense', Cooper wrote in the second issue under his editorship, 'but we have a serious object in view'[32] The *Illuminator* finally came to an end in May 1841. Cooper had been responsible for keeping the journal alive for so long, and twice he had saved it from closure – first when Bown gave up the editorship and subsequently when he took over the ownership from the shareholders. But there was little he could do when Cockshaw refused to print any further editions. Cooper, discounting the *Illuminator's* debts, sought out an explanation for its demise, and found it in the Whigs, often the victims of bitter censure in the pages of his journal, whom he now claimed had brought pressure to bear on Cockshaw. Working-class hatred of the Whigs, responsible for the 1834 Poor Law, the transportation of John Frost, Zephaniah Williams and William Jones, and the imprisonment of many Chartists, was intense in summer 1841, and, in the weeks following the final issue of the *Illuminator*, Cooper's biting attacks continued in full spate.[33] The *Illuminator*, however, was gone: Cooper was left with an impressive collection of back copies, a large debt, and an immensely strengthened position as a leader of Leicester Chartism.

For the rest of 1841 Cooper continued to press ahead with his efforts to establish a successful Chartist journal in Leicester. The *Illuminator* was succeeded by the ephemeral *Chartist Rushlight*, a halfpenny journal whose sharp anti-Whig tone ensured that it sold well amongst local Tories during the election excitement of summer 1841, and then, from July to November 1841, by the *Extinguisher*, which, like the *Illuminator*, made a financial loss.[34] On the very first issue Cooper lost ten shillings, a debt which increased every week until, after twenty-two numbers, he was compelled to call a halt. Cooper had tried hard to make the *Extinguisher* pay: the price had been reduced from three half-pence to one halfpenny, and collections had been made to support the journal. Thomas Duncombe, the radical MP for Finsbury, also donated ten pounds, but most of this was used to pay off some of the *Illuminator's* debts.[35] Sales of the *Extinguisher,* however, remained inadequate. In Melton Mowbray, Gideon Cooke sadly reported to Cooper in October 1841, there was 'a verry slack sale' (sic).[36]

In his autobiography Cooper refused to discuss his bitter arguments with John Markham in winter 1841-2.[37] This should not surprise us. His escape from the Potteries in August 1842 made far more exciting reading. Besides there seemed little point in recollecting old quarrels. The Chartists, he believed, deserved bet-ter than to be remembered for their arguments. Though Cooper could set aside his rupture with Markham, an historian cannot. The immediate background to the dispute lay in Cooper's growing ascendancy in the local movement. Since early 1841 he had been in effect a full time Chartist organiser, unlike Markham, who remained a shoemaker. He began to preach and to lecture, and also devised a plan to reorganise the local Chartist body.[38] At first the old leaders welcomed the new vigour which Cooper brought to Chartism. 'I was the greatest man he ever saw', Cooper recalled of Markham's attitude. 'He thought it quite provi-dential that such a man should have come among the Chartists'.[39] There were only two dissenters, John Seal and William Burden, active Chartists from the beginning, who objected to Cooper's enthusiastic endorsement of O'Connor's Chartist-Tory alliance, a tactic advanced by Cooper on the grounds that the Whigs would be 'driven to the Charter ... by the Tories being placed in office'.[40] Doubtless Seal and Burden also caught wind of Cooper's financial dealings with the Tories: 'a considerable sum'[41] of Tory money, probably about one hundred pounds, passed through his hands in order that he could secure Chartist (and other) support for the Tory candidates in the borough and county elections. None of this money Cooper retained for himself, though he had no hesitation in accepting a number of unspecified personal payments from individual Tories.[42] To Seal these arrangements only 'prostituted their principles at the shrine of Toryism ...'[43] The upshot was that, on nomination day in Leicester in June 1841, he publicly denounced Cooper, an act which earned him a vehement reply, and severed all connexions with the local Chartists.[44] Ironically, nearly two years later, in March 1843, Cooper himself was to identify the Tory alliance as a chief cause of Chartism's failure.[45]

It was evident by autumn 1841 that all was not well between Cooper and Markham. By this time Cooper had taken effective control of the local move-ment, though Markham had, to some extent, conceded this to him, and had not been just shouldered aside. Markham had stood 'aloof from active exertion',[46]

declining, for example, Cooper's invitation to assist him in his Sunday preaching, an activity which contributed substantially to Cooper's growing popularity
with the Leicester Chartists. It was clear that such lack of assistance irritated
Cooper, and helped prepare the ground for his confrontation with Markham.
There was, however, another factor: Cooper's devotion to O'Connor. Hero worship came easily to him, and, even if he was not alone in Leicester in his admiration for O'Connor, he certainly led the way. To Cooper, O'Connor 'possessed ...
greater political foresight than all the other leaders of Chartism put together',[47]
though such an assertion, he declared, 'is not the language of personal idolatry.
It is simply a candid confession of proper and deserved attachment ...'[48] As
early as March 1841 Cooper had demonstrated the strength of his attachment
to O'Connor by organising a Leicester petition, which Duncombe had agreed
to present to the House of Commons, to secure the Chartist leader's release
from York Castle. Two months later he conceived a plan for O'Connor to stand
in Leicester at the next election, together with Perronet Thompson. Feargus'
candidature was enthusiastically proclaimed in the *Illuminator*.[49] Markham,
however, did not share Cooper's excitement, and kept his 'hands ... at his awl
and would not budge one inch to help me'.[50] 'I'll raise such a hell of a row about
your ears',[51] Cooper threatened, but to no avail. O'Connor was not destined to
stand in Leicester, and neither was Thompson, who instead took himself off to
be defeated elsewhere. Cooper, however, was by no means discouraged by this
setback. When O'Connor was released from York Castle in August 1841, after
eighteen months, Leicester rejoiced in no uncertain terms: Cooper decorated his
shop in High Street with flowers, flags and a portrait of Feargus, and organised
a jamboree of eating, dancing and singing which went on until early morning.
Markham joined in the celebrations, even if he did not share Cooper's considerable admiration for O'Connor. Markham in fact held Lovett in great esteem,
and, earlier in the year, had even considered writing him a letter of consolation
after O'Connor had secured his ejection from mainstream Chartism. It was
Markham's sympathies for Lovett, his lukewarm support for O'Connor's proposed candidature and his refusal to assist with Sunday preaching that finally
led Cooper to fix on him the public appellation of 'Judas', though Cooper subsequently claimed that this sobriquet pre-dated his own arrival in Leicester. 'I
am willing to work with you as before', Cooper declared, '[though] it is but little
that you have worked with me'.[52] Markham responded in a series of aggrieved
private letters. 'Your attempts to injure me in the estimation of friends', he wrote
to Cooper early in December 1841, 'are still continued by representing me as an
unreasonable man, determined to perpetuate strife in the society'.[53] Cooper,
however, had no doubts that justice was on his side. 'Can you divine no reason',
he asked Markham, 'why I used the epithet "Judas" with regard to you?'[54]

By January 1842 bitter public recrimination had broken out between Cooper
and Markham. Cooper continued to assert what he saw as Markham's disloy-

alty to the Chartist cause. For his part, Markham accused Cooper of dictatorial behaviour. Cooper, he claimed, had flouted the constitution that he himself had written, and had often threatened to divide the local Chartists. George Wray, who was to remain a prominent Leicester Chartist into the 1850s, supported Markham in a public letter to Cooper:

> 'You cannot but remember when Scotton voted for Markham being secretary, how you lifted up your hands, with eyes turned up, and cried out, "Now I must leave you. I cannot act for you. Mr Scotton has voted against me. I must leave you"; which raised a general cry among the women and boys as usual, "No, Mr Cooper, you must not leave us"; and then you repeated the old feeler, "Will you support me?", and that has been your constant cry since you came among us'.[55]

Markham also accused Cooper of financial irregularity, a sensitive issue amongst Chartists. Cooper was quick to deny these charges. He had 'never received a farthing from O'Connor ... Let Judas ask him',[56] and, as for approaching the Tories for money for the *Illuminator,* it was 'a lie ... gratuitous and unqualified'.[57] There could be no disavowal, however, of Markham's charge that Cooper had sought to impose his own leadership on the Leicester Chartists. Cooper's reply in fact was remarkable both for its honesty and its degree of self knowledge:

> 'I am a despot in nature, that is perfectly true; and every strong willed man is a natural despot; but a despot is not always a tyrant, nor am I one. I cannot help feeling strongly: my constitution was given to me by my Maker. I cannot help my tendency to prefer my own views to other people's. I have acquired all I know amidst suffering and privation, and in the face of opposition and scorn. A self educated man is always strongly opinionated – for he feels he owes his mental superiority to no other man's teaching. Such a man is ever jealous of other people's control – and is never likely to seek fetters for his opinions'.[58]

There can be no doubt that, convinced of his own 'mental superiority', Cooper did seek control of Leicester Chartism, and experienced great difficulty in working in unison with others. It should also be recognised, however, that, in spite of any earlier threats he may have made, he did not wish to cause division. Cooper was anxious to maintain unity around his own leadership in Leicester, and that of O'Connor nationally, and envisaged Markham and the other old leaders serving as loyal lieutenants. He made several attempts to seek reconciliation with Markham at the end of 1841, but on each occasion was met by 'refusals ... to take my hand when I offered it to him'.[59] A permanent breach had now become inevitable, and, in mid-January 1842, Cooper himself advocated just such a step. One week later O'Connor visited Leicester, and Markham and his supporters were excluded from the platform.[60] The N.C.A. made an attempt to end the .quarrel by sending John Campbell to Leicester, but without success.

Leicester Chartism was now divided into two unequal groups. Significantly, it was Cooper's Shakespearean Association which retained the loyalty of most Chartists.

In the months which followed Cooper tried to reunite the local movement. A deputation was sent to Markham's All Saints Chartists in April 1842, but the olive branch was rejected.[61] Even when Cooper stood up in the middle of a lecture by Dean Taylor, organised by the All Saints Chartists, the following month to urge unity and to accept some of the blame for the division himself, he was spurned. The action also cost him the support of J.G. Brooks, secretary of the Hinckley Chartists:

> I do not approve of … your conduct in disturbing the lecture of Mr Taylor & branding him as a man hired by the Whiggs [sic] to sow discord amongst us and destroy Chartism. Your general conduct is too arbitrary & tyrannical, & on these accounts I must discontinue my contributions to your paper. I cannot approve of tyranny in any shape'.[62]

To the All Saints Chartists, content with the connexions with such O'Connorite dissidents as Bronterre O'Brien and Henry Vincent and their membership of 168,[63] Cooper became known as 'King Tom, the tyrant'. Not until Cooper's arrest was there a thaw in relations between the two groups.

IV

Cooper's radicalism was of a very emotional nature. He had been spurred into advocacy of Chartism by exposure to the plight of the Leicester stockingers:

> '…'twas gnawing hunger's pain
> I saw your lank and fainting forms reveal,
> Poor trampled stockingers! – that made me feel
> 'Twas time to be in earnest, nor regard
> Man's freedom merely as a theme for zeal
> In hour's of emolous converse, or for bard
> Weaving rapt fancies in pursuit of Fame's reward'.[64]

In Lincoln Cooper 'never knew what poverty was … I could not have believed that such squalid degredation, such intense misery, existed …'[65] But now, in 1842, he received letters which told the full story of the stockingers' misery:

> 'Friend, think what must have been my feelings on last Sunday morning to lay in bed and here my wife sighing and lisping, well Sunday's here & nothing to eat. And then the poor little infant crying for suck and there was none, no the little nourishment was dried up & gone & had it not been for a friend who brought a little not one morsel should we have had with the Exception of a mouthful of Bread, & that

friend was next neighbour for we had neither meat, flower, Potatoes, milk, Tea, Sugar, Coffee nor nothing else & no money not even one halfpenny to come to school with' [sic].[66]

Such hideous poverty greatly distressed Cooper, and he became increasingly angry. His speeches grew fiercer. At the head of his Shakespeareans he began to march through the streets of Leicester in early evening, defiantly singing Chartist hymns and striking genuine fear into the hearts of local shopkeepers. Those who, in Cooper's eyes, sought to divide and weaken Chartism at a time of such great suffering did not escape his wrath. Both Bronterre O'Brien, in June 1842, and Henry Vincent, the following month, had their meetings in Leicester, organised by the All Saints Chartists, broken up by Cooper's Shakespeareans, much to the delight of George Julian Haney: 'How nobly you tackled O'Brien. What a treacherous humbug he is …'[67]

Though not himself a stockinger, Cooper was able to convey to his followers a very real sense of identification. At the same time he gave an impression of superiority, probably most obvious in the way he spoke and which the stockingers encountered only in their employers. Cooper's frequent references to the Bible and the struggles of the past served to strongly legitimize the Chartist cause His radical sermons and the hymns of William Jones and John Henry Bramwich gave Leicester Chartism strong religious overtones, one of its most distinctive features. To Cooper the struggles of the Commonwealthsmen and the Chartists were almost interchangeable. 'Our cause is one with that for which "Hampden bled in the field and Sydney died on the scaffold", he wrote in July 1842, 'We think too meanly of it by far'.[68] He saw himself (in an early draft of the *Purgatory* written in autumn 1842) as a latter day Commonwealthsman:

'Hampden and Pym and Eliot – product rare …
I burned to reinstate that lofty time
Those lofty deeds – within my fatherland
Once more …'[69]

The Leicester Chartists became very familiar with the struggles of the Commonwealthsmen. Within little over a month of becoming editor of the *Illuminator* Cooper had begun a lengthy series of romanticised front page portraits of Hampden, Eliot and Pym.[70] His most ambitious (and best) Chartist journal, which included letters from Feargus, an abundance of verse and an account of the untimely demise of Charles I, was even named after his heroes. This harmonizing with the past, however, did not guarantee the *Commonwealthsman* success.[71] In all twenty issues were published, intermittently, between December 1841 and June 1842. At first the journal sold well enough, but, after the early issues had appeared, sales began to fall off. The circulation in Melton Mowbray, for example, which in December 1841 had stood at twenty-one a week, had declined by April 1842 to just four a week.[72] The *Commonwealthsman* was not the only means Cooper used to remind his fellow Chartists of those who had gone before them. He lectured on the lives of his heroes, and Hampden, Sydney, Pym and Milton all had classes named after them in his adult school. The point was certainly not lost on some Leicester Chartists who, after Cooper's departure from the town, organised a Hampden section amongst their own numbers.[73]

From the Commonwealthsmen Cooper derived his belief in the ultimate triumph of the Chartist cause, and his support for republicanism and a defensive use of force.[74] Like most Chartists, Cooper believed that it was legitimate to fight in self defence against violent repression by the ruling class. The Commonwealthsmen, he asserted in the *Illuminator,* had believed in the right of resistance.[75] He asked in one Chartist hynm in 1842:

'God of power! – is it true,
"We are many, they are few"?
Why, then, drag we still the chain?
Better to be with the slain …

Better like brave Hampden die,
With the sword upon our thigh;
Better like brave Sydney fall,
Bold and blithe, at freedom's call …'[76]

There is no evidence, however, that Cooper's rhetoric of fighting and martyrdom ever served as an impetus for arming amongst the Leicester Chartists; possibly, it may actually have held that in check. Certainly Cooper himself never handled a weapon during his period of leadership there. Moreover, he spoke of the insurrection at Newport in November 1839 in disapproving terms, though, very likely, his attitude would have been different had it not ended so disastrously.[77]

In the localities the Chartist struggle was sustained on a week-to-week basis by a variety of cultural activities. Schools, lectures, readings from the *Star* and tea parties were widespread, ensuring that, for many, their commitment to the Chartist cause became a part of their everyday lives. Leicester, under Cooper's leadership, provides one of the most interesting examples of this cultural side of the Chartist movement. Typical of the leisure activities organised by the Leicester Chartists were the lectures, recitations, tea parties, dancing and singing which celebrated Christmas 1841 and Whitsuntide 1842. Cooper was especially concerned to foster feelings of intellectual self-respect amongst his followers. The back page of the *Illuminator* was filled each week with extracts from the works of William Hazlitt, Mary Wollstonecroft, Thomas Paine and many others. From March 1841 he began to deliver regular lectures. History, literature, geography and geology were the main subjects for these discourses. He did, however, make some forays into more unusual areas, including astronomy and phrenology, the latter of which was subsequently developed to include demonstrations of mesmerism. Cooper's lectures were well received: the Chartists 'wedged the room'[78] where they met to hear him, and one anonymous correspondent felt sure that the lectures would 'elevate the minds of the working classes and fit them for the exersise of every right and privilidge man is heir to' (sic).[79] Even Markham, it seems, was moved to 'ecstatic delight'.[80]

On 16 January 1842 Cooper opened his adult school, funded in part by a weekly subscription of one halfpenny, but mainly by donations obtained from local shopkeepers and householders after personal visits by Cooper: of the £10 4s. ½d. raised in the school's first six weeks only £3 2s. 0d. came from the Chartists themselves. From the figures provided by Cooper for subscriptions collected in the school it is possible to calculate the numbers who attended the first six meetings:[81]

	Subscriptions	Attendance
16 January	7s.1d.	170
21 January	10s.9d.	258
6 February	11s.1d.	266
13 February	11s.5d.	274
20 February	11s.5d.	280
27 February	10s.0d.	240

The classes were named after Cooper's heroes from the past and leading Chartists, including James Leach, Peter McDouall, and Frost, Williams and Jones. Cooper himself taught a teachers' class, named, predictably enough, after O'Connor. Some books were donated to the school, but the bulk had to be bought. The first books purchased were fifteen copies of William Cobbett's *Legacy to Labour*, together with six dozen copies of his spelling book, twenty six copies of William Channing's *Self Culture*, thirteen copies of his *Elevation of the Labouring Class*, twenty six copies of Thomas Paine's *Common Sense*, and twenty copies of John Campbell's *Examination of the Corn Laws*. This expenditure, totalling £7 11s. 3d., together with payments for rent, repairs and fires, ensured that, by the end of February, the school was 17s. 3d. in debt. Soon after, probably in May 1842, as the hardship confronting the stockingers grew worse and they lost all interest in learning, the whole enterprise had to be abandoned.[82]

A fuller and more lasting expression of the intellectual self-awareness Cooper sought to inspire amongst his Shakespeareans came perhaps in his creation of a small cell of Chartist poets. The *Shakespearean Chartist Hymn Book*, which first appeared in summer 1842, collected together thirty or so Leicester hymns, mainly written by Bramwich and Jones.[83] Bramwich, a soldier-turned-stockinger, died of consumption at the age of forty-two in 1846, 'a system-murdered man'[84] in his own words. He wrote a genuinely poignant hymn which was sung at the graveside of Samuel Holberry, who died incarcerated in York Castle in

June 1842, but unfortunately little else of his verse has survived.[85] Jones, a glove-hand in his early thirties in 1841-2, was an abundantly productive working-class poet.[86] He continued to produce verse long after Cooper's departure from Leicester, culminating in the publication in 1849 of his extended poem, *The Spirit; or A Dream in the Woodlands,* and, four years later, of his non-combative *Poems.*[87] He died in January 1855, aged forty seven.[88]

Cooper himself appears to have written little verse during his time in Leicester. Although widely credited with the introduction of Chartist hymn signing, he published just three hymns[89]. The Chartists believed, however, that he was also the author of probably the most famous Chartist song, the paean to O'Connor, the 'Lion of Freedom'. The song first appeared in the *Star*, without any identification of author, in September 1841, at the time of O'Connor's release from York Castle.[90] If Cooper was responsible, it was unlike him not to append his name. He subsequently denied authorship in fact, attributing the song to an unknown Welsh female Chartist.[91] It is possible, however, that Cooper may well have written the song, though there can be no certain proof of this. The choice of words seems to suggest him. He also did an immense amount to popularize the song, giving every impression that it was one of his own. He concluded nearly all his Leicester meetings with a rousing chorus, included the song in his *Shakespearean Chartist Hymn Book,* and sang it wherever he went in 1842. By 1848 the 'Lion of Freedom' was sufficiently the property of the Leicester Chartists for Jones to re-write it.[92]

V

On 9 August 1842 Cooper left Leicester at the beginning of his ill-fated journey to the Chartist conference in Manchester.[93] He was already in a state of great excitement. His tour of the north in mid-July had been greeted with great enthusiasm and, at the beginning of August, together with O'Connor and the Chartists, he had supported Joseph Sturge in the second Nottingham by-election.[94] In the Potteries, which he travelled through on his way to Manchester, Cooper reached a fever pitch of emotional excitement. At last he could sense Chartism coming to a head, and was determined to play a decisive role in that climax. 'Now do not be alarmed, my dear love, if they take me a prisoner', he wrote to Susanna, his wife, 'Run away, I cannot. Latimer would not – Christ would not. My sweet love will not expect me to act cowardly'.[95] Passionately he called, on the Crown Bank in Hanley on the morning of 15 August, for a dramatic show of numbers in support of the Charter, though he genuinely did not expect the turnout to lead to the destruction of property.[96] 'The Queen thinks everything shd. be done to apprehend this Cooper ...',[97] Victoria wrote to Sir Robert Peel the day after the outbreak ended. Cooper was duly arrested, and, on 11-12 October, stood trial for arson. He was acquitted. 'This trial has been one of great interest for they panted for his blood', Thomas Winters, leader of the Leicester stockingers, wrote to Susanna. 'As soon as the verdict was given, I went and had a glass of Brandy … Excuse writing more for I am up to the neck in joy and so we all are'.[98] As if to demonstrate his resilience, Cooper returned to Leicester immediately after his release from Stafford Gaol in November 1842. Here he spent the remaining four months of his freedom.

In Leicester Cooper resumed his lectures, informing the stockingers, on one occasion, about Chinese history.[99] The Shakespeareans also performed several plays, including John Home's *Douglas* and, with Cooper in the title role, *Hamlet*.[100] It was during these months that Cooper and Markham took the first steps towards renewing their former friendship, undoubtedly brought about by the fate which had befallen Cooper. When a fund was set up for Cooper in Leicester in November 1844, Markham made a generous contribution.[101] There was, however, discord in the ranks of the Shakespeareans in winter 1842-3, which Cooper found difficult to quell. The dissension of Robert Jackson, one of Cooper's main lieutenants, and James Duffy, an Irish Chartist imprisoned after the abortive Sheffield rising in January 1840, was perhaps an early indication of how attitudes amongst some Shakespeareans to Cooper were to change during his long imprisonment.[102]

The arrest and first trial of Cooper had finally confirmed him as a national leader of Chartism, and, during the months before his second trial, he turned his mind increasingly to the future of the movement. He was determined, he wrote in one of a number of letters published in the *Star,* to see Chartism grow in strength.[103] For a time he believed that this might be accomplished by an alliance with Joseph Sturge's Complete Suffrage Union.[104] Cooper had in fact initially been hostile to the C.S.U., denouncing in the *Commonwealthsman* those Chartists who supported the new group.[105] During his first imprisonment, however, he experienced a change of mind. The strikes of the summer had been defeated, and, after conversations with Arthur O'Neill and William Prowting Roberts, both of whom had a signed a declaration supporting Sturge's initiative, he became convinced, for a short period, of the value of an alliance between middle class and working class radicals. O'Connor remained opposed to any alliance with the C.S.U., and Cooper's flirtation was soon over. His attempts to establish cordial relations with the C.S.U. in Leicester ended in complete failure. He was denounced for his support for O'Connor, and for his involvement in the outbreak in the Potteries. 'His reckless violence will doubtless not be forgotten at his trial', the Revd. J.P. Mursell, the local C.S.U. leader, declared. 'Nor, we trust, in his sentence'.[106] The Leicester supporters of the C.S.U. refused to join with the Chartists in sending delegates to a C.S.U. conference in Birmingham in December 1842. 'I will not sit in a conference where Cooper is', Mursell pronounced. 'I will have no share in a deputation with such a fellow, and I know he will be elected'.[107] The Birmingham conference, which Cooper attended as a delegate, was also to end in failure. 'My old and severe policy of opposing the hollow Sturgites root and branch', Cooper was ruefully concluding by the end of the year, 'was founded on the strictest propriety'.[108]

Found guilty of seditious conspiracy at this second trial in March 1843, Cooper was imprisoned in Stafford Gaol for two years. His period of Chartist leadership had ended not, as he had expected in summer 1842, in victory for the Chartists, but in his own imprisonment. 'My conscience tells me I have acted for the best', he was still able to write. 'If I erred, I cannot blame myself'.[109] Cooper was never again to return to Leicester as a resident. In his final few months in prison he fell out over money with the Chartist lecturer and journalist, Jonathan Bairstow, who also managed to turn some of the Leicester Chartists against him.[110] There was also the need to find a publisher for the *Purgatory*. It was therefore to London that Cooper went on his release from prison in May 1845. The links with Leicester, however, could never be broken. He spent the weeks before his expulsion from the Chartist conference in Leeds in August 1846 in his old stronghold. Terrible indigence persisted amongst the stockingers. For Cooper the six points seemed as vital and relevant as they had five years earlier.[111] In June 1849 he put himself forward as a parliamentary candidate for Leicester. He intended to stand in support of the Charter. Markham offered support, but, lacking money, Cooper was forced to withdraw his name.[112] Several months later he agreed to speak at a radical meeting in the town. Ill health, however, prevented his attendance. There were, Markham declared, 'great numbers who were disappointed in consequence of the non-appearance of Thomas Cooper'.[113]

Acknowledgements

Crown-copyright material in the Public Record Office is reproduced by permission of the Controller of Her Majesty's Stationary Office. I am also grateful to the Bishopsgate Institute, the British Library and Lincoln Reference Library for permission to quote from material in their possession. Thanks to Dorothy Thompson, who supervised the thesis-research on which this article is based.

Notes

[1] See Thomas Cooper, *Life of Thomas Cooper, Written by Himself*, (1872), pp.133-231 (hereafter, Cooper, *Life*).

[2] Robert Conklin, *Thomas Cooper, the Chartist 1805-1892*, (Manila, 1935).

[3] A. Temple-Patterson, *Radical Leicester: A History of Leicester, 1780-1850*, (Leicester, 1954), pp. 315-31(hereafter, Patterson, *Radical Leicester*); J.F.C. Harrison, 'Chartism in Leicester', in Asa Briggs, ed. *Chartist Studies* (1959), pp.99-146 (hereafter, Harrison, 'Chartism in Leicester'). Jack Simmons, *Leicester Past and Present*, (1974), I, pp.162-6 offers a brief (and unfair) account of Cooper's Leicester years.

[4] See Patterson, *Radical Leicester*, p.320.

[5] Ibid., See *Lincolnshire Chronicle*, 11 May 1929 (hereafter *L. C.)* for the letter which Patterson mentions. The sentence about 'a future struggle' in London refers to Cooper's literary ambitions.

[6] See Bishopsgate Institute (hereafter B.I.), Thomas Cooper to Thomas Chambers, 1 June, 2 June 1868 for references to Cooper's illegitimacy.

[7] Public Record Office (hereafter PRO), T.S. 11/600, John Yeats to Cooper, 7 July 1842. Also see T.S. 11/601, Ann Anderson to Cooper, 8 March, 8 April, 25 April 1842.

[8] See Cooper, *Life,* pp.22, 33-5, 42-66.

[9] For a full discussion of the *Purgatory* see Stephen Roberts, 'Thomas Cooper: Radical and Poet, c. 1830-1860' (unpublished M.Litt. thesis, University of Birmingham, 1986), pp. 298-329.

[10] See Cooper to R.G. Gammage, 26 February 1855, in Gammage's *History of the Chartist Movement* (1969 edn.), p.405 (hereafter Gammage, *History).* For Shakespeare's importance to Cooper see Roberts, thesis, pp.31-3.

[11] See Roberts, thesis, pp.49-54.

[12] See ibid, pp.55-7.

[13] See ibid., pp.58-60.

[14] See ibid., pp.60-1.

[15] See Harrison, 'Chartism in Leicester', p.141.

[16] See Roberts, thesis, pp. 61-2.

[17] See *Lincoln, Rutland and Stamford Mercury,* 28 December 1838.

[18] See ibid., 30 June, 7 July, 3 November 1837.

[19] For Cooper's endeavours to get a novel published in 1839 see Roberts, thesis, pp.63-4. The novel – eventually published in 1850 – is discussed in ibid., pp.284-9.

[20] See *Kentish Mercury, Gravesend Journal and Greenwich Gazette,* 30 May, 11 July, 8 August, 15 August 1840.

[21] See Roberts, thesis, p.66.

[22] See *Northern Star,* 3 September 1842 (hereafter *N.S.); The Times,* 27 August 1842.

[23] B.I., Cooper to Chambers, 8 February 1867.

[24] Cooper to T.J.N. Brogden, 7 December 1842, reprinted in *L.C.,* 11 May 1929.

[25] See Patterson, *Radical Leicester,* p.317. Also see letter from John Bowman in *Leicestershire Mercury,* 5 March 1842 (hereafter *L.M.).*

[26] *L.M.,* 5 March 1842. Shares in the *Illuminator* cost one shilling, and local Chartists had been free to buy as many as they wished.

[27] Cooper states in ibid., 19 February 1842, that his salary as editor of the *Illuminator* was two pounds a week, though in the autobiography (Cooper, *Life,* p.146) this is reduced to thirty shillings. No copies of the *Illuminator* under Bown's editorship have survived. The file at Colindale begins with the issue dated 13 February 1841, almost certainly the first Cooper edited: it is labelled a new series, and contains extracts from *Gideon Giles, the Roper,* a novel just published by Cooper's childhood friend, Thomas Miller.

[28] See British Library (hereafter B.L.), Add.MS 27,835, fos.165-8, John Seal to Francis Place, 15 July 1841; *Leicester Chronicle,* 26 February 1842.

[29] Robert Barnes, 'The Midland Counties Illuminator. A Leicester Chartist Journal', *Transactions of the Leicestershire Archaeological and Historical Society,* XXXV, (1959), pp.68-77. Barnes bases his claims on the fact that John Seal, and not Cooper, is identified on the back page of the *Illuminator* as its publisher until the issue of 22 May 1841, though he neglects to consider that this may have been in recognition of Seal's position as a small bookseller and Chartist newsagent or simply an oversight.

[30] See *Midland Counties Illuminator,* 24 April 1841 (hereafter, *M.C.I.).*

[31] See ibid., 20 February, 13 March, 20 March, 3 April, 17 April, 1 May 1841.

[32] Ibid., 20 February 1841.

[33] See, for example, *L.M.,* 17 July 1841; *Leicester Journal,* 4 June 1841.

[34] Unfortunately no copies of these two journals have survived. Both were printed by Thomas Warwick, a small Tory printer.

[35] See PRO, T.S. 11/601, Thomas Duncombe to Cooper, 31 December 1841; Thomas H. Duncombe, ed. *The Life and Correspondence of Thomas Slingsby Duncombe* (1868), I, p.303. Also

see T.S. 11/601, Duncombe to Cooper, 8 January 1842 for a further sum sent to Cooper for his own use.

[36] PRO, T.S. 11/600, Gideon Cooke to Cooper, 21 October 1841. Cooke was agent for Cooper's Chartist journals in Melton Mowbray.

[37] See Cooper, *Life*, p.163.

[38] See *M. C. I.*, 24 April 1841. The plan included the creation of a teetotal section amongst the Leicester Chartists. For Cooper's conversion to teetotalism see *L. M.*, 3 April 1841.

[39] *L.M.*, 5 March 1842.

[40] Ibid., 19 February 1842.

[41] Ibid.

[42] See ibid. Cooper claimed the Tories gave him this money to prevent the Whigs succeeding in their plan to drive him from Leicester.

[43] Ibid., 25 September 1841.

[44] See ibid., 3 July 1841. Seal was agent for the *Star* in Leicester, and his break with the local Chartists deprived him of the revenue from the sale of the newspaper, a major loss. Cooper took over this role.

[45] See ibid., 11 March 1843.

[46] Ibid., 19 February 1842.

[47] *M.C.I.* 17 April 1841.

[48] Ibid.

[49] See ibid., 8 May 1841. Also see *N.S.*, 8 May, 15 May 1841.

[50] *L.M.*, 5 March 1842.

[51] Ibid., 12 February 1842.

[52] Ibid.

[53] PRO, T.S. 11/600, John Markham to Cooper, 3 December 1841. Also see T.S. 11/600, Markham to Cooper, 6 December 1841, 19 January 1842.

[54] *L.M.*, 12 February 1842.

[55] Ibid., 5 March 1842.

[56] Ibid.

[57] Ibid., 19 February 1842. Markham subsequently changed his mind, claiming that it was the *Extinguisher* which Cooper had sought Tory money for. Cooper also denied this.

[58] Ibid.

[59] Ibid.

[60] See ibid., 29 January 1842. Also see PRO, T.S. 11/601, Jonathan Bairstow to Cooper, 3 May 1842: 'Feargus says, after the refusal of the Markham party to unite with you, that he shall not come to lecture for them. Pretty Chartists — to refuse union with their fellows ...'

[61] See PRO, T.S. 11/601, Markham to Shakespearean Association, 25 April 1842; *L.M.*, 23 April, 7 May 1842.

[62] PRO, T.S. 11/600, J.G. Brooks to Cooper, 22 May 1842. See *L.M.*, 7 May 1842 for a report of events at Taylor's lecture. Cooper, it seems, as well as seeking reconciliation with Markham, had 'found considerable fault with the lecturer'.

[63] See PRO, T.S. 11/601, William Hill to Cooper, 22 June 1842. The All Saints Chartists had claimed a membership of 168, but Hill doubted the figure and wrote to Cooper for confirmation. There is an All Saints Chartists' report in *N.S.*, 30 April 1842.

[64] Thomas Cooper, *The Purgatory of Suicides. A Prison Rhyme* (1851 edn.), X, v.22 (hereafter, Cooper, *Purgatory*).

[65] Cooper to Brogden, 7 December 1842, reprinted in *L.C.*, 11 May 1929.

[66] PRO, T.S. 11/600, Anonymous to Cooper, n.d. The name has been removed. See Cooper, *Life*, p.172, for the delivery of the letter. Also see T.S. 11/600, Nathias Norton to Cooper, 12 May 1842, explaining why poverty had forced the writer to spend the few pence he had collected for the Chartists; *Douglas Jerrold's Weekly Newspaper*, 15 August 1846, for an account by Cooper of conditions in Leicester in 1841-2 (hereafter *D.J. W.N.*); Thomas Cooper, *Wise Saws and Modern*

Instances (1845), I, pp.201-34, for the two stories about the suffering stockingers.

[67] PRO, T.S. 11/600, George Julian Harney to Cooper, 17 June 1842. For disapproval of Cooper's conduct at O'Brien's lectures see T.S. 11/600, J.B. Smith to Cooper, 15 August 1842. Full details of the disruption of both O'Brien's and Vincent's lectures can be found in *L.M.*, 4 June, 11 June, 30 July 1842; and *N.S.*, 11 June, 18 June, 30 July 1842.

[68] *English Chartist Circular*, no.76 (hereafter *E.C. C.*).

[69] Lincoln Reference Library, unpublished draft MS of the *Purgatory*. Also see Cooper, *Purgatory*, II, vs. 12-13.

[70] See *M.C.I*, 20 March-17 April, 1 May, 15 May, 29 May 1841.

[71] See PRO, H.O. 45/260, fos., 422-5, 449-52 for two copies of the *Commonwealthsman*, 2 April, 18 June 1842. The point of the name was lost on one Chartist, at least: see PRO, T. 5. 11/601, B. Chaloner to Cooper, 16 January 1842.

[72] See PRO, T.S. 11/600, Cooke to Cooper, 17 December 1841, 30 April 1842. The *Commonwealthsman* was succeeded very briefly by the *Chartist Pioneer*, Cooper's last Leicester journal.

[73] See *N.S.*, 16 November 1844, 18 January, 25 January 1845. There had been a Hampden Club in Leicester after the Napoleonic Wars.

[74] For Cooper's support for republicanism see Roberts, thesis, pp.39-40.

[75] See *M.C.I*, 6 March, 8 May 1841.

[76] *E.C.C.*, no.75. The second line is taken from Shelley's 'Mask of Anarchy'.

[77] See *M.C.I*, 6 March, 3 April 1841.

[78] *N.S.*, 21 August 1841.

[79] PRO, T.S. 11/601, Anonymous to Cooper, 29 November 1841.

[80] *L.M.*, 5 March 1842.

[81] The receipts and disbursements of the school from 16 January to 28 February 1842 were published in *ibid*. Figures for attendance at the first two meetings of the school can also be found in *N.S.*, 22 January, 29 January 1842. These record that 128 attended on the first morning, 148 on the first afternoon, and 226 attended the second meeting. It will be seen that there is some discrepancy between these figures, and those extrapolated from subscriptions published in *L.M.*

[82] The All Saints Chartists also opened a school. See *L. M.*, 5 March 1842. There is a reference to an adult school in Leicester in *N.S.*, 30 November 1844.

[83] Unfortunately this little volume seems to have now completely disappeared.

[84] *N.S.*, 4 April 1846. The obituary, written by Cooper, is continued in *ibid.*, 18 April 1846.

[85] See Gammage, *History*, pp.214-15; PRO, T.S. 11/601, Bairstow to Cooper, 22 June 1842, inviting the Leicester poets to write hymns for Holberry's funeral. Other examples of Bramwich's verse can be found in *Commonwealthsman*, 2 April, 18 June 1842; *E.C. C.*, no.115; *N.S.*, 5 January 1850.

[86] For examples of Jones' verse see *E.C.C.*, nos.75, 77, 81, 91, 92, 97, 103, 104, 113, 122, 130; *Chartist Pilot* (in Cambridge University Library), 9 December, 16 December, 30 December 1843, 6 January, 20 January 1844; *N.S.*, 21 August 1841, 28 June 1845, 15 June 1850; *Leicestershire Movement*, 9 February, 16 February, 2 March 1850; *Cooper's Journal*, 17 January, 9 February, 16 March, 8 June 1850.

[87] A copy of Jones' now rare anthology can be found in Cambridge University Library. Verse written in the early 1840s is not included.

[88] See *L.M.*, 3 February 1855 for Jones' obituary.

[89] See PRO, T.S. 11/600, Smith to Cooper, 15 August 1842; *E.C.C.*, nos.74, 77.

[90] See *N.S.*, 11 September 1841.

[91] See Gammage, *History*, pp.203, 407; Cooper, *Life*, p.160.

[92] See *N.S.*, 13 May 1848.

[93] For an account of Cooper's role in the outbreak in the Potteries and his subsequent trials see Roberts, thesis, pp.109-25.

[94] See *N.S.*, 23 July 1842; PRO, T.S. 11/602, Cooper to Susanna Cooper, 3 August 1842.

[95] PRO, T.S. 11/602, Cooper to Susanna Cooper, 12 August 1842.

[96] Cooper did not see the rejection of the second petition in May 1842 as the end of the constitutional process. See *N. S.,* 9 July 1842 for his call for mass demonstrations in support of the Charter.

[97] B.L., Add. MS 40, 434, Peel Papers, CCLIV, fos.318-19, Queen Victoria to Sir Robert Peel, 17 August 1842.

[98] B.I., Thomas Winters to Susanna Cooper, 12 October 1842.

[99] See *N.S.,* 3 December, 10 December, 17 December, 24 December 1842, 14 January 1843; *L.M.,* 18 February 1843.

[100] See *N.S.,* 10 December, 24 December 1842, 14 January 1843, *L.M.,* 17 December 1842.

[101] See *N.S.,* 16 November 1844, 3 May 1845.

[102] See *L.M.,* 7 January 1843. Duffy does not seem to have stayed in Leicester very long.

[103] See *N.S.,* 17 December 1842.

[104] For a plan Cooper also conceived at this time to reorganize the N.C.A. see Roberts, thesis, pp. 127-8.

[105] See *Commonwealthsman,* 2 April 1842.

[106] *N.S.,* 17 December 1842. Mursell had indicated his support for the Leicester Chartists earlier in 1842. See Cooper, *Life,* p.181.

[107] *N.S.,* 17 December 1842.

[108] Ibid.

[109] Cooper to Brogden, 7 December 1842, reprinted in *L.C.,* 11 May 1929

[110] See Roberts, thesis, pp.144-6.

[111] See *D.J.W.N.,* 1 August, 22 August 1846.

[112] See Roberts, thesis, pp.236-8.

[113] *Leicestershire Movement,* 16 February 1850.

Chartism, 1838-1858:
Responses in Two Teesside Towns*

Malcolm Chase

POLITICS HAS BEEN LARGELY IGNORED by historians of early Victorian Teesside. This is particularly true of Middlesbrough, where in the view of its principal historians (including, curiously Asa Briggs), political life hardly began even with the incorporation of the Borough in 1853, and is presented as only taking shape with the award of parliamentary representation in 1867. The standard history of Stockton-on-Tees dismisses the possibility of Chartism ever having taken root there, and finds it 'difficult ... to understand why the Mayor and leading citizens of the town should have been concerned enough to have issued a public notice warning against Chartism'.[1] 'Economic' interpretations of Chartism have encouraged the view that 'the new Victorian boom town' of Middlesbrough was devoid of political activity in the 1840s. Chartism's 'complete absence' has been alleged in the cases of two other new communities in the North, St Helens and Crewe.[2] The same view has been advanced for Middlesbrough, also citing 'the heterogeneous nature of the community' as preventing 'the development of any political awareness'. Activity in Stockton during 1839-40 has been noted; yet the conclusion drawn is still that 'it failed to take any serious root'.[3]

This article opposes this interpretation. Popular political activity on Teesside in the early Victorian period has simply gone unnoticed. Convinced of the improbability of Chartism ever taking root in its economically fecund soil, partly perhaps because of the historiography of the movement, historians have simply failed to consult relevant primary sources with the area in mind. Chartist activity in this area (generally seen as an inimical, on account of its location, and its economic and social structure) suggests that we have not yet fully understood the character of either Chartism or Teesside. For all its 'boom town' reputation, Middlesbrough's economy actually faltered in the late 1830s and early 1840s as the completion of a national railway network undermined its original *raison d'etre* as a coal-shipping port. The Cleveland iron industry had barely emerged, and the town's main employers enjoyed indifferent fortunes. The Darlington & Middlesbrough Sailcloth, Shoe Thread and Patent Rope Company's mill was on short time, for example, in 1842; and the entire workforce at the Middlesbrough Pottery was laid off in 1843. The docks were as yet unfinished, and were only completed after a serious anti-Irish riot, indicative of volatile local demand for unskilled labour: Middlesbrough's population contained a surfeit of former agricultural labourers, attracted by the prospect of ready work, whose presence tended to depress wage rates in any but boom years.[4]

Nor was Stockton exempt from the uneven economic fortunes of the period. Though its decline as a port, due to the emergence of Middlesbrough, has been exaggerated, it was conspicuously tied to the Durham coalfield (only ten miles away at its nearest point). This was a major consideration in the critical years of 1839 and 1842. It was also the centre of a declining handloom canvas and sail-cloth weaving trade. This industry shared the slow demise of the domestic linen weaving trade of the North Riding (also represented in Stockton), in the face of mechanization and increasing Scottish and Irish output. The larger of the Tees-side towns, Stockton's working population was mainly crammed into decaying seventeenth- and eighteenth-century dwellings, grouped in a confined area ad-joining the riverside wharves. This acute spatial segregation of social classes lent impetus and drama to the emergence of Chartism, and was a key factor in shaping the contrasting character of the movement in the two Teesside towns. Such social zoning was far less apparent in Middlesbrough, the smaller size of which in any case mitigated its effects.

The older town also had a history of radical agitation, which quickened with the depression post-1815. The traducers of Queen Caroline were burnt in effigy in Stockton in 1819, and the circulation of 'atrocious handbills' supporting her was noted. The Reform Agitation was socially divisive, with attempts being made by certain employers to dismiss known radicals from their service. The 1832 Act lent a certain vigour to local political life, however, through the forty shilling freehold franchise. It has been observed of County Durham at this time that 'it did not take much more than a paddock and a pigsty to qualify'. Though this was more true of the northern than the southern division at this early date, nevertheless, the effect in Stockton an expanding urban area without the status of parliamentary borough was initially striking. It secured, for example, a visit from Cobbett dur-ing the election campaign of 1832. He stayed at the home of William Milburn, who, twelve years before, had been prominent among local supporters of Richard Carlile.[5]

Adjacent to Stockton, on the Yorkshire bank of the Tees, lay the smaller community of Thornaby (usually called South Stockton at this time). It had been dominated since 1825 by a substantial pottery, which brought a distinctive political flavour to the area. The company recruited its workforce largely from Staffordshire, attracting as it did so trades union activists no longer able to find employment in the Potteries. Inadvertently it thus helped to create one of the most active branches of the National Union of Operative Potters outside Staf-fordshire, apparently larger by 1834-35 than the lodges of Derbyshire, Sunderland, or Newcastle. Delegates were regularly sent to meetings of the Union in Hanley, whilst a protracted dispute at Thornaby in 1836 was considered important enough for both parties to advertise their respective cases in the Staffordshire press. By contrast, Middlesbrough's pottery, founded in 1834, recruited at a time of relative strength for the Staffordshire unions and therefore enjoyed better industrial relations. Yet it too relied on Staffordshire immigrants for a large proportion of its skilled hands, who brought with them experience of labour organization otherwise lacking in the town. Middlesbrough Chartism suffered a considerable setback in 1843 when, during the pottery's prolonged closure, many of its workforce returned to Staffordshire.[6]

The emergence of Chartism in the Teesside region is therefore hardly surprising. As early as February 1838 the secretaries of the Stockton Conservative Association noted with dismay 'that Newspapers and Tracts of an objectionable and mischievous tendency are almost exclusively circulated among the lower classes of Society'. The Chartist press was available in Middlesbrough from May 1838, and within twelve months 'a good society' had been established there. In the spring of 1839 Peter Bussey, the Chartist Convention's missionary to the North Riding, used nearby Stokesley as a base for a tour of the linen-weaving villages of Cleveland and the northern Vale of York (communities which provided a similar constituency to the Chartist heartlands of the Pennine domestic weaving areas, albeit one whose economic base was in an even greater state of decline).[7]

The greatest impact, however, was felt in Stockton. A team from the Durham Charter Association toured Stockton and Hartlepool during Easter 1839, preaching 'the plain but unspeakably important doctrines of democracy' to an audience variously described as 'about 700 persons' (by the Chartist *Northern Liberator)* and as 'a small mob' (by the Tory *Sunderland Herald)*. A Charter Association was formed immediately.[8] From its inception it clashed with Stockton Corporation, which was plainly unnerved by even the mildest Chartist activity. The publican of the Turf Inn was threatened with the loss of his licence if Chartist meetings did not cease; and when these moved to a nearby schoolroom its master, too, fell foul of authority. It was also alleged that activists' correspondence was being delayed and tampered with. A few weeks after the inaugural meeting, the mayor, Thomas Jennett, sent to the Home Office a detailed account of a rally at which 'the speaker … Called the Queen, Lord John Russell, and Earl Fitzwilliam Tyrants … he said we have now got the Tyrants by their throats and we will struggle with our lives before we will let go'. Unnerving as this may have been to a middle-class audience, the rhetoric was in itself unexceptional, and it was the authorities' inexperience in dealing with boisterous political demonstrations that prompted them to contact Whitehall.[9]

Activity and counter-activity centred on Stockton's market cross where a right of free assembly was popularly believed to be an ancient privilege. Certainly, a notice issued by the mayor, vicar, and magistrates of the town could only 'request that all peaceable and well disposed Inhabitants in Stockton will refrain from attending any Meeting of the Chartists'. In May, however, the *Northern Star* alleged that only the size of the assembly, gathered to hear the Sunderland Chartist George Binns 'preaching a sermon', had deterred the police from forcibly dispersing it; and in June a formal application for the Mayor to call a public meeting on the state of the country was refused. The meeting went ahead in defiance, adopting the manifesto of the Convention, which called among other things for all Chartists to obtain arms, for a run on the savings banks, and for the implementation of a strategy of exclusive dealing.[10]

As the Convention's proposed 'Sacred Month' [general strike] grew imminent, serious social and economic instability seemed likely. Some Durham pits had already struck by mid-July. It was feared that the complete closure of the coalfield would let loose large numbers of unemployed seamen in Stockton. Moreover, there was no way of knowing at this juncture how seriously local Chartists would take the Convention's call to obtain arms. On 17 July an informer attended a crowded meeting at the Chartists' 'Council Room'. Between eighty and a hundred were present, 'chiefly of mechanics and the labouring classes, some females were also present'. There was a detailed discussion on how to obtain arms. Jennett immediately requested the Home Office that, 'a military force ... be stationed in this Town'.[11] The following evening, at a meeting held in the midst of Stockton's annual Cherry Fair (always a time of boisterousness and licence) William Byrne of Newcastle urged his audience (estimated by the *Northern Liberator* at 5,000)

> to buy arms and to have them in readiness against the struggle; the speaker went on to state that it was possible the Magistrates might send the Police Officers to search for arms [so] they the People ought to secrete them in such places as even their bosom Friends did not know where they were but so as they themselves could lay their hands upon them at a moment's notice.[12]

A witness's sworn deposition was promptly dispatched to London, arriving the same day as a letter from Hartlepool predicting that 'every House would be pillaged and even human life sacrificed', should striking pitmen enter the town. The following week Stockton magistrates swore-in 235 special constables, divided into four divisions each commanded by one of the borough's policemen. It was a critical and divisive action. Although there were a number of working men among the specials, their bulk was made up of the professions and the better class of tradesmen, along with all the town's Customs men, the managers of the Thornaby Pottery, twenty two 'Gentlemen', and the Poor Law Relieving Officer.[13]

Yet opinion among the Chartists was by no means unanimous. Two key figures particularly stood out against arming: Thomas Whalley, a potter; and Henry Heavisides, a journeyman printer and leading Stockton radical. Both 'strongly condemned the violent proceedings', which, Heavisides believed, 'retarded the progress of reform'. 'Denounced as a traitor' in consequence, Heavisides left the movement, in which he played no further part. This division, however, inspired no confidence in Stockton's authorities. Contrary to the advice of General Napier (officer commanding the army's northern division, and responsible for military precautions against a Chartist rising), the Home-Office acceded to Jennett's request for troops: two companies of the 77th Foot were dispatched to Stockton on 27 July, the National School being turned over to accommodate them.[14]

The indefinite postponement of the Sacred Month on 6 August cut little ice with the Stockton magistracy. 'Until the convention is broken up', wrote the chairman of the bench, 'I am afraid the danger will rather increase than diminish'. By 14 August the entire Durham coalfield was at a standstill. Two days later, as the Chartists announced a mass rally in support of the Birmingham Bull Ring rioters for 19 August, a small cache of arms was found at the home of William Brown, a bellman and frequent speaker at Chartist meetings.[15] A state of near-panic now existed in certain quarters. Leading inhabitants of Middlesbrough issued an address predicting 'riot and bloodshed' if Chartism went unchecked in the locality. With Stockton rumoured to be a 'town in tumult', public spirited residents of nearby Yarm tried to turn travellers back at the bridge over the Tees. The *Gateshead Observer* reported the circulation of a rumour among North Yorkshire farmers that 'there were 11,000 Chartists in the town'. More seriously, the core of Stockton's special constables, numbering about a hundred, formed a quasi-military 'association for the protection of the lives and property of Her Majesty's Subjects'. Providing themselves with 'a dress not unlike the police force of the town', they met for cutlass drill in the Stockton Assembly Rooms under the direction of one of the 77th's sergeants. On the admission of their captain, Robert Henderson (who was also both Clerk to the Justices and the Stockton police inspector), they wished 'to become a Rifle Corps [to] act as Military body in case of any sudden break out of insurrection among the persons calling themselves chartists.' Rifles and cutlasses were requested of the Home Office, but were refused. In the long term the Association seems to have done no more than provide a target for subsequent local authors to lampoon. Yet it was indicative of an extraordinary degree of incipient social conflict in Stockton, whose existence makes more intelligible the determination of the authorities to suppress Chartism at almost every point.[16] The pattern of events, and extent of official preparation, on 19 August suggests that a decision had been taken to force the issue. The 77th Foot were brought by train from Darlington (where they had been waiting in readiness for meetings in support of the Convention), and placed on stand-by at their barracks. At the appointed time of the meeting Jennett read the Riot Act to a far from disorderly assembly. 'A great number of special constables, armed with swords, pistols, and lance-wood staves, in addition to the regular police force, attacked the people in a most furious manner', reported the *Northern Liberator*. The Whig *Gateshead Observer*, on the other hand, observed that, 'The swords, drawn by the armed specials had a magical effect on the crowd, causing the brave fellows round the speaker to vanish like lightning.' William Byrne was arrested before he had uttered a word, not for illegal assembly but for the remarks he had made during the Cherry Fair. Some stones were thrown, and six other Chartists arrested; but the crowd otherwise dispersed peaceably and the infantry were never called from their barracks.[17]

Byrne's arrest was followed by that of a local leader and basketmaker, James Ball Owen, also for previous seditious remarks. Owen admitted he had been delegated, 'to attend meetings of parties who had struck for wages'. Unable to find bail and sureties totalling £300 (an offer from two shopkeepers was refused by the magistrates 'on account of [their] professing reform principles') he was remanded in custody along with Byrne and two Darlington Chartists, Brown and Batchelor.[18] There was a further arrest the following month after a lecture by John Watkins, a Whitby Chartist who had urged his audience to fight for the Charter 'like heroes [and] die for it like martyrs', whereupon a warrant was immediately issued. As a Chartist victim, Watkins was a distinct contrast to Durham working men like Byrne and Owen. He was a determined self-publicist, who studiously declined all offers of bail while his father (the squire of Aislaby in Eskdale) made personal representations to the Home Secretary, Lord Normanby, whose seat at Mulgrave Castle made him a near neighbour. 'The fact is, the Stockton magistrates ... were in a panic and violently prejudiced against all chartists', observed Watkins later. 'The judge had no private pique to gratify nor any political animosity'. The case was dismissed. The incident earned for Teesside Chartists a greater share of national attention than the trial of Byrne and Owen; and it made Watkin's political reputation, on the strength of which he moved to London. His contribution towards discrediting opponents of Chartism in the area should not be underestimated, but he did not otherwise have any lasting impact upon the movement on Teesside.[19]

The events in Stockton during the summer of 1839 are instructive for several reasons. They demonstrate how, outside the main urban centres, the threat Chartism presented was as much in the eye of nervous officialdom as anywhere else. The Durham Chartist executive had in fact concluded that the southern part of the county was insufficiently prepared for the Sacred Month even before it was postponed. In so far as a threat to social stability existed, it came from middle-class elements like the uniformed core of Stockton's special constables. Arguably, had this 'middling' class of shopkeepers, professionals, and tradesmen occupied a less conspicuous place in the political and cultural life of the town, Chartism would have been construed as much less obvious a threat. The contrasting experience of Middlesbrough, four miles away, provides almost a counter-factual model for this hypothesis.

Middlesbrough, with a disproportionately male population crammed into hastily erected housing (mud huts are mentioned in the 1851 census), had an awesome reputation for casual violence. To wear the radical's 'white hat was a public challenge to anybody and everybody to combat'.[20] Within seven months of the Chartist affray in Stockton the new town had had a real riot: yet it was one which at least two Chartists helped, as special constables, to contain. Middlesbrough's police force of two officers was a quarter the size of Stockton's. Yet public meetings of the Chartists were easily avoided in 1839-40, and as easily policed thereafter. Yet the town had a vigorous Chartist organization, even if superficial impressions suggest the opposite.

In a different way from Stockton, the development of Chartism in Middlesbrough reveals the problems of legal assembly. Until 1841 its Chartists met in each other's homes. Restrictions imposed by the Owners of the Middlesbrough Estate precluded open air meetings. Their control over what, effectively, was a company town was such that Chartists were denied the use of any licensed premises or hall, and offers of lectures by touring speakers were turned down for want of adequate accommodation. One way of circumventing these problems, however, lay in the town's temperance movement, which was almost indistinguishable from Chartism. In the early months of 1841, for example, it organized torchlight meetings in the market place, addressed by the Durham Chartist missionary, Deeghan. Meetings were also held to consider the issue of Church rates, again with Chartist speakers. After July 1841, however, Middlesbrough Chartists won permission in their own right to hold public meetings in the market place, a notable victory when one considers the experience of Stockton, and surely an indication of less social tension.[21]

This is evident, too in middle-class participation in the Middlesbrough branch. Those few major employers actually resident in the town, who might be characterized as an upper-middle class, were never involved with Chartism; but in Middlesbrough the movement received significant support from members of that social strata who, in Stockton, most implacably opposed it. Take, for example, responses to the Corn Laws. In contrast to Stockton, the Anti-Corn Law League made no headway in Middlesbrough: but in 1841 a series of meetings on the issue was held in the Chartist Working Men's Reading Room. A sizeable middle-class contingent heard a local grocer debate the issue with the branch secretary (an iron-foundry labourer), and a platemaker from the pottery. 'Several shopkeepers' stayed to join the branch, among them Joseph Bermond, the grocer, who appears at a subsequent meeting 'demanding extension of the field of labour, and a system of national education'. The most prominent middle-class Chartist was a printer and stationer, John Jordison. The only Teesside Chartist to appear in the 1851 census keeping a servant, he is one of two Chartists known to have served as special constables in the aftermath of the anti-Irish riot in 1840. One has difficulty imagining a similar situation in Stockton; the same comment applies to the appointment of a Chartist as one of the town's census enumerators (a function filled by the Middlesbrough hairdresser, newsagent, and bookseller, James Medd).[22]

To a considerable extent the explanation for the absence of social conflict in Middlesbrough, compared with Stockton, lies in the relative strengths of their lower middle class. This in turn was rooted in contrasting patterns of landholding, and therefore of the distribution of political power, in the two towns. Working and 'middling' class were united in Middlesbrough in at least one respect: both were excluded from the exercise of significant political power. The absentee Owners of the Middlesbrough Estate exercised almost total control over the town, either directly as owners, employers, and financiers, or through the convenants they placed on the properties they had sold (always in large parcels). Even after the establishment in 1841 of an Improvement Commission, it was three further years before a fully elected body emerged (the initial commissioners having been nominated by Act of Parliament); and then the qualification for election was to be either rated at more than £25 per annum, or in receipt of annual rents or profits exceeding £20. In spite of these obstacles several supporters of the Charter stood for election, and two of them, Jordison and David Jackson (a tailor), were successful in 1848 and 1849.[23]

In the borough of Stockton, on the other hand, the 'shopocracy' dominated local politics, the bench and the guardians. In place of Middlesbrough's closed oligarchy of absentee owners there were numerous freeholders and tenants of substantial copyholds. There were a few from both groups among the Chartists of the town, but they tended to be small dealers or skilled artizans, employed rather than employers, and in no way associated with the local establishment which the printer Jennett epitomized (he was among other things an honorary officer of Stockton's Mechanics' Institute, Oddfellows' Lodge, and Literary Society). Entrenched behind its firmly-established political power, this group were highly sceptical of Chartism's essentially constitutional claims, in contrast to Middlesbrough where the right of free assembly was won from the Owners and never subsequently challenged.[24]

Further developments in Stockton during the early 1840s reveal this antagonism further. After a temporary retreat into classes and 'street societies', and a campaign to raise funds for the defence of local Chartist prisoners, public meetings resumed early in 1840. Fund-raising parties were held in the Brunswick Arms, but because of pressure from the magistracy the landlord would not permit speeches. In the spring meetings were once again convened at the market cross, in the full knowledge that they would be prohibited. The result was political theatre: a crowd would gather, and then disperse on the appearance of the police. It would then reassemble a few yards over the borough boundary (which was within the urban area), and march in solemn procession beyond Durham jurisdiction, across the Tees into the North Riding. A meeting would then be held on Thornaby Green, an expanse of common some two miles from the centre of Stockton. In clement weather it was an agreeable demonstration of aggrieved popular rights: but it left unresolved the problem of a permanent meeting place for committee meetings and lectures.[25]

The answer to such problems was found in a 'large and commodious room belonging to the Joint Stock Provision Store', an ancillary benefit of a move into co-operative retailing. This solution to the issue of lawful assembly revived the political and cultural life of the branch in the wake of its suppression the previous summer. Here the Chartists held meetings, lectures, and festivals, for example a 'testimonial tea' to John Owen on the eve of his standing trial at Durham Assizes. A Middlesbrough engine-driver 'Mr Man addressed the meeting in a most eloquent manner, for about an hour and a quarter, after which dancing and singing commenced, and at about half-past four in the morning the company separated', with three cheers each for Owen, Feargus O'Connor, and the Newport prisoners.[26]

The co-operative was a logical development from the policy of exclusive dealing, advocated by the 1839 Convention, which Stockton had enthusiastically endorsed.

> Co-operation is the most practical form of exclusive dealing . ... the speediest means of working out our political regeneration. Let this be employed in establishing grocery and provision, drapery, hardware and book and news stores, it will place us in a position in which we can battle with the wholesale merchants, the great commercial gods.[27]

The decision to establish a co-operative had been made in the immediate wake of the meeting on 19 August, and trading had begun in December. Subscriptions were opened 'in every factory, workshop, shipyard, and wherever a few honest working men may be found', with the overt political aim 'to raise supporters to that independent position in society which will enable them to treat with contempt, all the malevolence of aristocratic and shopocratic tyranny'. The Stockton Chartists were also among the first nationally to discuss co-operative manufacture and wholesaling, with a proposal for a corn-mill, inspired by the example of the Whitby Union Mill. In the late 1840s 'Flour Societies' became a prominent feature of northern co-operation; but in Stockton the idea never proceeded beyond the planning stage, even when revived with the support of Middlesbrough Chartists in 1847.[28]

Though several stores survived to take their place in the later cooperative movement, Stockton's (and this is true of the North-East generally) was not among them. In 1842 lawyers were sought to resolve a dispute between the manager and shareholders of the store. Yet even this failed scheme may be seen as constituting part of the apprenticeship of the subsequent co-operative movement. Furthermore, the very existence of such an initiative is a revealing indication of working-class hostility to the town's 'shopocracy', scarcely less dramatic an expression of social antagonism than the market cross confrontations which preceeded it. Stockton's example followed in the nearby village of Bishopton, but there was never any attempt by Chartists in Middlesbrough to involve themselves in co-operative retailing, reinforcing the contrasting relationships between working and middle class in the two Teesside towns.

The other significant area of development in the Teesside Chartist movement at this time was educational. From the beginning Stockton Chartists had 'supplied themselves with a few books and newspapers ... exchanging these books and papers with one another, and nightly discussing ... the information they had gleaned throughout the day, in the brief intervals from labour which the hard lot of British artizans allows'. By May 1841 a reading room was established, which courted clerical displeasure by being open for discussion on Sundays. Stockton, however, was only following the lead of Middlesbrough, where the Chartists' reading room and library anticipated by several years the formation of a Mechanics' Institute in the town. The pronounced educational tone of Chartism in Middlesbrough is additionally significant given the social character of the young community. That the earliest educational provision for adults in the town should have emerged out of the Chartist movement gives some indication of the frailty of the middle-class cultural presence there in these years. From the Reading Room, the local Chartists pursued a definite O'Connorite line:

A spirited meeting of the Chartists of this place was held in the Working Men's Reading Room, Newcastle Row, on Wednesday night week, when spirited addresses were delivered on the present state of the country and the prospects of the people, by Messrs Sutherland, Hollinshead and Maw. The different speakers advised their hearers to abstain from intoxicating liquors, and join the Working Men's Library, which is already established; and likewise for the people not to be led away by any new move, whether it was commended by real enemies or pretended friends, and as far as the Chartists of Middlesbro' are concerned they are determined to struggle for the Charter and nothing less.[29]

This account is worth considering in detail. Education and temperance were at the very centre of the New Move – the attempt, notably by Lovett, Collins, and Henry Vincent, to realign Chartism after 1840. However, the Chartists of the Teesside region were implacable in their support for O'Connor and the National Charter Association, against whom the New Move was very largely directed. The New Move, in the words of a Stockton resolution, was 'a deviation from the principles of the Charter ... This meeting repudiates as leaders, and deems unworthy the spirit of Chartists, those individuals who sanction the principles contained therein'. What happened on Teesside in response to the New Move – the rejection of the concept but simultaneous embrace of its constituents – was not at all unusual. Conventional histories have been right to contrast the New Move with O'Connor and mainstream Chartism, but not because the latter rejected temperance or education; rather, as Dorothy Thompson has argued, proponents of 'Knowledge Chartism, Christian Chartism and Temperance Chartism ... appeared to be putting forward their programmes as *alternatives* to the National Charter Association rather than as organizations under the general Chartist umbrella'.[30]

Education lay at the heart of Teesside Chartism. Stockton Charter Association kept open its 'Mechanics' Reading Room' (the very title implies an antagonism with the town's Mechanics' Institute) until the movement entered the doldrums of 1844-45. The Middlesbrough reading room seems to have closed then too; but when the National Charter Association branch reformed in 1848, the forty odd members met 'in Mr Alcock's school room, which is open every Saturday night, at six o'clock, and Sunday from ten in the forenoon'. Alcock's was a working-class day school (he lodged with a coal trimmer), opened in competition with the nearby premises of the British and Foreign School Society. A similar relationship with autonomous workers' schooling existed in Hartlepool.[31]

Chartist culture in Middlesbrough was distinctively masculine. In reports of Chartist activity women are as conspicuously absent there as they are present in Stockton. The earliest accounts of Chartism in the Durham town noted the involvement of women, not peripherally but conspicuously in events in the market place, and at meetings where arming was discussed. At one early market cross meeting a commercial traveller, heckling from the side-lines, was jostled by a group of Chartist women who 'slapped his jaws'. He was so incensed by the episode that he wrote directly to the Home Secretary, though he studiously neglected to mention the sex of his assailants. More serious scope for the women's involvement came with the changing pattern of activity from 1840. Stockton females made their own separate collections, for example in aid of John Frost's wife. Co-operative retailing was obviously an area to which they could make a decisive contribution, as was the burgeoning branch social life of tea parties and festivals. This, it must be stressed, is not to belittle their involvement. The social life generated in the Chartist branches was itself a political statement, a counter culture which promoted solidarity and underpinned instrumental politics. It was customary for women to take a leading role in the testimonials organized in honour of Chartist prisoners. When J. B. Owen was finally bailed from Durham Gaol he was met on arrival at Stockton station by 'the females of Stockton-on-Tees', and presented with 'an elegant plaided silk scarf, with the inscription in large gilt letters, "Liberty"'. George Binns, the Sunderland Chartist missionary who had visited Teesside in 1839, and was gaoled for a speech made at Darlington, returned to Stockton on his release to a reception headed by a brass band, 'and an elegant and extensive assortment of silk banners, with various inscriptions suitable for the occasion'. Elizabeth Robson, 'a female Chartist' from a family of handloom canvas weavers, presented him with a pair of gloves, whilst one of her colleagues christened her new-born baby, 'George Binns Newby after that virtuous and unflinching advocate of the people's rights'.[32]

None of this, not even young George Binns Newby, was unique to Stockton, or to Chartism. The movement borrowed and adapted from 'Owenite' socialist culture, and from the ritual and practices of friendly societies: all the elements of Binn's reception, band, banners, and gloves were thus derived. There was a branch of the Owenite Association of All Classes of All Nations at Darlington, and a considerable number of female-only friendly societies in the region, including at least five in the Stockton area itself. A number of male Chartists were also friendly society activists. Some overlap, arguably, is only to be expected: but in Middlesbrough quite senior figures in local Oddfellowships were active Chartists and vice versa: John Anderson, the Chartists' secretary; James Hollinshead, their treasurer, one of the founders of the Middlesbrough district of the Manchester Unity and a 'Noble Grand'; the secretary to the town's premier lodge, David Ward, like Hollinshead a potter; and most notably William Gendle (a house-carpenter), Provincial Grandmaster of the Middlesbrough District and a delegate to national conferences of the order. There appears to have been less overlap in Stockton, though the local Oddfellows' Hall was used for meetings in the late 1840s (significantly after the death of Jennett).[33]

However, by the time of these meetings in the Oddfellows' Hall, Chartism on Teesside had changed considerably. During the 1840s it was Middlesbrough which supplied the regional leadership, notably in the person of a bricklayer's labourer, James Maw, whose self-education eventually enabled him to become a coal agent's clerk. At one point early in 1840 Maw was reported to be giving three or four speeches a day. A Methodist, he used his network of circuit contacts to arrange venues and hospitality when lecturing in the region: one Hutton Rudby class leader was dismissed by the Wesleyan Circuit Meeting for entertaining him.[34]

The Middlesbrough leadership nursed ambitious plans for a regular regional delegate conference from Chartists both sides of the Tees. Effectively the result was limited to the establishment of a group in the Cleveland village of Stainton, and the revival of activity in Hartlepool.[35] Yet 1842 had started well with a lecture in the Stockton Theatre by Bronterre O'Brien, who was to represent Northumberland and Durham at the forthcoming Convention. Soon afterwards the *Northern Star* claimed, plausibly, 1,200 signatures to the national petition from the Stockton area (including, presumably, Middlesbrough). In Stockton however Chartism was now largely contained by the authorities, who avoided open confrontation. In 1839, faced by frontal attack and direct repression, the movement had thrived. Now it was peculiarly vulnerable, not least to disappointment. Parliament's rejection of the petition on 3 May coincided with the difficulties of the Provision Store. Reaction in the branch was immediate. On 21 May it was listed in the *Northern Star* as having failed to pay its share of O'Brien's Convention expenses; the next month it failed to poll in the elections for a new national executive. By 1844 even the Chartist Mechanics' Reading Room had disappeared, apparently along with Middlesbrough's. In 1844-45, no reports of Chartist activity in either town appeared in the Chartist or local press.[36]

These were doldrum years for the movement generally. Several local reasons can be advanced for the downward spiral. In Stockton the social base for the movement was eroded by the continued decline of the weaving trades. Middlesbrough was profoundly affected by the deteriorating fortunes of the Pottery: Hollinshead was only the most notable of those who returned to Staffordshire in the winter of 1843. This period of dereliction was followed, however, by a quickening in the pulse of the town's economy, as the long term benefits of the new iron foundries and the docks were felt, whilst the building trades benefited from the burgeoning civic pride of 'this Carthage in miniature'.[37]

It is difficult to assess how far the absence of newspaper reports reflected actual conditions. Formal organization need not have evaporated in the face of a poor press. Very little coverage of either Durham or Tyneside Chartism appeared in, for example, the *Gatehead Observer* in this period, yet these were areas where activity, albeit at a lower ebb than before, is known to have persisted in the mid forties. The absence of reports in the *Northern Star* is perhaps a better indicator. Having moved to London from Leeds in November 1844 it lost its distinctive northern flavour (throughout the first seven years of its life, for example, it had carried market reports from Thirsk and Darlington). At a time when its political coverage was inevitably lacklustre, there was then even less incentive on the part of correspondents of smaller northern branches to send in reports. Activity of some kind was presumably contingent on the candidacy of a Chartist tailor, David Jackson, in the 1844 election to the Middlesbrough Improvement Commission. Equally, one may assume a collapse after a humiliating defeat with just one vote cast in his favour. In general there may have been a return to highly informal classes and street societies, taking little notice of the London based National Executive. The latter had ceased to notice Teesside. In October 1845, when Christopher Doyle toured the North on its behalf, he failed to stop *en route* from the West Riding to Sunderland.[38]

Collections set-up by Stockton seamen the following year for 'Veteran Patriots and Exiles' initiated a revival, which the emergence of the Chartist Land Plan then reinforced. The local response to the latter was initially sluggish: Stockton's first contribution in April 1846 was 4d: but in 1847-48 regular recorded contributions were averaging £5. Locally and nationally, as branch correspondents and O'Connor himself argued, the land campaign gave Chartism a new lease of life. It furnished the means of financing an effective executive and missionary team, enhanced the provincial circulation of the *Northern Star,* and in towns like Middlesbrough and Stockton created once more the need for formal organization. It also brought to the area for the first time since 1842 a prominent national figure in the movement: Peter McDouall. He reported a 'doubling of numbers' in Stockton, 'rapidly gaining strength' in Middlesbrough, and also visited Hartlepool, Stokesley, and, remarkably, Redcar.[39]

Nationally, the Land Company numbered some 70,000 shareholders. It is therefore not surprising to find large numbers enrolled from Teesside. Joint stock company law required registering companies to provide details of a majority of shareholders upon registration. Names, addresses, and occupations of 128 Stockton members, and 73 and 24 from Middlesbrough and Thornaby respectively, survive in the registration documents. The latter cover, however, no more than a quarter of the total shareholding (registration procedure was never completed, partly because of the daunting number of members to be recorded). Membership on Teesside may therefore have approached 700, rather more than three per cent of the total population. The occupational backgrounds of the local members differed hardly at all from those of Chartists earlier in the decade. They did tend, though, to be slightly younger and have smaller families. Large numbers were lodgers – 45 per cent in Stockton, possibly as many as 74 per cent in Middlesbrough – often sharing accommodation with parents and 'in laws'.[40] These features are not unexpected, though they imply that many members' perception of the scheme was closest perhaps to that of a building society. There can be no denying the appeal of a scheme which potentially offered a home and self-sufficient smallholding to its members. The pace of local interest certainly quickened when two Stockton sail-cloth weavers, Joseph Bennett and William Ableson, were awarded holdings on the 'Charterville' estate near Minster Lovell, Oxfordshire.[41]

Early histories of Chartism tended to assert that the Land Plan fragmented the movement. As the experience of Teesside shows, however, it was a powerful reviving and unifying force. In its emphasis on the dignity, and the claims to independence and self determination, of labour it reflected central concerns of the movement. With these factors in mind, the predominant participation of certain occupational groups becomes more intelligible. In Stockton the largest group (some 17 per cent) were canvas and sailcloth weavers, a skilled and traditionally independent group in a declining trade. In Middlesbrough, by contrast, more than a quarter of recorded shareholders were labourers: nationally, however, labourers constituted no more than 14 per cent of the overall membership, and in the longer established economy of Stockton their participation was below even this figure. These figures are consistent with information on the condition of unskilled labour, originally attracted into the town by the prospect of ready work, in Middlesbrough at this time.

In all three Teesside communities pottery workers were conspicuous subscribers (more than 17 per cent of the total regional membership). Their workplace autonomy, and ability to negotiate a favourable list price for the tasks they performed, was rapidly undermined in the eighteen-thirties and forties. Another key group, shoemakers (just under 10 per cent), were involved in a trade which was contracting under the impact of a growing and highly competitive Midland industry, in which division of labour was more extensive. On the other hand, the buoyant industries of the Teesside economy are indicated in low enrolments from engineering and shipbuilding (each less than 3 per cent) and the building trades (bricklayers, painters, and house-carpenters: collectively below 5 per cent). The national pattern of low enrolment among agricultural workers is reflected in the Plan's failure to make any headway elsewhere in the North Riding.

Important as it was, however, the Land Plan never totally dominated activity. Teesside Chartism was assuming significant additional dimensions. Stockton, for example, was in correspondence with the Democratic Committee for Poland's Regeneration, a key internationalist group which was mainly responsible for the distribution in Britain of propaganda concerning the Polish struggle against Russia. The Middlesbrough branch swelled through an influx of Irish supporters. The library in Alcock's school took not only the *Northern Star* but also the *United Irishman* (the militant republican weekly and advocate of armed insurrection), extracts 'being generally read amidst loud applause'. Given the earlier history of Anglo-Irish relations in Middlesbrough this was a moment of some significance.[42]

In 1848 the pattern of convention, petition, and rebuttal was again repeated. Two thousand signatures were reportedly collected in the area for the national petition presented on 10 April. If this figure is accepted, and the spurious estimates of attendance at Stockton demonstrations in 1839 discounted, it represents the peak of support for the movement on Teesside: slightly more than 10 per cent of the total population of Stockton, Middlesbrough, and Thornaby in 1851. Furthermore, the advance on the 1,200 signatures claimed in 1842, is of a greater proportion than the growth of the region's population during the decade. Clearly these are rough figures, using obviously rounded, totals for the two petitions. However, given the overall pattern, and the social base, of Chartism of Teesside they are not implausible; and the strength of local support for the Land Plan, already referred to, bears them out. It is a debateable point whether they substantiate a claim for Chartism on Teesside being a mass movement, but it was certainly one which had taken root among the populace. Furthermore in 1848, unlike 1842, momentum was maintained after the petition was rejected. On Teesside, as elsewhere, the persistence of Chartist activity beyond 10 April 1848 exposes the inadequacy of any interpretation which sees in the Kennington Common demonstration the 'collapse' of the movement. (Regular meetings in Hartlepool did not commence until a month later). Appropriately, among the first references to Chartism in the region after 10 April is the christening in Middlesbrough Parish Church of 'Feargus O'Connor Tate', son of an ironmoulder and Land Plan shareholder. A Durham and Yorkshire delegate assembly, similar to that attempted in 1841-42, was convened in June; and in Stockton the Chartists were once more involved in a game of cat-and-mouse with authority. On Whit-Tuesday, 13 June, for example, fifty additional police were drafted in to prevent a meeting in the market place. Perhaps the most notable incident of the summer, however, was a local election success in Middlesbrough.[43]

David Jackson, bottom of the poll in 1844 with just one vote, captured 154 votes out of a possible 194 in the elections to the Improvement Commission in July 1848, including the votes of all but two of the twenty-six known Chartist activists and Land Plan members who polled. However, John Jordison's success the following year was achieved in spite of securing only half the votes of the fourteen known Chartists appearing in the pollbook. Jackson, moreover, had resigned, and a second Chartist (Sutherland) who offered himself for one of the four seats came bottom of the poll. Possibly the 1849 election was an early indication of the decline of Chartism in Middlesbrough, or at least of the accord between working and middle-class reformers. It should however be noted that Jordison was comfortably elected to the new Council shortly after its incorporation in 1853.

From this date, however, Middlesbrough Chartism drops from sight. After 1851 both there and in Stockton activity was only sporadic. It is clear that certain Teessiders continued to call themselves Chartists right up to the final demise of the movement nationally in 1858: but collectively they functioned only intermittently, and as a formal organization hardly at all. As early as the first quarter of 1851 the National Charter Association's balance sheet reveals the cessation of contributions from Teesside. Yet delegates continued to attend north-eastern regional meetings 'to effect a better organization'; and when the 'Northern District Union' of the National Charter Association (revived once more under the leadership of O'Connor's former lieutenant Ernest Jones) was launched in Newcastle in June 1851 it explicitly embraced Teesside.

The continuation of Chartist activity was now most apparent in the sphere of trades' organization. Participation in Chartism had enhanced inter-trades' awareness. It had brought organized workers into regular contact with non-unionized trades, and it ensured through the pages of the Northern Star an awareness of labour issues nationally. In December 1841, for example, Middlesbrough Chartists organized a public meeting and subscriptions from the trades and local publicans, in support of masons striking at the half-completed Houses of Parliament. Workplace collections were regularly made for Chartist prisoners and their families.[44] In 1847 Teesside workers were 'represented by letter' at the conference of the United Tailors Protection Society, reports of which initially reached them via the Northern Star. Trades activity particularly accelerated in 1851. In June, at the inaugural meeting of the Seamen's National Conference Middlesbrough was represented by Eneas McKenzie, another working-class day-schoolmaster. The Hartlepool representative was one of those delegated by conference to lobby Parliament and address meetings of the metropolitan labour movement later that year.[45]

One of the consequences of this national initiative was the Miners' and Seamens' United Association. This attempt at general union had been directly inspired by the Northern Chartist Union, and on Teesside 'large and enthusiastic meetings' were held in its support. At gatherings in October collections were made for the defence of a group of Wolverhampton tin plate workers, awaiting trial for conspiracy (their trade had practised 'rattening', a form of physical intimidation of those who accepted low wage rates). The vehicle for northern involvement in the dispute, like others, was the National Association of United Trades for the Protection of Industry. Hartlepool was particularly involved, and its banner much in evidence at meetings; 'the English flag on the right, the American flag on the left, with the significant motto between of "Which shall we take?"'. At the end of the year all three towns again sent delegates to a national conference organized in Hull.[46]

The initiative, however, was shortlived. Its frailty underlines the contrast with the situation a few years before. The Miners' and Seamen's United Association is an interesting indication of a strategic switch by key Chartist activists on Teesside; but it cannot be said that it was either successful or, while it lasted, widely-supported. Furthermore, in contrast to neighbouring Darlington, no attempt appears to have been made at this time to reform under the umbrella of the National Charter Association. Unlike Newcastle and the north-eastern coalfields, Teesside was never a focal point for sustained Chartist agitation in the mid 1850s. When the Tyneside Chartist R. G. Gammage sought to arrange meetings in the area early in 1853 on behalf of the national executive, he failed to find any local Chartists willing to help him; and in a tour of the region that July Ernest Jones visited only Darlington.[47]

It is possible that the local temperance movement offered asylum and refuge to Chartism, just as it had done more than fifteen years before. Henry Vincent drew crowds of unprecedented size to his lectures at Middlesbrough Mechanics Institute in 1854, and when the Stockton branch of the National Charter Association was at last reformed in February 1856 it operated from the town's Temperance Rooms. It seems, though, to have mustered only twelve members, and was defunct by June, when one of its committee reported 'the absence of any local organization' to the national Chartist *People's Paper*. Soon after, however, a series of public meetings at the market cross and the Temperance Rooms was held on the issue of bread prices in the town, 'because the corn and flour are altogether in the hands of one or two individuals who monopolize all that comes into the market'. A committee was formed, but nothing came of the proposal advanced once again to set-up a union mill in Stockton. It was to be a further ten years before the proposal came to fruition, and with it the birth of a new Co-operative Society in Stockton.[48]

The failure of both the union mill initiative and the revived branch still left a small group whose political aspirations remained focused on Chartism. 'It may not be said that Stockton could not either send a delegate or assist others', wrote one of them in July 1857 in response to Jones' announcement of a national reform conference. South Stockton raised a subscription towards the cost of a north-eastern representative; but a similar fund to support Ernest Jones' bid to recapture O'Connor's old parliamentary seat of Nottingham was an embarrassing failure. No less critical was the failure to send a representative to, or even correspond with, the north-eastern subscribers' assembly convened to select and mandate a delegate to the conference. A complaint by Newcastle Chartists about the apathy of Stockton towards this issue, shortly before the conference convened in February 1858, effectively marks the end of Teesside Chartism.[49]

The deficiency of explanations for the decline of Chartism which rest, wholly or in part, on a supposed fiasco in 1848 means that the causes of the movement's demise need to be re-examined. On Teesside, as elsewhere, Chartism did not collapse in 1848. It faded during the eighteen-fifties, partly as the energies it had done so much to create found further outlets in trade organizations, temperance, secularism, co-operation, education and perhaps especially municipal politics. Neither Middlesbrough nor Stockton was a parliamentary borough, and therefore the development of a Radical-Liberal constituency body was retarded – in contrast to many communities of the West Riding and Lancashire. However in both towns the reconstruction of local government (an Extension Act for Stockton in 1852, and incorporation for Middlesbrough the following year), coincided with the decline of Chartism, and absorbed raw political energy which, had the circumstances been less novel, might well have sustained the Chartist movement on Teesside. Instead, what amounted to a revolution in local government offered a partial – and for the time being apparently sufficient – answer to Chartist claims to participate in constitutional processes. The Stockton Act gave the predominantly working-class residents of that part of the town which lay beyond the ancient borough, and the commercial heart, a role in local government at last. Fifteen, or even five, years before Stockton Chartists might well have been in a position to exploit this opening. As it was the early elections in the reformed Borough were boisterous, even bad-tempered, but seem not to have mobilized supporters on class or party lines.[50]

The relationship between the working and middle classes of the two towns was also crucial in the timing of the local decline of Chartism. It is noticeable that insofar as Chartism endured on Teesside in the 1850s it did so in Stockton, but not in Middlesbrough, where the residual effects of the *rapprochement* first cemented as the town's inhabitants chafed under the rule of the original Owners seem to have continued. Furthermore it is no crude economic reduction to recognize that the expansion of the local economy, led by the iron industry, was likely to draw much of the sting from continued agitation. The dramatic growth of Middlesbrough, following the opening of the Cleveland main ironstone seam in the nearby Eston Hills, also rescued Stockton from the stagnation that had seemed poised to overtake it in the late 1830s.

A significant recent essay in 'Rethinking Chartism' stresses the extent to which it was redundant from the mid 1840s.[51] Yet the picture on Teesside, especially when the later years of the movement are considered, is more complex than this re-evaluation will permit. Gareth Stedman Jones rightly criticizes the tendency of local studies to produce atomized pictures, conveying neither the strengths, nor the real weaknesses, of the Chartist movement as a whole. But local studies of Chartism are not henceforward redundant. The case of Teesside demonstrates how superficially similar communities a few miles apart could have very different experiences of the movement. It further reveals a capacity to penetrate ostensibly unpromising localities in sufficiently comprehensive a way as to suggest that our knowledge of the extent of the Chartist experience is still imperfect. It also offers a measure of support for Stedman Jones's thesis that it was official accommodation as much as economic stability that finally killed-off Chartism: in Stockton decline was matched by diminished municipal hostility; and in both towns reform in local government paralleled, and arguably contributed to, the movement's local demise.

Lastly, Teesside reveals the resilience of Chartism. It may be some time before the history of popular politics there during the 1850s and 1860s can be traced with any certainty: and ultimately it may still be difficult clearly to delineate where Chartism ended and other forms of activity began. In July 1857, in a letter to the *People's Paper,* a South Stockton Chartist, Matthew Lishman, drew an important distinction: 'There are not many of us, but we are of the right sort ... [however] there are plenty of Democrats here'. Research into the still neglected mid Victorian period is long overdue: it ought to establish how influential 'the right sort' were, and how plentiful the Democrats. As 'An Old Chartist', surveying the remnants of the movement in this locality, wrote in 1852:

> It is true that when certain speakers visit the district, meetings are got up, which are generally striking failures. Such, sir, is the true state of this locality, and yet we are not yet without hope; I believe, Sir, that a real People's Party is now forming which will secure the confidence of the great mass ... But you will say, what are you doing? I answer, we are forming ourselves into Local Societies, we are getting ourselves on the Register of Municipal Electors. We think this is a step in the right direction. It is true that we are not brawling and making a noise, but we have begun to work.[52]

Notes

* I am grateful to Ray Challinor, Shirley Chase, Bob Fyson, John Marlow, and Jim Turner for their comments and suggestions; also to members of Cleveland History Workshop, and of the day school on Chartism held in May 1987 at the University of Leeds Adult Education Centre, Middlesbrough.

[1] W. Lillie, *The History of Middlesbrough* (Middlesbrough, 1968); A. Briggs, 'Middlesbrough: The Growth of a New Community', *Victorian Cities* (1963); R.P.Hastings, 'Middlesbrough: A new Victorian boom town in 1840-1', *C(leveland and) T(eesside) L(ocal) H(istory) S(ociety), Bulletin,* 30 (1975-76); T. Sowler, *A History of the Town and Borough of Stockton-on-Tees* (1972), p. 150.

[2] W. H. Chaloner, *The Social and Economic Development of Crewe, 1780-1923* (Manchester, 1950), pp. 148-50 (yet p. 234 seems to contradict this); T. C. Barker and J. R. Harris, *A Merseyside Town in the Industrial Revolution: St Helens, 1750-1900* (1959), p. 323 (but see D.Thompson, *The Chartists* (1984), p.363, for evidence of Chartism in St Helens).

[3] R. P. Hastings, *More Essays in North Riding History* (North Yorkshire County Record Office, North-

allerton, 1985), p. 106; idem, 'Chartism in South Durham and the North Riding of Yorkshire, 1838-1839', *Durham County Local History Society Bulletin,* 22 (1978),13. This omission regarding Teesside is not the fault of regional historians alone. The seemingly exhaustive appendix on the geography of Chartism in Thompson, *The Chartists* underestimates its strength in Stockton, overlooks Middlesbrough prior to the Land Plan, and ignores Hartlepool. This, however, is the only book on Chartism to mention the area.

[4] Public Record Office, Home Office Papers, HO 40/57/421, 428, 432; *G(ateshead) O(bserver), 1* May 1842.

[5] *Cobbett's Weekly Political Register,* vol. 78, 7 and 8 (17 and 24 Nov. 1832); H. Heavisides, *Annals of Stockton-on-Tees* (Stockton, 1865), reprinted in *The Centennial Edition of the Works of Henry Heavisides* (London, 1891), pp. 349-50, 383, 393-94; Hobhouse to Hardy, 23 Aug. 1821, PRO, HO 41/6 fo. 281; T. J. Nossiter, *Influence, Opinion and Political Idiom in Reformed England: Case Studies from the North-East, 1832-74* (Brighton, 1975), p. 58; M. S. Chase, 'Atheists and Republicans in early 19th century Cleveland', *CTLHS Bulletin,* 47 (1984), and 'Deadly effluvia and atheistical glare', *N(orth) E(ast) L(abour) H(istory),* 19 (1985).

[6] Sowler, pp. 358-59; T. Richmond, *Local Records of Stockton and its Neighbourhood* (Stockton, 1868), pp. 182-83; M. Williams, *The Pottery That Began Middlesbrough* (Redcar, 1985); *North Staffordshire Mercury,* 2 April-17 Aug. 1836, passim; *GO,* 25 March 1843.

[7] Durham C[ounty] R[ecord] O[ffice], Londonderry Papers, D/LO/C 445-48 (correspondence with the Stockton Conservative Association, 14 Feb., 1838); *N(orthern) S(tar),* 16,30 March, 20 April 1839; *N9orthern) L(iberator), 26* May 1838.

[8] *NL, ii,* 76 (30 March 1839), 77 (6 April 1839); *Sunderland Herald,* 30 March 1839.

[9] PRO, HO 40/42/107, Jennett to Home Office 18 April 1839; *NL ii,* 104 (12 Oct. 1839).

[10] *NS,* 18 May, 8 and 22 June, 3 Aug. and 5 Oct. 1839; C(leveland) C(ounty) Archives Department), Pargeter Papers [Acc 1250], Stockton Corporation handbill. Similar disputes over the right of assembly in the market place arose in Thirsk and Northallerton, see *NS,* 27 July 1839. The Stockton Chartists had begun exclusive dealing several months before, *NL, ii,* 80 (27 April 1839).

[11] Jennett to Home Office, PRO, HO 40/42/229,17 July 1839.

[12] *NL ii,* 92 (20 July 1839); deposition of James Ward. PRO, HO 40/42/431,18 July 1839.

[13] Thomas Powell to Home Secretary, PRO, HO 40/42/241; Stockton magistrates to Home Office, enclosing list of special constables, HO 40/42/407-10; see also Hastings, 'Chartism', p. 11.

[14] *GO,* 27 July; Napier to Phillipps, PRO, HO 40/53/561-4; *NS, 3* Aug. 1839; on the regional context of these events see W. H. Maehl, 'Chartist disturbances in north-eastern England, 1839', *International Review of Social History,* 8 (1963), pp. 389-414

[15] Stockton magistrates to Home Office, PRO, HO 40/42/323, 29 July 1839; Marshall Fowler to Home Secretary, HO 40/42/395,14 Aug. 1839.

[16] E. M. Heavisides, *Poetical and Prose Remains* (Stockton, 1850), pp. 74-75; Raine to Russell, PRO, HO 40/42/423 and 443, 18 and 22 Aug. 1839.

[17] *NL, ii,* 98 (31 Aug. 1839); *GO,* 27 July, 24 and 31 Aug. 1839; *Durham County Advertiser,* 23 Aug. 1839; Richmond, 182; cf. (J. W. Ord), 'Memoir of the late Thomas Jennett', in T. Pierson, *Roseberry Topping, a Poem* (Stockton, 1847), p. xii.

[18] Depositions of Harewood and Owen, PRO, HO 40/42/471, 29 Aug. 1839; Nl ii, 98 (31 Aug. 1839); *GO,* 31 Aug. 1839.

[19] *NS,* 1 June and 5 Oct. 1839; J. Watkins, *The Life and Career of George Chambers* (1841), p. 177.

[20] R. Henderson, *Incidents in the Life of Robert Henderson; or, Extracts from the Autobiography of Newcassel Bob' (A Tyneside Rake)* (Carlisle, 1869), p. 18.

[21] *NS,* 19 Oct. 1839, 5 Sept., 28 Nov., 1840, 20 Feb., 10 July 1841; *NL, i,* 32 (26 May 1838),ii, 79 (20 April 1839), 122 (15 Feb. 1840); *GO,* 6 March 1841.

[22] *NS,* 25 Sept., 2 and 16 Oct. 1841; *GO,* 6 March 1841 and 20 Aug. 1842; 1851 Census, PRO, HO 40/57/421, 428, and 432; CCA, CB/M/C 17/3: pollbooks for elections to the Middlesbrough Improvment Commission, 14 July 1849 and 13 July 1849. (Henceforward *Pollbooks).* On Jordison ('His weakness was for vegetarianism, teetotalism, and radicalism'), see W. H. Burnett, *Old Cleveland, being a collection*

of papers: local writers and local worthies, section one (Middlesbrough, 1886), pp. 119-48.

[23] D. Pattenden, 'Joseph Pease and the Owners of the Middlesbrough Estate', *CTLHS, Bulletin* 41 (1981), 26-30; Lillie, pp. 79-80; Briggs, pp. 241-47.

[24] Sowler, pp. 486-93.

[25] *NS*, 15 Feb., 20 and 27 June, 26 Dec. 1840.

[26] Ibid., 29 Feb., 1 Aug. 1840.

[27] *NL*, 7 Sept., 1839.

[28] *NS*, 28 Sept., 7 Dec., 1839. 20 June 1841,27 March 1842; *Charter*, 8 Sept., 1839; *GO*, 16 Jan, 1841 and 27 March 1847. See also R. C. N. Thornes, 'The early development of the Co-operative Movement in West Yorkshire, 1827-1863' (unpub, D.Phil. thesis, Sussex Univ. 1984); M. Purvis, 'Co-operative Retailing in England, 1835-1850: developments beyond Rochdale', *Northern History*, xxii (1986), 198-215: R. Challinor, 'Chartism and Co-operation in the North-East', *NELH*, 16 (1982), 34-39; J. Tann, 'The Whitby Union Mill Company: a case of early co-operative production', *Business Archives*, 39 (1973), 32-38.

[29] *NS*, 8 June 1839, 21 May 1841.

[30] Ibid., 1, 8 May 1841; Thompson, p. 260.

[31] *NS*, 11 Nov. 1843, 8 April, 20 May, and 1 July 1848.

[32] Deposition of Stagg, PRO, HO 40/42/229,17 July 1839; Mason to Home Office, HO 407 42/311, 18 July 1839; *NS*, 3 Aug. 1839, 14 March, 31 Oct. 1840, 20 Feb. 1841.

[33] *NS*, 22 June 1839; *GO*, 19 Nov., 1842; K. Wilson, 'Owenite Socialism in Darlington', *NELH*, 18 (1984); C. Postgate, *Middlesbrough, its Environs and History*, pp. 117-18;Joseph Warburton Lodge, *Centenary Booklet* (1935); J. J. Turner, 'Early Friendly Societies in North Yorkshire and South Durham', *CTLHS Bulletin*, 50 (1986), 66-68. See also E. M. Yeo, 'Robert Owen and Radical Culture', in *Robert Owen: Prophet of the Poor*, ed., S. Pollard and J. Salt (1971), pp. 102-08.

[34] *NS*, 19 Oct. 1839; *NL*, 122 (15 Feb. 1840).

[35] NS 28 Nov. 1840; 25 Sept., 2 and 16 Oct., 6 and 13 Nov., 11 and 24 Dec. 1841:19 March, and 24 Sept., 1842.

[36] *NS*, 15 and 2 Jan. 7, 14 and 21 May, 25 June, 9 July, 3, 17 and 24 Sept.,1,15 and 22 Oct.1842.

[37] *GO*, 25 March 1843, 7 Feb. 1846.

[38] CCA, *Pollbooks*, 12 July 1844; PRO HO 40/57/432; Jackson was another special for the anti-Irish disturbances of 1840, and also an Oddfellow. See Lillie, p. 93; Warburton Lodge, p. 6.

[39] *NS*, 11 Oct. 1845, 24 Jan. 7 and 14 March, 2 and 23 May 1846; 10 July and 20 Nov. 1847;

[40] *NS*, 24 April, 1 and 29 May, 10 June, 10 July 1847; PRO, National Land Company, Registration Documents, Board of Trade Papers, BT 41/474-76; *NS*, 14 Aug. 1847, 12 Feb. 1848. (Data on residence and occupations taken or verified from: the 1851 census; CCA *Pollbooks*, 9 July 1847; Durham CRO, EP/STO 62 U/ST 94, 'An Assessment upon all and every the owners and occupiers of Lands Houses and tenements within the parish of Stockton upon Tees ...' (17 Aug. 1847). Hastings, *Essays*, p. 95, estimates from the 1841 census that 18 per cent of Middlesbrough's population were lodgers. Shareholders also seem to have been more mobile: e.g. of the 128 Stockton members only 62 are listed in the 1851 census, and of these 33 are shown at a different address. However, there is a lack of general work on working-class residential mobility by which to judge this data.

[41] Neither Ableson nor Bennett remained at Charterville long. Ableson had disposed of his holding by 1851, and although Bennet is listed in the Tithe Apportionment for Minster Lovell in 1851, he was not listed in the Census return two months later; see K. Tiller, 'Charterville and the Chartist Land Company', *Oxoniensia*, 50 (1985), 262. In the ensuing paragraphs comparison has been made with the national sample of shareholders in D. J. V. Jones, *Chartism and the Chartists* (1975), pp. 134-37.

[42] *NS*, 22 May 1847, 6 May 1848; on the Democratic Committee see H. Weisser, *British Working Class Movements and Europe, 1815-48* (Manchester, 1975), passim.

[43] *GO*, 22 April 1848; *NS* 20 May, 10 and 24 June, 1 and 8 July 1848; 20 Jan., 14 July, 25 Aug., 6 Oct. 1849; 5 and 12 Jan., 13 April, 11 May 1850; 4, 11 and 25 Jan., 1 Feb., 5 April, 31 May, 21 June, 19 and 26 July 1851; CCA, Po*llbooks*, 14 July 1848, 13 July 1849.

[44] *NS*, 28 Sept., 21 Dec. 1839; 25 Jan. 1840, 29 Feb., 14 March, 23 July, and 31 Oct. 1840: 24 Dec. 1841; 14 March 1846; 5 Aug. 1848.

[45] Ibid., 18 Dec. 1841, 17 April 1847; 7 and 14 June 1851.

[46] Ibid., 27 Sept., 11 Oct., 8 Nov., 20 Dec. 1851. For the scaling down of the Miners' and Seamen's United Association into a regional body for the North-East, see *Star of Freedom*, 15 May 1852, and also for its subsequent activities *P(eople's) P(aper)*, 11 Dec. 1852, 30 July 1853.

[47] *PP*, 3 July 1852; 5 Feb., 12 March and 16 July 1853.

[48] *Annual Report of the Yorkshire Union of Mechanics' Institutes* (Leeds, 1854), p. 90; *PP, 9, 16*, 23 Feb., 1, 8 March, 28 June, 12 and 19 July 1856. For the early history of the subsequent Stockton Co-operative Society see M. Heavisides, *A Condensed History of Stockton-on-Tees* (Stockton, 1917), p. 73

[49] *PP*. 11 July, 22, 29 Aug., 5 Sept., 7, 14, and 21 Nov. 1857; 9 and 16 Jan. 1858.

[50] Stockton Central Library, Local Collection, ephemera for the 1852 and subsequent elections. By contrast, a Chartist presence could be sustained in a parliamentary borough largely because of the opportunities for agitation this presented: see K. Tiller, 'Late Chartism; Halifax, 1847-58', *The Chartist Experience: Studies in Working Class Radicalism and Culture, 1830-60*, ed. J. Epstein and D. Thompson (1982), pp. 311-44. Such opportunities were simply denied in county constituencies; moreover elections in South Durham were uncontested between 1841 and 1857, and in the North Riding between 1835 and 1857.

[51] G. Stedman Jones, 'Re-thinking Chartism', *Languages of Class Studies in English Working-Class History, 1832-1892* (Cambridge, 1983), pp. 90-138. There is also an abridged version in Epstein and Thompson, pp. 3-58.

[52] *Star of Freedom*, 25 Sept. 1852.

Postscript (2003)

Contrary to the claim in note 41 above, Bennett did remain at O'Connorville; but as he told a Parliamentary Commissioner in 1868, 'it has taken me twenty years to learn how a man can live without victuals, and I've just about come to it', quotation in Malcolm Chase, '"Wholesome object lessons": the Chartist Land Plan in retrospect', *English Historical Review* 475 (Feb. 2003), p. 65. For details of the careers of two other Chartists featured in this article see the entries for James Maw and John Watkins in the Dictionary of Labour Biography, volumes 10 (2000) and 11 (forthcoming, 2003) respectively. These also note other relevant recent secondary works.

Chartism Remembered:
William Aitken, Liberalism, and the Politics of Memory

Robert G. Hall

Early one Sunday morning, in August 1839, `a very authoritative knock' on the door awoke the young Chartist William Aitken and his family. After a thorough search of his house for `revolutionary and seditious documents,' the chief constable and his men placed Aitken under arrest and marched him through the silent streets of Ashton-under-Lyne. Recalling his sense of distress and anguish some thirty years later, Aitken tried to find solace in the ultimate triumph of his principles, in his conviction that `the cause of liberty is eternal, and that the principles of democracy, which are now becoming universal, must be right and must in the end prevail.'[1] This optimistic reaffirmation of his life's struggle for `bread and liberty' appeared in the fifth installment of his autobiography in the *Ashton News*, a Liberal newspaper. Unfortunately, the tone of quiet confidence and hope that pervaded his autobiography apparently masked a growing sense of private despair and ever deepening bouts of depression. Some two weeks before the publication of this installment, his wife, Mary, had found Aitken lying on the bedroom floor, `with a fearful gash in his throat.'[2]

That many thousands of working men and women `thronged the streets' on the day of his funeral was hardly surprising. The son of a Scottish cordwainer and later sergeant-major, Aitken came from, as the *Ashton News* put it, `the people' and `knew intimately their feelings and their wishes, and could express what the many felt with fullness and point.'[3] His own identification with the working class came through clearly in the title of his autobiography, `Remembrances and Struggles of A Working Man for Bread and Liberty.' And yet, for most of his adult life, Aitken was not a member of the manual working class. In many ways, his decision to describe himself as `a working man' was a revealing one; it pointed to the intertwining of class and gender and, above all, to the role of imagination and empathy in the creation of his sense of self. This form of self-portrayal certainly did not fit, in any straightforward way, the social and economic realities of his life over the previous three decades. Blacklisted for his role in the Ten Hours movement during the early 1830s, he left forever the world of mule spinning as a young man and turned, with few regrets, to the more agreeable (and profitable) livelihood of schoolmaster. From time to time, he also supplemented the family income through work as an accountant and the `trade of agitation' and turned his hand to versifying and writing fiction and essays for newspapers and friendly society magazines.[4]

In 1869 there was no consensus in Ashton about either the meaning of his melancholy death or his life of struggle for 'bread and liberty.' Some, like the poet and free-thinking radical James Hindle, looked to the young Aitken, the Chartist militant, as a source of inspiration for the future generations that would carry on his 'unfinished' work. In contrast, Hugh Mason chose to remember the Aitken of later years, as someone who had 'rendered essential Service to Free Trade and to Liberal Politics.'[5] The fact that Aitken's autobiography appeared in the columns of the Liberal *Ashton News* lends apparent support not only to Mason's assessment of Aitken's legacy but also to the 'currents of radicalism' interpretation of Chartism and Liberalism. Building on the accepted wisdom of the Victorians (especially those of the Gladstonian Liberal persuasion) as well as the work of later scholars, Eugenio Biagini and Alastair Reid have raised important questions about the currents of continuity, in terms of ideology and outlook, between Chartism and popular Liberalism; moreover, they have rejected the emphasis on a sharp discontinuity in popular politics around 1850 and have moved away from the idea of class as a basis for Victorian politics. Biagini and Reid have also pointed to biographical studies of mid-Victorian radicals, like Robert Lowery and George Howell, as examples of 'the personal continuities from early nineteenth-century radicalism, through Chartism, and into the Liberal party.'[6]

Although approaching the question from a very different theoretical position, Gareth Stedman Jones and Patrick Joyce have put forward a similar line of argument about radicalism and class. Placing the movement for the Six Points within a long tradition of radical opposition that stretched back to the 1770s, Stedman Jones has emphasized that radicalism was, above all, 'a vocabulary of political exclusion whatever the social character of those excluded.'[7] Joyce has likewise criticized the 'fixation' on class as an analytical category and has described how Aitken's career and style of leadership 'spanned both radicalism and Liberalism, cementing their shared vision of the world.' Joyce has gone on to argue that Aitken's autobiography was a classic expression of this shared vision. 'It is clear,' Joyce noted, 'from his autobiography that he saw no fissure between the two: Liberalism was completing the business of Chartism, and both were yet one more step in the history of liberty.'[8]

This very literal reading of his autobiography overlooks the often subtle ways in which he struggled, through the writing of his life story, to construct a stable, coherent sense of self through the careful selection and presentation of his 'remembrances' about his public life.[9] Even then, despite his efforts to reconcile somehow his Chartist past with his Liberal present, he was acutely aware of the problems that this involved. Throughout his narrative, there was a tension between his stated goal of telling the truth about his public career as a radical working man and his desire to create what Jerome Buckley has called 'a continuity of self.'[10] To strike this delicate balance, Aitken took a highly selective approach to his memories of the 1830s, especially in the case of his portrayal of the movement for the People's Charter, 'that much abused and misrepresented embodiment of the people's political rights.'[11] While remaining silent about his own connection to and defence of the insurrectionary side of the Chartist movement in 1839, he frankly acknowledged, however, the existence of mass support for the physical force strategy and the general strike. By placing his emphasis on the hostility of 'the higher and middle classes' to democratic reform, he also chose to give the term 'the people,' in the case of his account of the 1839 campaign, distinct class overtones.[12]

My rereading of Aitken's autobiography thus points to some of the difficulties inherent in any attempt to place Chartism and Liberalism within a shared radical tradition. Just as Aitken downplayed or omitted altogether many of the inconvenient aspects of his own Chartist past, so the proponents of the 'currents of radicalism' approach have tended to accentuate the similarities between the two traditions and to minimize the very real differences. This is not to say that their perspective does not provide some valuable insights into reform politics of the mid-nineteenth century. After all, radicalism, and later Chartism, intersected Liberalism at a number of points. Although they often clashed over trade unionism, 'class legislation', and the question of universal suffrage, Chartists and advanced Liberals generally agreed on the need for some sort of suffrage extension, the ballot, and a redistribution of seats and shared a common hostility toward aristocratic privilege, the Established Church, and the centralization of political power as well as a common interest in humanitarian and libertarian issues.[13] What gave Chartism a separate and distinct political identity in the late 1830s and 1840s was the way that its activists and leaders chose to define their reform programme and their strategy for winning political power. Along with their emphasis on the Six Points, and especially universal (male) suffrage, as the solution to 'class legislation', the Chartists defined their movement through their use of the mass politics of the platform, with its confrontational strategy of 'peacefully if we may, forcibly if we must', and through their identification with the cause of labour and the working classes. For the Whiggish historian and politician Thomas Macaulay, one of the movement's many critics, all this meant that Chartist democracy was synonymous with 'rebellion', 'the destruction of all property', and 'ignorant labouring men'.[14]

The process of carefully selecting and interpreting memories of things past, especially those of a controversial nature, was central to Aitken's creation of a sense of self through all 'the battles of a chequered life.'[15] The writing of his autobiography was never a simple case of retrieving timeless, unchanging memories of his individual past and fitting them into a narrative form. Memory involves forgetting as well as remembering; with the passage of time, details of long ago conversations and events fade and change. Over the years, ongoing discussions and arguments with family members, friends, and neighbours about episodes and personalities of the collective past also affect how individuals remember their own pasts.[16] By its very nature, the genre of autobiography likewise pre-cluded the possibility of telling the entire story of Aitken's life, in all its richness and variety, and forced him to impose some kind of order on his memories. His life story, like all autobiographies, was, consequently, at best an incomplete and very selective account of his past. Aitken's personal circumstances in 1869 and the political and cultural context within which he organized and published his 'remembrances' were also crucial in determining how he told his readers the story of his life and gave it meaning. A creative and present-minded act of self-expression, the writing of his autobiography was thus mediated through and was influenced by the selective nature of memory and autobiography itself and by his relationship to the means of publication, the *Ashton News,* and to his audi-ence. Together, these influences, some cultural, others personal and political, profoundly shaped Aitken's attempt to tell the truth about his life and one of its most dramatic episodes: the first great campaign for the People's Charter.

Memory and the Art of Autobiography

In the late 1860s the word 'autobiography', like the genre itself, was still relative-ly new. As a literary genre, with its own distinctive style and conventions, it had only begun to emerge by the late eighteenth century; but, after 1800, the number of autobiographies published in Britain increased dramatically. This develop-ment pointed to a new belief in the relevance of what Jerome Buckley has called 'the subjective impulse, the writer's assumption that he or she may or even must confess, explain, divulge, or simply display an innermost self to a putative audi-ence'.[17] In his own way, Aitken tried to follow the conventions of the new genre. Written in the first person, his autobiography took the form of a narrative about his past, from childhood and first memories onward. With the exception of a lengthy account of an 1862 trip to London during the early days of the 'Cotton Famine', his narrative proceeded chronologically up to his arrest in August 1839. There it ended abruptly; this was all that Aitken had written before his suicide. His autobiography was thus, in the most literal sense, an autobiographi-cal fragment, one that left the story of much of his life untold and his final word on its meaning unsaid. And yet, the very title that he chose, 'Remembrances and Struggles of a Working Man for Bread and Liberty', suggested something of his perspective on his life and its meaning. His autobiography sought, above all, to tell the story of 'a working man' and the political struggles of his public life.[18]

Precisely because the autobiography was a relatively new literary form, Aitken found himself with few models to draw on in the writing of his narrative. This was particularly the case, since he chose to tell the story of a radical and 'a working man'. The most well-known and influential model of his day, the spiritual autobiography, had its obvious attractions. He, like many of the men and women of his generation, understood the development of the individual in moral terms; in his narrative he turned repeatedly to the importance of 'moral courage' and stressed the virtue of compassion and 'humane and Christian feelings' for fellow human beings, especially the poor and unfortunate. And yet, despite his respect for 'the simple and ennobling principles' of Christianity, he chose to avoid this model.[19] This decision by Aitken reflected, in part at least, his own uneasy relationship to the Christian faith. As a life-long critic of 'priestcraft and superstition' and someone of 'no particular religious sect', his life story did not match up very well with many of the conventions of the spiritual autobiography.[20] By the late 1860s, there was, however, an alternative model that closely fit the outlines of Aitken's life: the radical, and later, Chartist autobiography. Even here, though, the examples were few and far between. Of these, the best known in Aitken's Lancashire was, no doubt, the two-volume autobiography of Samuel Bamford, the weaver-poet, whose radical career unfolded during the stirring days of the Blanketeers and Peterloo.[21]

Drawing on a jumbled mass of memories, some intense, some half-forgotten, about persons, places, events, and books and poems, Aitken tried to create, through his narrative, a sense of stability of self.[22] It was his decision to portray his life story, in the words of his title, as the 'struggles of a working man for bread and liberty' that gave his narrative coherence and unity. By choosing to portray himself as 'a working man', Aitken moved beyond the material circumstances, if not of his childhood and youth, of his adult years as a 'highly respectable' schoolmaster and part-time accountant and writer.[23] His decision to adopt this persona enabled him to define himself as a working man and made the act of self-expression a political act, one that was consistent with a lifetime of struggle to gain political power and the right of self representation. In making his own a genre that had been reserved, like political representation itself, for the wealthy and powerful, Aitken proudly announced the entry of a new figure in the corridors of power as well as the pages of history. 'All things have a history,' he defiantly asserted in the opening lines of his autobiography. 'And the struggles of many of the working men of this country, if placed upon paper, would read as well, and be as interesting, as the lives of many a coronetted lord.'[24]

The sense of self-identity that this self-proclaimed 'working man' constructed out of his 'remembrances' took at once a very public and a radical form. It was significant that he described himself, not as a worker or a member of 'the working-classes', a term that he rarely used, even in its plural form, but as 'a working man'. His choice of words here suggested the extent to which the intertwining of masculinity and class informed his sense of self-identity.[25] Throughout his retelling of his activities as 'a working man', he stressed in fact the centrality of manly exertion to the workplace and political conflicts of the 1830s; again and again, he praised the role of the 'moral courage', the heroic spirit of self sacrifice, and 'the becoming fortitude' of those men who were 'engaged in a noble struggle for freedom'.[26] His was also a radical story of a lifetime of struggle for 'bread and liberty' that was based on 'moral power' and power of the spoken and written word, not 'brute force and secret mischief'.[27] Highly critical of the advocacy of political violence, whether by the Whiteboys or by trade unionists and Chartists, Aitken roundly condemned their appeal to physical force as well as state violence and war making. 'Monarchial and aristocratic tyranny and ambition', he noted with disgust, had led to the steady growth of the military throughout Europe and 'needless wars of aggression'.[28]

Telling his story in this way inevitably meant that Aitken had to leave out certain memories about his personal life and family. He ultimately chose, like Bamford and the other radical autobiographers, to privilege the public and political over the private and personal; consequently, women, and children as well, were too often, as Eileen Yeo has noted, a 'missing presence' in his and other Chartist life stories.[29] Following the conventions of the autobiographical genre, Aitken discussed in some detail his childhood and 'first remembrances', but he said nothing about his mother and her family or about the 'mysterious', and no doubt traumatic, disappearance of his father in 1836. For the most part, he was even more reticent on the subjects of his own marriage and family and his private life as husband and father. Although the outgoing, sociable Aitken gave the names of many friends, personal and political, in his autobiography, he never mentioned his wife, Mary, by name; he never discussed their courtship or their life together and only alluded, in the most indirect way, to her contribution to his radical career. Nor did Aitken ever refer to their children in his autobiography.[30]

By their very nature, Aitken's memories about his public self were also highly selective; his attempt to understand and interpret the present in 1869 clearly shaped, to a certain extent, his 'remembrances' of the past.[31] Aitken tended to select, from among the sometimes conflicting memories of his past, the memories that most closely fit his emphasis on the role of 'moral suasion' in his struggles as 'a working man'. If the memories dealt with controversial events or undercut his interpretation, he typically only alluded to them indirectly or omitted them altogether. 'I have been told of acts of violence', Aitken frankly admitted about local trade unions, 'and of violence contemplated, at which the mind shudders, but it is well to let them repose in the brain, and not bring them in here in these remembrances'.[32] One such set of memories that Aitken never directly mentioned dealt with the bitter 1830-31 strike in the Ashton and Stalybridge area. The *Ashton Reporter* obituary told a dramatic story of how the very young Aitken had used his body as a shield to protect radical mill owner Charles Hindley from a group of angry strikers, armed with 'a considerable number of pistols'. For Aitken the autobiographer, keen to emphasize the triumph of 'moral power' and the 'the growing intelligence of the many', the best approach was simply to pass over this, and similar episodes from his own Chartist past, in silence.[33]

By selecting certain memories, and setting aside others, Aitken thus tried to create a persona that he defined as that of 'a working man' who was radical in his political goals and moral in his political methods. Telling the story of the unfolding of this public self also involved something more: a search for a sense of purpose and meaning. What was the point of his years of sacrifice and hard work? Looking back over his life, he discovered a possible answer to this question in the 'healthful signs of progress' that he saw everywhere. Through his struggles, and the struggles of others like him, 'year after year', he argued, 'a little is gained for the happiness of man'.[34] Throughout his narrative, Aitken paused to point out yet another example of the progress and changes that he had witnessed and indeed had contributed to over the course of his life: the passing of factory legislation, 'the growing intelligence of the many', the rise of rational trade unions, an end to taxes on knowledge and the corn laws, and the spread of democracy.[35]

What had made all this possible was the lonely struggles, often against enormous odds, of 'enthusiasts' and heroic individuals. 'It is well, indeed', Aitken asserted, 'there are such beings born in the world, or where would progression seek for a shelter or a place to lift her all-ennobling head?'[36] For Aitken, and indeed many of his fellow Chartist activists, this turn to the Romantic cult of the hero came quite naturally. 'He had read much', the *Ashton News* obituary noted about Aitken, 'and was familiar with history and popular science, and he was extensively acquainted with the writings of our best poets, with many of the best passages of which he was accustomed to adorn his speeches'.[37] In a similar fashion Aitken inserted lines and sometimes verses of poetry by Byron, Goldsmith, Burns, and Cowper in the text of his autobiography.[38] In doing so, he was hardly unique. Running throughout many of the working-class autobiographies of this period was a fascination with poetry and the personalities of great poets, especially Byron, 'that wonderful and wayward child of nature'.[39] There was as well, among those who were politically active, a tendency to cultivate a certain Romantic style of dress and oratory. The darkly handsome Peter Murray McDouall, one of Aitken's close friends, liked to dress in black and wear a cape; this gave him, as W. E. Adams noted, the look of 'a hero of melodrama'.[40]

This emphasis on the role of the heroic, self-sacrificing individual was intimately linked to his own distinctive view of progress. In some cases, like that of the Ten Hours Act, progress came, he argued, as the result of 'the exertions of the working men themselves, and many others'. Here Aitken was careful to bring out the contributions of 'others', like the mill owner Charles Hindley and the earl of Shaftesbury, to this great victory of 'the people'.[41] In other cases, the crucial figure was the high-minded patriot, aided only by 'the powers of his eloquence and the prowess of his pen', who struggled against the tyranny of the few and the apathy of the many. His was, Aitken believed, indeed an age of progress, but progress occurred only through the efforts, the sacrifices, and the 'moral courage' of the radical patriot, or hero: 'It has not been by timidity or fear that the battles of liberty have been won, but by a moral courage equalling, if not surpassing, the hero.'[42]

Autobiographer and Audience

To set down on paper the story of one's life is a solitary, creative act of imagination and recollection, the usual object of which is to discover and interpret the meaning of one's life. This does not mean, however, that autobiographies represent purely individual accounts of past events; they involve the interplay between private memories and public representations and between past experiences and present situations.[43] 'It is in society,' as the sociologist Maurice Halbwachs has pointed out, 'that people normally acquire their memories. It is also in society that they recall, recognize, and localize their memories.'[44] Aitken's 'Remembrances' certainly underline Halbwachs's point about the role of collective memory. In his search for the truth about his life, Aitken the autobiographer ultimately came to understand his past through a dialogue with his own present and with his prospective audience. His own difficult situation in 1869 inevitably affected his effort to create a sense of self and perhaps to reconnect, in some way, with the people and ideals that recurred in the telling of his life story. The medium of publication, a series of 'letters' in the Liberal Ashton News, and his awareness of the audience for his 'remembrances' also shaped how he told and understood the struggles of his past.

Alienated from Ashton Liberalism and many of his old friends by his support for the Confederacy during the American Civil War and by 'habits and associations' that he had formed, Aitken increasingly withdrew, in his final years, from public life. Well known 'in his brighter days' for his wit and energy as a speaker and conversationalist, he was no longer able to speak in public for more than twenty minutes at a stretch; even reading, one of his great pleasures, was now a difficult chore. The waning of his intellectual powers and stamina, together with ill health, deepened his 'low desponding state' and forced him to give up in August 1869 his once flourishing school. The growing frequency of his bouts of depression and disturbing signs that 'his reasoning powers were leaving him' had begun to raise serious concerns among family members, friends, and neighbours. 'On the Friday before his death,' the Ashton News obituary noted, 'he called at the office of the News for a few minutes, and was apparently as cheerful and collected as usual, but his voice had a strange tone in it, and his eyes had a restless look'.[45]

It was against this background of bad health and a growing sense of personal and political isolation that Aitken set out to tell the story of his life. That he decided to do so reflected, in part, his long-standing belief in the importance of history to the struggle for political power. History, claimed Aitken in a lecture on Feargus O'Connor and democracy, 'was the light by which we could look upon past ages – the landmarks of what has gone before us; and by studying which with intentness, they would become wiser and more able to take part in the management of their country than they would be otherwise'.[46] Years later, this passion for history remained strong. In 1869, about the time that he began his autobiography, he published a cautionary but sympathetic account of the early years of the French Revolution; in this melodramatic tale, Aitken held up Camille Desmoulins, his central character and perhaps alter ego, as the voice of moderation, the very embodiment of the English tradition of 'liberty without licentiousness'.[47]

The autobiographical urge also represented in part an attempt to re-establish a connection to the people and ideals of his past and to establish a sense of stability of public self through all the twists and turns of a life in politics. To a certain extent, indeed, Aitken had come to see, by 1869, his career in politics as part of the unfolding of the Liberal vision. Speaking to a small meeting of Liberal activists on the eve of the 1868 general election, he described himself as 'an advocate of liberal principles when it was treason to love and death to acknowledge them'. He went on to praise the Liberal party for its consistent support for 'progressive measures' and for lowering taxes and establishing free trade. 'He was proud,' he concluded, 'to live in this grand historic age, and to help in improving the laws, so that the people might be better and happier in every respect. It was to the Liberals we were also indebted for liberty of conscience, free speech, and a free press, and he hoped those who had now the franchise for the first time would rally around the men who had consistently advocated those principles'.[48]

By reinterpreting the 'battles' of his public career as a struggle for 'liberal principles', Aitken fell in line with a political trend that had first emerged in his hometown in the mid-1850s, with the founding of the *Ashton Reporter*. This radical-liberal weekly, under the proprietorship of the impeccably radical Hobson family and its patriarch, the ex-Chartist Edward Hobson, pushed an ambitious, 'ultra' liberal reform agenda and, as one editorial proudly noted, 'never failed to assert the rights of combination and co-operation, which the law allows equally to the masters and to the workmen'.[49] The *Reporter* took equal care, however, to graft the history and traditions of radicalism onto Liberalism. Through carefully selecting, muting, and reinterpreting key episodes, like Peterloo and the war of the unstamped, and ideas of the radical past, the paper began the process of converting old radicals and Chartists into what one editorial called 'The New Liberals':

> Fifty years ago the charge of being a liberal was sufficient to consign a man to legal persecution and social ruin. Nay, within forty years the yeomanry of Lancashire rode down and sabred at Peterloo a meeting held to advocate the principles now so popular. A suffrage which should comprehend the masses; a ballot scheme

which should protect the voter; and a curtailment of office which should restrain the representative, were then the cries only of men branded as revolutionaries or as dreamers of a political Utopia. What a change since then!... Nothing short of ultraliberalism is now possible; and the men who have all their lives strenuously resisted these reforms, are now loudest in demanding them.[50]

By 1869 the *Reporter* even eulogized the late Ernest Jones as an honest and sincere member of 'that section of the Liberal party for many years of which Mr. Feargus O'Connor was the leader'. Jones, the paper went on to admit, had been a follower of O'Connor, 'that noisy democrat', but he ultimately came to see 'the folly' of Chartism and took up 'the principles laid down by the advanced Liberals'.[51]

This interpretation of the life and career of Ernest Jones, with its remarkable transformation of Chartism into a 'section of the Liberal party', provides an invaluable insight into how 'advanced Liberals' tried to come to terms with the Chartist past. By distancing themselves from the noise and 'folly' of Chartism, its 'unruly meetings' and 'foolish songs' and appeals to physical force, they rendered the movement suitable for inclusion in the Liberal tradition and were also able to tap into 'the inert strength of that party'.[52] As Aitken cast about for models and themes to give a sense of unity and continuity to his public career, this way of tying together his life story had an obvious appeal. Once he decided to turn to the columns of the Liberal press as the forum for telling his story, the interpretative pull of this approach was, no doubt, almost irresistible.

But, despite his long history with the Hobson family, Aitken did not publish his autobiography with the *Reporter,* the oldest and most widely circulated local paper in the Ashton and Stalybridge area. He turned instead to the *News,* a rival Liberal paper, a new weekly with financial ties to the wealthy and powerful Mason family.[53] The layout for page three, where each of his five installments appeared, underscored, in a symbolic way, the extent to which his memories were embedded in and were shaped by the politics and business of Liberal journalism and by the interests and lives of his readers. Squeezed in between advertisements for Epps's Cocoa and Holloway's Ointment and Pills, local poetry and sensational fiction, articles on reform and free trade, and reports of local meetings and friendly society dinners, Aitken's life story made its public appearance in the form of a series of weekly 'letters'.[54] This very format, serialized weekly 'letters', as Aitken described them, imposed certain conventions and limitations on how he told his story. The serialization of autobiographies, as David Vincent has noted, often reinforced the tendency to divide one's life into self-contained episodes; however, at the same time, serial publication required the autobiographer always to keep in mind the overall design and purpose of the narrative. This format also forced Aitken to meet deadlines and word counts and emphasized the importance of ending each episode at some dramatic, gripping point.[55]

Serialization in a local newspaper, in the form of weekly 'letters,' almost inevitably made for a close relationship between autobiographer and audience. This kind of format, as E. P. Thompson has pointed out, enabled readers to challenge points or to add new information and perspectives in the next weekly installment. The audience that the *Ashton News* targeted was, like those that Thompson described, a highly localized and politicized one; almost all, if not all, of the paper's readers lived in the immediate Ashton and Stalybridge area, or one of the outlying towns and villages, like Mossley, Hyde, Denton, and Droylsden. In this period, there was a growing sense of local patriotism that took the form of a new interest in dialect poetry and the history and 'folk' traditions, like Riding the Black Lad, of the area.[56] Aitken was well aware of the existence of this well-informed local audience for 'remembrances' about his public life. In the second sentence of the first installment, he thanked the editor of the *News* for the opportunity 'to give your readers remembrances of the battles of a chequered life.'[57] But, he did not merely give his readers his own, individual memories of the past; over the years, he had discussed and argued with the men and women of Ashton in their homes and in the pubs and public streets and markets of their town about the personalities and events of their collective past. To a considerable degree, then, the 'remembrances' of his autobiography were deeply enmeshed in and were influenced by the memories of those who made up his audience.

At two crucial points, Aitken the autobiographer in fact paused and directly addressed his readership about events that loomed large in the collective memory of the townspeople of Ashton. The first of these had to do with the passing of the Ten Hours Act of 1847. Here Aitken explicitly referred to an issue that had cropped up during the 1868 general election in Ashton: 'which party carried the bill?' His answer, then and now, Aitken argued, was 'that all parties alike, extreme Tory, Whig, Liberal, Radical, or any other name, added their weight, their eloquence, and their power to carry it.'[58] Two issues later, he once again stopped to address his 'gentle reader'; this time his subject was popular views about 'the absurdity of the men of 1838-39' and the first great mass campaign for the People's Charter. This was, even from 'the long vista of thirty years', still a living and controversial memory for Aitken and many of his 'gentle' readers.[59]

Chartism Remembered

Turning to the turbulent, hungry days of the late 1830s, Aitken the autobiographer was acutely aware of the intensity of Chartist memories in Ashton and its environs. No doubt many of his readers age forty and upward had signed one of the petitions for the Six Points or had attended the mass meetings at Hyde or Kersal Moor that he described in his last two 'letters'. Over the course of the 1850s and 1860s, 'a few choice spirits' continued to display black flags on August 16 to commemorate the Peterloo massacre and met at public houses and inns to celebrate the birthdays of Henry Hunt and Thomas Paine and to toast 'The

People's Charter' and 'the immortal memory of Feargus O'Connor'.[60] Through these kinds of commemorative events and rituals, and through participation in local politics and lectures and tea parties at the Chartist Institute or at the meeting room of the Ashton Secularist Society, a small but determined band of radical activists and plebeian intellectuals had struggled to keep alive the values and practices of Chartist democracy and an alternative set of memories about the recent past.[61]

Aitken clearly hoped to do justice to this very different set of collective memories of the movement and to give an honest account of what he called 'that much abused and misrepresented embodiment of the people's political rights'.[62] At several points, there was, however, clearly a tension between these goals and his desire to maintain a continuity of political self. Telling the truth about Chartism inevitably involved selecting some of the memories of the collective past and discarding or downplaying others. Even a cursory reading of the narrow columns of the Liberal *News* where he gave his 'remembrances' revealed a Chartist world that was masculine and public in its politics and moral in its methods. In portraying the movement in this way, he tried to bring his Chartist past into line with the persona that he had so carefully crafted in his earlier 'letters'. And yet, even though this approach made Chartism more fit for inclusion in the Liberal tradition, Aitken was careful to stress aspects of the movement that were very much at odds with the Liberalism of his later years; he continued to emphasize, above all, the distinctiveness of the Chartist democratic vision and ultimately defined 'the people', in his account of 1838-39, in class terms.

For all his determination to give an honest account of that `much abused' movement, Aitken struggled, sometimes quite openly, over which `remembrances' to include in his narrative of the 1839 campaign. On the one hand, he said almost nothing about the very public role of Ashton women in Chartism. There were, on the other hand, several allusions, though always in very general terms, to mass arming and the debate over the general strike, or `SACRED MONTH,' but he was careful to avoid any mention of the names of those local militants who had taken part in the insurrectionary side of the movement. One controversial memory that Aitken did discuss, though again without naming names, dealt with what he called `a miserable dispute' between two of the leaders of `the people.' It had, he sadly noted, `serious consequences' for the movement, but he refused to go into the details of this incident. `It would gratify,' he admitted, `a morbid curiosity to know what it was, but that also will remain in the recesses of the brain, and shall never be printed with my sanction.'[63]

This `thunder storm in a tea pot,' as Aitken euphemistically described it, drew its power from the ways in which gender and politics intertwined in sexual scandal. In late June 1839, despite the efforts of Aitken and others to keep the matter quiet, Peter Murray McDouall publicly accused the Rev. J. R. Stephens, champion of family values and the sanctity of the working man's cottage, of making improper advances to a young lady. McDouall went on to imply that Stephens had a hand in McDouall's near arrest a few weeks earlier. Several hours after this meeting Abel Williamson, a local leader and surety for both Stephens and McDouall, turned McDouall over to the Ashton police.[64] These two episodes touched off an internecine quarrel among the Chartists throughout Ashton, Stalybridge, and Hyde. This infighting over sexual impropriety, personalities, and the 'unEnglish conduct' of Williamson, as Aitken later put it, reinforced and intensified growing divisions over strategy. McDouall wholeheartedly supported the national holiday, but Stephens actively opposed 'the delusion of a National Holiday' and bitterly attacked those who supported it.[65]

The fact that J. R. Stephens was still alive and well in 1869 no doubt contributed to Aitken's reticence here, but his silence was also consistent with his tendency to portray politics as a very masculine world that dealt with public, not private, matters. With the exception of his passing reference to the role of Mary Hobson in the war of the unstamped, Aitken the autobiographer in fact never even alluded to the involvement of women in the radical politics of the 1830s.[66] He made no mention of the presence of women at the great Kersal Moor demonstrations or at the rowdy 20 April meeting at the marketplace in Ashton. Nor did he discuss their role in collecting the National Rent and organizing exclusive dealing campaigns or their willingness to support the mass platform's strategy of confrontation and intimidation.[67] These omissions in Aitken's account of 1839 were all the more striking because of his own introduction to radical culture. His earliest memory of Ashton radicalism, as he recalled in January 1869, was 'a Radical banquet of potato pies and home brewed ale' to commemorate Peterloo at 'Owd Nancy Clayton's.'[68]

This 'missing presence,' to borrow Yeo's phrase, of women in Ashton Chartism was consistent, however, with Aitken's views on femininity in his autobiography and his definition of the political arena and workplace as masculine domains. Throughout his narrative he used adjectives like 'kind,' 'loving,' and 'gentle' to describe women. Clearly, the proper place for 'frail women' was not the coal mine or the cotton mill.[69] Looking back on a visit to Wigan as a teenager, Aitken recalled with horror the sight of two miners, a husband and his 'gentle' wife, who had just returned to their home:

> Had it not been that the woman was suckling a child about six months old, I could not have told but that they were both male colliers. Yes, there this woman sat, dressed in the garb of a collier, and had been working the mine all day wagoning for her husband, yoked to coal wagons with a strap and chain like a beast of burden. As I had not then heard that females were employed in the mines, it startled me the more coming on this exhibition so suddenly. It is needless to remark on the cruelty of such a system as that was, or the vast evils it inflicted on what should be gentle woman. It almost transformed woman into man, and took away that gentleness which is so high an attribute of her sex. This giant evil is now done away

with, and I took a part with others, in after years, in laying these things before Parliament.[70]

For Aitken, indeed, the Ten Hours campaign had taken the form of `a great moral effort' by men, like himself, to put an end to `the evils of the long-hour system' and to protect `frail women, and frailer children.'[71]

What was also `missing' in his account of 1839 was any real discussion of the insurrectionary side of the movement. The emphasis by Aitken on the role of public meetings and the open, constitutional side of the movement was clearly one way of revising, or at least avoiding, the most painful and controversial of the collective memories of Ashton Chartism; it reflected as well his conviction in 1869 about `the folly of attempting to put down a Government like ours by physical force.' The proper way to bring about political change, he believed, was through moral power, `the power of eloquence, the pen, and the press.'[72] This was possible in England, Aitken believed, because of its history and constitutional traditions. `I hold that in a country like ours,' he wrote, `where we have liberty of speech, liberty of the press, and what we call liberty without licentiousness, any means to accomplish a given end, however good it may be, other than moral power, must ultimately fail.'[73] For Aitken, the agent of moral change was, of course, the manly, self-sacrificing hero who struggled courageously against great odds in the cause of the people:

> All men who have hitherto taken the people's side of the question have had to sacrifice their own money and time. Their homes have been made desolate, themselves looked upon too often with scorn by the wealthy classes of society, their motives entirely mistaken, and they have been ostracised from what is called good society. Imprisonment and exile have too often been the lot of the men who have hitherto advocated the political and social rights of the people, but those days let us hope in this country and all others are gone.[74]

The consistency of Aitken the autobiographer's views on moral power and his identification with `a country like ours,' however, were at odds with the political actions and opinions of his own Chartist past. While acknowledging `a great many wild things said and done,' Aitken chose to pass over in silence the drilling on secluded spots in the parish or the open sale of cutlasses, guns, and pike heads in the shops and market stalls in Stalybridge and Hyde. In a similar fashion he avoided any reference to `*secret meetings*' at Bush Inn, owned by James Duke, or to the involvement of fellow activists, like Timothy Higgins, in the mass arming campaign.[75] Unlike his close friends, Duke and McDouall, Aitken apparently steered clear of any direct involvement in 1839 in the buying and selling of firearms; however, Aitken, like most Chartist activists, made no hard and fast distinction between `moral' and `physical' force and always upheld the right of the people to bear arms.[76] Worried that `the Government of this country intends to establish a military reign of despotism,' Aitken urged his fellow Chartists to support the National Convention and to rely on 'the strength of your own right arm' to win their rights; he also defended mass arming as a way of applying pressure to the Whig government, 'the most bloodthirsty set of scoundrels in existence,' and of preventing arbitrary arrests and another Peterloo massacre.[77] During the torchlight campaign in autumn 1838, his speeches took on an even more violent, threatening tone. 'Any man that would abuse my parent, kinsman, or child—(hear)—,' Aitken told his audience at a radical dinner, 'as those worthy Britons were treated at Peterloo, that man shall surely fall by my hand, let the consequence be what it may. (Loud cheers).'[78]

Dismissive alike of 'our *glorious* Constitution' and of the legitimacy of the Whigs' claim to political power, Aitken declared that it did not matter which faction was voted into office. 'Under the existing franchise,' he defiantly asserted in 1841, 'I consider it signifies nothing to the people who is returned to Parliament.'[79] These sentiments, expressed so forcefully by Aitken during the contentious parliamentary election of that year, clearly clashed with his later identification with the Liberal party and England as 'a country like ours.' They also put into perspective his willingness in 1839 to explore the potentially revolutionary question of the 'SACRED MONTH,' or general strike, a tactic that he dismissed in the autobiography as a 'wild scheme.'[80] That summer Aitken was in fact at the centre of the debate among the Ashton and Stalybridge Chartists over the crucial issue of 'ulterior measures.' Early on, in June, he apparently came out in favor of 'a cessation from labour for one month.' As the original day for launching the general strike, 12 August, drew close, Aitken continued to speak out and added his voice to the growing debate over this popular but controversial tactic.[81] His exact role during the chaotic three-day general strike in August remains unclear, but shortly after its conclusion he was arrested on charges of seditious conspiracy and speeches and unlawful assembly.[82]

By editing out these kinds of 'remembrances,' Aitken began the process of bringing his interpretation of Chartism into line with the values and outlook of Ashton Liberalism and its own distinctive perspective on the recent Chartist past. But, at the same time, despite his description of the People's Charter as 'a document drawn up by five members of Parliament and five working men,' he made no real attempt to recast the movement in the image of the cross-class reform alliance of the Liberal party.[83] Thereafter, in his narrative of the 1839 campaign, he paused at several points to draw a distinction between 'the people' and what he variously referred to as 'the higher and middle classes' or 'the higher and well to do classes' or simply as 'the middle classes.'[84] In making this distinction, Aitken fell in line with a common contemporary usage of the phrase. 'The people,' as Thomas Wright remarked in *Our New Masters*, was often used in the early 1870s 'as a synonym for the working classes.'[85]

The hostility of the 'higher and middle classes' to democracy, the people's cause, was in fact, as Aitken the autobiographer pointed out, a formidable obstacle to reform both then and in the present. This was particularly true for the earlier period. 'Prejudice ran very high at that time,' he stressed about 1839, 'among the middle classes against the Chartists.'[86] And yet, such prejudice was still alive and well at the time that Aitken wrote down the final lines of his 're-membrances.' When describing the ambitious, 'sweeping' democracy of the Six Points, he drew explicit parallels between middle-class 'prejudice' toward the People's Charter in the late 1830s and the continued strength of such feelings in the late 1860s:

> It was a document that provided for the election of members of Parliament on an equitable basis. In brief, a most extensive reform bill, going much further than the one we have just obtained. That the higher and middle classes of this country were not ready for so sweeping a measure of reform thirty years since, may easily be imagined, from the strong opposition we have seen within the last few years to the bills that have been before the country.[87]

One such liberal member of 'the higher and middle classes,' John Stuart Mill, clearly found the coming of democracy deeply disturbing. Worried about the rights of 'minorities' (as well as the security of property) under majority rule, he was convinced that 'class feelings' would inevitably influence, if not determine, the politics of 'the wages-receiving class.'[88]

Conclusion

For Aitken the autobiographer, 'the higher and middle classes' as a whole were not part of 'the people' in 1839. This did not mean, of course, that in his autobiography 'the people' always equaled 'the working class.' At several points, Aitken used the term as a sort of synonym for 'Chartists,' thus including, perhaps intentionally, individuals of 'a high social position,' like John Frost or McDouall, who embraced and identified with the people's cause. If anything, then, his use of language in his autobiography points to the need to avoid univocal interpretations of this and other recurring tropes in radical rhetoric and to the importance of context in determining meaning.[89] His life story also clearly underlined the ways in which empathy and imagination influenced the creation of individual and collective identities, like 'the people' or 'working man.' In defining himself in the latter way, Aitken transcended the social and economic realities of his daily life over the last thirty years and consciously chose, no doubt, this persona as a symbol of his democratic commitment and as a way of presenting and interpreting himself and his life story. This decision to portray himself as 'a working man,' at once radical and moral in his politics, shaped how he told his story.

His relationship to the audience for his 'remembrances' and the medium of publication also affected how he ordered and interpreted his memories of a life in politics. Determined to create a continuity of public self, he downplayed or ignored some memories, selected other memories, and reinterpreted all of them in light of his Liberal present in 1869 and the collective memories of Ashton's recent past. The Ashton men and women who made up his audience inevitably influenced his 'remembrances' of his struggles for 'bread and liberty,' for, as the *Ashton News* stressed, Aitken had devoted his life to giving voice to 'what the many felt.'[90] Reaching out to this highly politicized and local readership through the columns of the Liberal *News,* Aitken also quite naturally began to lean toward the increasingly popular view of Chartism as a 'section of the Liberal party.'[91] This interpretation gave a sense of unity, mission, and consistency to his public self and also allowed him to smooth over many of the controversial (and illegal) aspects of the movement and to bring his life story into line with the prevailing Liberal perspective on the Chartist past.

One such example of this often subtle process of reinterpretation occurred in his retelling of a story about an exchange that took place between himself and Colonel Wemyss in the Ashton marketplace in May 1839. In his autobiography, he recalled the incident almost with fondness:

> A troop of dragoons had been over here and one piece of artillery on the Saturday previous, in consequence of anticipated disturbances which never took place. The troop was under the command of Colonel Wemyss, a fine, soldierly, kind, old gentleman as I have ever met with in all my travels. After he saw there was no occasion for this military display, he sent the soldiers back to Manchester, and on horseback he gathered the people round him and spoke to them of the constitutional methods to be used for the gaining of what they wanted. I being close to the Colonel got hold of his bridle, which hung loosely on his horse's neck, and he and I entered into a long discussion on the general topics which were then agitating the country, the Poor Laws, the Ten Hour's Bill and the Charter. The gallant old Colonel rode off with many compliments, good advice and the ringing cheers of the people.[92]

Aitken left his readers with a sense that 'the people' and 'the gallant old Colonel' had engaged in rational, far-ranging discussion of 'the constitutional methods to be used for the gaining of what they wanted.' A contemporary account in the *Northern Star,* reported by Richard Oastler, who was present at the scene, gave a somewhat different version, one that varied significantly from Aitken's 're-membrance.' The recent arrest by the Ashton police of four Chartists for drilling had created, Oastler noted, a tense situation in the town. Worried about the fate of the young men, all working men in their early twenties, crowds of men and women 'in great numbers' had begun to collect in the streets of Ashton on this wet, rainy Saturday; at least some of those who were present had heard rumors about plans for a rescue attempt. This volatile situation alarmed the Ashton magistrates, who sent out an urgent request to Manchester for troops. This was the immediate context for the 'conversation' in the marketplace between

Wemyss and Aitken. For all the obvious reasons, Aitken the autobiographer chose not to recall his description, on this occasion, of the Ashton mill owners as `a bloodthirsty set of monsters' or his curt dismissal of Wemyss' s defense of English liberty. `Liberty! The people of England,' he declared, `have liberty to be worked to death in a cotton mill, and when they get so that they cannot perform the work required, to be starved to death in a Poor Law Bastile.' Nor did Aitken mention to his readers his final warning to Wemyss, amid `great cheering' from the crowd, that `the Government cannot put down the united voices and determination of the people of Great Britain.'[93]

This striking divergence between the account in the *Northern Star* and Aitken's own recounting of the incident some thirty years later underscores the changing, subjective nature of his `remembrances' and points to some of the problems in trying to use the later careers and autobiographies of Chartist activists, like Aitken, as evidence for the `currents of radicalism' approach to Chartism and Liberalism. On the one hand, he and other Chartist autobiographers selected and interpreted their memories of this period of their lives in light of their Liberal present; they also realized that in the case of certain painful or divisive `remembrances,' the best approach was simply to try to forget. `Let the middle and the working classes then … unite,' urged the former Chartist R. J. Richardson in 1848, `let bygones be bygones; let Peterloo even be forgotten.'[94] On the other hand, Aitken and many of his fellow Chartist autobiographers often ignored Richardson's words of advice and instead went on to remind their readers about episodes, ideas, and traditions that fit uneasily with the Liberal vision of society and politics. For all his hard words about the National Convention and `the very indiscreet conduct and language' of the Chartist leadership, he was candid about the `state of incipient rebellion' in 1839 and the mass support for the Newport uprising; he was also critical of the heavy-handed response of the Whig government, especially of Lord John Russell, to the Chartist challenge.[95]

The entry of Aitken and other former Chartists into the world of Liberal and Conservative party politics was also a more troubled passage than Biagini and Reid and like-minded historians have suggested. Their interpretation of Liberal politics overlooks, above all, the extent to which the mass movement for the Six Points transformed and radicalized the nature and practice of local and parliamentary politics in former militant Chartist towns, like Ashton and Stalybridge. The integration of plebeian intellectuals and activists into the party politics of the 1850s and 1860s was a two-way process, one that involved conflict as well as cooperation and affected the politicians of the emerging mass party system as well as `owd' Chartists. While the Chartists drew back from the insurrectionary spirit and class confrontation of the late 1830s and early 1840s, many of the leaders of the Liberal Party retreated from their exposed ideological position as proponents of the harsh, utilitarian side of political economy and adopted some of the Chartist demands as well as some of the Chartists' methods of mobilization and forms of action. Out of this interplay between resistance and compromise and between forgetting and remembering, grew the conflict-ridden but stable society of mid-Victorian England.[96]

Notes

[1] Robert G. Hall and Stephen Roberts (eds.), *William Aitken: The Writings of a Nineteenth Century Working Man*, Tameside, 1996 (hereafter cited as *William Aitken*), pp. 40-41.

[2] *Ashton News*, 2 October 1869; *Ashton Reporter*, 2 October 1869.

[3] *Ashton News*, 2 October 1869.

[4] *Ashton News*, 2 October 1869; *Ashton Reporter*, 2 October 1869; *Parliamentary Papers*, Special Report from the Select Committee on the Sale of Liquors on Sunday Bill, 1867-68, [402] XIV, pp. 382-83; Public Record Office (PRO), Home Office (HO) 20/10, Interview with William Aitken. In the latter source the prison inspector estimated that Aitken's school brought in about three pounds a week. For the rise of the 'trade of agitation,' see Paul A. Pickering, *Chartism and the Chartists in Manchester and Salford*, London, Macmillan Press, 1995, pp. 139-58.

[5] *William Aitken*, p. 55; Manchester Central Library, George Wilson Papers, M20/1868-69, Mason to Wilson, 19 November 1869.

[6] Eugenio F. Biagini and Alastair J. Reid (eds.), *Currents of Radicalism: Popular Radicalism, Organised Labour, and Party Politics in Britain, 1850-1914*, Cambridge, Cambridge University Press, 1991, pp. 1-2; Eugenio F. Biagini, *Liberty, Retrenchment, and Reform: Popular Liberalism in the Age of Gladstone, 1860-1880*, Cambridge, Cambridge University Press, 1992, pp. 2, 10-11; see also the classic work Brian Harrison and Patricia Hollis, 'Chartism, Liberalism, and the Life of Robert Lowery,' *English Historical Review*, vol. 82 , July 1967, pp. 503-35; and F. C. Mather (ed.), *Chartism and Society: An Anthology of Documents*, London, Bell and Hyman, 1980, pp. 39-45. For recent attempts to place Chartism in southeast Lancashire within the tradition of popular Liberalism, see Peter Taylor, *Popular Politics in Early Industrial Britain: Bolton, 1825-1850*, Keele, Keele University Press, 1995; and Michael Winstanley, 'Oldham Radicalism and the Origins of Popular Liberalism, 1830-52,' *Historical Journal*, vol. 36, no. 3, September 1993, pp. 619-43.

[7] Gareth Stedman Jones, *Languages of Class: Studies in English Working Class History, 1832-1982*, Cambridge, Cambridge University Press, 1983, p. 104.

[8] Patrick Joyce, *Visions of the People: Industrial England and the Question of Class, 1840-1914*, Cambridge, Cambridge University Press, 1991, pp. 37-38, 1-15.

[9] Jerome Hamilton Buckley, *The Turning Key: Autobiography and the Subjective Impulse since 1800*, Cambridge, Harvard University Press, 1984, pp. vii, 14-15, 19, 45; and Charles Rycroft, 'Viewpoint: Analysis and the Autobiography,' *Times Literary Supplement* (27 May 1983), p. 541.

[10] Buckley, *Turning Key*, p. 45.

[11] *William Aitken*, p. 28.

[12] Ibid. See also, Dorothy Thompson, 'Who Were "the People" in 1842?' in Malcolm Chase and Ian Dyck (eds.), *Living and Learning: Essays in Honour of J. F. C. Harrison*, Aldershot, Scolar Press, 1996, pp. 118-32. For a very different perspective on Aitken's use of 'the people,' see Patrick Joyce, *Visions*, pp. 37-38, 60, 103, 108, and *Democratic Subjects: The Self and the Social in Nineteenth-Century England*, Cambridge, Cambridge University Press, 1994, p. 132.

[13] Harrison and Hollis, 'Robert Lowery,' pp. 503-35; and Mather, *Chartism and Society*, pp. 39-45.

[14] Macaulay to Greig, 30 January [1846] and Macaulay to the Secretary of the Committee for the Liberation of Frost, Williams, and Jones, 16 February [1846], in Thomas Pinney, (ed.), *The Letters of Thomas Babington Macaulay*, vol. 4, *September 1841-December 1848*, Cambridge, Cambridge University Press, 1977, pp. 291-93; and Robert G. Hall, 'Work, Class, and Politics in Ashton-under-Lyne, 1830-1860,' Ph.D. dissertation., Vanderbilt University, 1991, pp. 137-41.

[15] *William Aitken*, p. 14.

[16] For the growing literature on history and memory, see Popular Memory Group, 'Popular Memory: Theory, Politics, Method' in Richard Johnson et al (eds.), *Making Histories: Studies in History-Writing and Politics,* Minneapolis, University of Minnesota Press, 1982, pp. 205-52; David Lowenthal, *The Past is a Foreign Country,* Cambridge, Cambridge University Press, 1985, pp. 193-210; Alistair Thomson, 'The Anzac Legend: Exploring National Myth and Memory in Australia' in Raphael Samuel and Paul Thompson (eds.), *The Myths We Live By,* London, Routledge, 1990, pp. 73-82; John R. Gillis (ed.), *Commemorations: The Politics of National Identity,* Princeton, Princeton University Press, 1994; Pierre Nora, (ed.), *Realms of Memory: Rethinking the French Past,* vol. 1, *Conflicts and Divisions,* trans. Arthur Goldhammer, New York, Columbia University Press, 1996; and Emily Honig, 'Striking Lives: Oral History and the Politics of Memory,' *Journal of Women's History,* vol. 9, no. 1, Spring 1997, pp. 139-57.

[17] Buckley, *Turning Key,* pp. vii, 3, 14-15, 19; and David Vincent, *Bread, Knowledge, and Freedom: A Study of Nineteenth-Century Working Class Autobiography,* London, Methuen, 1981, pp. 1-38.

[18] *William Aitken,* p. 14. For the 1862 trip, see *Ashton Reporter,* 23 August 1862. See Robert Folkenflik, 'Introduction: The Institution of Autobiography' in Robert Folkenflik (ed.), *The Culture of Autobiography: Constructions of Self-Representation,* Stanford, Stanford University Press, 1993, pp. 12-16.

[19] *William Aitken,* pp. 14, 17, 21, 40. See also, William Aitken, 'Franklin's Maxims,' *Oddfellows' Magazine,* April 1859, p. 79; Vincent, *Bread, Knowledge, and Freedom,* pp. 14-15; Linda H. Peterson, *Victorian Autobiography: The Tradition of Self-Interpretation,* New Haven, Yale University Press, 1986, pp. 1-3.

[20] William Aitken, 'Life of Hofer,' quoted in Aitken's obituary, *Ashton Reporter,* 2 October 1869; PRO, HO 20/10, Interview with William Aitken; *McDouall's Chartist and Republican Journal,* 10 April 1841; and William Aitken, *A Journey Up the Mississippi River from Its Mouth to Nauvoo, the City of the Latter Day Saints,* Ashton-under-Lyne, [1845], preface and pp. 25-30, 34-35, 38, 46.

[21] Samuel Bamford's autobiography was published as *Passages in the Life of a Radical* (1844) and *Early Days* (1849). The memoirs of Thomas Hardy came out in 1832; and the autobiographies of the Chartists John James Bezer and Robert Lowery were published, in serial form, in 1851 and 1856-57, respectively. See, Vincent, *Bread, Knowledge, and Freedom,* pp. 204-8. For a nuanced perspective on Bamford's life and career, see Martin Hewitt, 'Radicalism and the Victorian Working Class: The Case of Samuel Bamford,' *Historical Journal,* vol. 34, no. 4, December 1991, pp. 873-92.

[22] Buckley, *Turning Key,* p. 45.

[23] PRO, HO 20/10, Interview with William Aitken; *Parliamentary Papers,* Special Report from the Select Committee on the Sale of Liquors on Sunday Bill, 1867-68, [402] XIV, pp. 382-83; *Ashton News,* 2 October 1869; *Ashton Reporter,* 2 October 1869.

[24] *William Aitken,* p. 14; Vincent, *Bread, Knowledge, and Freedom,* pp. 27-29; and Eileen Janes Yeo, 'Will the Real Mary Lovett Please Stand Up? Chartism, Gender, and Autobiography' in Chase and Dyck (eds.), *Living and Learning,* pp. 163-64.

[25] For his use of the terms 'working men' and 'the working-classes,' see *William Aitken,* pp. 14, 19-22, 26, 28. In the last two installments, which deal with Chartism, he avoided both constructions, with one exception, in favor of the term 'the people.' He twice referred, however, to 'middle classes' on pp. 28 and 43.

[26] Ibid., pp. 14, 19, 30, 39-40, 42-43.

[27] Ibid., pp. 14, 27-28.

[28] Ibid., p. 40.

[29] Yeo, 'Mary Lovett,' pp. 164, 167.

[30] *Ashton Reporter,* 2 October 1869. During his imprisonment in 1840 and flight to the United States during 1842-43, she had to manage on her own; the 1851 census listed her as a schoolmistress. See *Northern Star,* 15 July 1843; and PRO, HO 107/2233.

[31] Lowenthal, *The Past Is a Foreign Country,* p. 210; Thomson, 'The Anzac Legend,' pp. 73-79.

[32] *William Aitken*, pp. 28, 14.

[33] *Ashton Reporter*, 2 October 1869; *William Aitken*, pp. 27-28.

[34] *William Aitken*, pp. 28, 40.

[35] Ibid., pp. 19, 28, 30, 41; Walter E. Houghton, *The Victorian Frame of Mind, 1830-1870*, New Haven, Yale University Press, 1957, pp. 27-53; and Vincent, *Bread, Knowledge, and Freedom*, pp. 197-200.

[36] *William Aitken*, pp. 39-40. For the cult of the hero, see Houghton, *Victorian Frame of Mind*, pp. 305-40; and Thomas Carlyle, *On Heroes, Hero-Worship, and the Heroic in History*, London, J. Fraser, 1841.

[37] *Ashton News*, 2 October 1869.

[38] *William Aitken*, pp. 15, 18, 22, 40.

[39] William Aitken, `Over the Atlantic, from the Mersey to the Mississippi,' *Oddfellows' Magazine*, April 1864, p. 371; and Vincent, *Bread, Knowledge, and Freedom*, pp. 182, 186-87.

[40] W. E. Adams, *Memoirs of a Social Atom*, New York, Augustus M. Kelley, 1967, pp. 211-12. See also P. Pickering and S. Roberts, `Pills, Pamphlets and Politics: The Career of Peter Murray McDouall (18 14-54),' *Manchester Region History Review*, vol. 11, 1997, pp. 34-43; John Belchem and James Epstein, `The Nineteenth-Century Gentleman Leader Revisited,' *Social History*, vol. 22, no. 2, May 1997, pp. 178-81; and Joyce, *Visions*, pp. 34-40.

[41] *William Aitken*, pp. 19-21, 24-25.

[42] Ibid., p. 14.

[43] Popular Memory Group, `Popular Memory,' pp. 241-43; Thomson, `The Anzac Legend,' pp. 77-79; and Honig, `Striking Lives,' p. 140.

[44] Maurice Halbwachs, *On Collective Memory*, ed. and trans. Lewis A. Coser, Chicago, University of Chicago Press, 1992, pp. 38-39.

[45] *Ashton News*, 2 October 1869; *Ashton Reporter*, 2 October 1869; and *Ashton Reporter*, 27 December 1862. See also *Oddfellows' Magazine*, July 1857, pp. 129-32. For Aitken's activities in the 1860s on behalf of the Confederacy, see Robert G. Hall and Stephen Roberts, `Introduction,' in *William Aitken*, pp. 10-11; and R. J. M. Blackett, `Pressure from Without: African Americans, British Public Opinion, and Civil War Diplomacy,' in Robert E. May (ed.), *The Union, the Confederacy, and the Atlantic Rim*, West Lafayette, Purdue University Press, 1995, pp. 83-84.

[46] *Ashton Reporter*, 10 November 1855. See also Aitken, *Journey*, p. 29.

[47] William Aitken, `A Story of the First French Revolution,' *Oddfellows' Magazine*, July 1869, pp. 203-4, and `A Story of the First French Revolution,' *Oddfellows' Magazine*, January 1870, pp. 284, 289. In his autobiography Aitken also used the phrase `liberty without licentiousness' (*William Aitken*, p. 27).

[48] *Ashton Reporter*, 3 October 1868. See also *Ashton Reporter*, 16 and 30 January 1869.

[49] *Ashton Reporter*, 8 September 1860. For an overview of the Hobson family's involvement in radical publishing, see *Ashton Reporter*, 17 August 1867.

[50] *Ashton Reporter*, 26 December 1857. Note the similarities to Aitken's October 1868 speech. For the war of the unstamped as part of the struggle for `Liberal principles,' see *Ashton Reporter*, 5 October 1861.

[51] *Ashton Reporter*, 30 January 1869.

[52] For explicit attempts to come to terms with Chartism in this way, see *Ashton Reporter*, 19 March 1859 and 20 September 1856.

[53] Founded in January 1868, the *Ashton News* apparently received crucial financial backing from Hugh Mason, red hot Dissenter (Independent) and Liberal; a former mayor of Ashton, the wealthy mill owner later served as M.P. for Ashton, 1880-85. Philip Martin Williams and David L. Williams, *Extra, Extra, Read All about It: A Brief History of the Newspapers of Ashton-under-Lyne, 1847-1990*, Ashton-under-Lyne, 1991.

[54] In the original text of his `letters,' obvious typographical errors and strange, erratic punctuation were common. The *News* only infrequently broke up the text into paragraphs. For instance, the 16 October installment contained only two paragraph breaks. In the 1996 edition, the obvious errors

have been corrected, and the text has been broken up into more frequent paragraphs. See *William Aitken*, p. 56

[55] Vincent, *Bread, Knowledge, and Freedom*, pp. 9-10. For a discussion of the challenges of serial publication, see John Butt and Kathleen Tillotson, *Dickens at Work*, London, Methuen, 1957, pp. 15-16, 21-25, 202-3; and John Sutherland, *Victorian Fiction: Writers, Publishers, Readers*, New York, St. Martin's Press, 1995, pp. 55, 87, 115-16.

[56] Frank Peel, *The Risings of the Luddites, Chartists, and Plug-Drawers*, with an introduction by E.P. Thompson, New York, Augustus M. Kelley, 1968, pp. viii-x. Samuel Hill listed, for the Ashton and Stalybridge area, around nine dialect poets who were active in the nineteenth century, the most famous of whom was Samuel Laycock (Samuel Hill, *Old Lancashire Songs and Their Singers*, [Ashton-under-Lyne, nd.], pp. 51-52). See also W. E. A. Axon, *The Black Knights of Ashton*, Manchester, [1870].

[57] *William Aitken*, p. 14.

[58] Ibid., p. 24; and *Ashton Reporter*, 16 and 30 January 1869.

[59] *William Aitken*, p. 36.

[60] *Ashton Reporter*, 14 November 1857, and 5 February and 20 August 1859; *National Reformer*, 13 February 1864. For radical dining during the 1820s and 1830s, see James Epstein, *Radical Expression: Political Language, Ritual, and Symbol in England, 1790-1850*, New York, Oxford University Press, 1994, pp. 147-65.

[61] *Ashton Reporter*, 27 October 1860 (local politics); *People's Paper*, 17 February 1855, *Ashton Reporter*, 10 March 1860 and 28 March 1868 (Chartist Institute); and *Ashton Reporter*, 6 December 1862 and 26 September 1863, *National Reformer*, 30 January 1864 (Secularist Society).

[62] *William Aitken*, p. 28.

[63] Ibid., p. 35.

[64] Ibid.; *Manchester Guardian*, 29 June 1839; *Manchester and Salford Advertiser*, 29 June and 6 July 1839; and *Stockport Advertiser*, 28 June 1839.

[65] Hall, 'Work, Class, and Politics,' pp. 155-56; and *William Aitken*, p. 38.

[66] *William Aitken*, p. 30.

[67] *Northern Star*, 2 February 1839. See also, *Manchester Guardian*, 24 April 1839; *Northern Star*, 27 April 1839; and *Operative*, 31 March and 28 April 1839.

[68] *Ashton Reporter*, 30 January 1869.

[69] *William Aitken*, pp. 15, 34, 16, 19.

[70] Ibid., p. 19

[71] Ibid., pp. 24, 23. For the tendency of the Ten Hours movement to portray women as dependents and to use 'the language of patriarchal protection,' see Robert Gray, *The Factory Question and Industrial England, 1830-1860*, Cambridge, Cambridge University Press, 1996, pp. 29-31, 36-37. See also Anna Clark, *The Struggle for the Breeches: Gender and the Making of the British Working Class*, Berkeley, University of California Press, 1995, pp. 243-44; and Carolyn Malone, 'Gendered Discourses and the Making of Protective Labor Legislation in England, 1830-1914,' *Journal of British Studies*, vol. 37, no. 2, April 1998, pp. 166-91.

[72] *William Aitken*, pp. 31, 27-28.

[73] Ibid., p. 27. For this same point, see Aitken, 'A Story of the First French Revolution,' *Oddfellows' Magazine*, July 1869, p. 204.

[74] *William Aitken*, p. 30.

[75] Ibid., p. 38; PRO, HO 40/37, Jowett to Your Lordship, 3 July 1839; and Hall, 'Work, Class, and Politics,' pp. 153-56.

[76] Dorothy Thompson (ed.), *The Early Chartists*, Columbia, University of South Carolina Press, 1971, pp. 16-27; James Epstein, *The Lion of Freedom: Feargus O'Connor and the Chartist Movement, 1832-1842*, London, Croom Helm, 1982, pp. 124-26; and Robert Sykes, 'Physical-Force Chartism: The Cotton District and the Chartist Crisis of 1839,' *International Review of Social History*, vol. 30, no. 2, 1985, pp. 211-17.

[77] *Northern Star*, 18 May 1839; *Manchester and Salford Advertiser*, 27 October 1838; PRO, HO

40/37, 'Meeting of Chartists at Ashton under Lyne, Held in the Market Place on Saturday Evening April 20th 1839'; and *Northern Star,* 11 April 1840.

[78] *Northern Star,* 17 November 1838.

[79] Tameside Local Studies Library, L322, William Aitken, 'To the Non-Electors and Electors of the Borough of Ashton-under-Lyne,' Ashton-under-Lyne, 1841. For a copy, see *William Aitken,* p. 33.

[80] *William Aitken,* p. 36.

[81] *Manchester and Salford Advertiser,* 22 June 1839; and *Manchester Chronicle,* 10 August 1839. See also, British Library, Francis Place Papers, Additional MSS 34,245B, Deegan to Fletcher, 6 August 1839.

[82] Hall, 'Work, Class, and Politics,' pp. 155-57; and *Parliamentary Papers,* Returns of Every Person Confined for Charges for Printing and Publishing Seditious or Blasphemous Libels, 1840, [600] XXXVIII, pp. 10, 12, 8. The day after the general strike of 1842 had begun, an Ashton meeting of striking factory workers appointed six delegates to spread the strike for a fair day's wages and the Charter: William Aitken, Alexander Challenger, Richard Pilling, Thomas Storer, George Johnson, and James Taylor. See PRO, Treasury Solicitor's Papers, TS 11/813/2677; PRO, Records of the Palatine of Lancaster, PL 27/11, part 2, Deposition of Joseph Armitage.

[83] *William Aitken,* p. 28.

[84] Ibid., pp. 28, 42-43.

[85] Thomas Wright, *Our New Masters,* New York, Augustus M. Kelley, 1969, p. 62.

[86] *William Aitken,* p. 43.

[87] Ibid., pp. 28-29.

[88] Mill to Kinnear. 19 August and 25 September 1865, in Francis E. Mineka and Dwight N. Lindley (eds.), *The Collected Works of John Stuart Mill,* vol. 16, *The Later Letters of John Stuart Mill,* Toronto, University of Toronto Press, 1963, pp. 1093-94 and 1103-4.

[89] *William Aitken,* pp. 31, 35; Epstein, *Radical Expression,* pp. 70-71, 97-99; and Thompson, 'Who Were "the People" in 1842?' pp. 118-19.

[90] *Ashton News,* 2 October 1869.

[91] *Ashton Reporter,* 30 January 1869.

[92] *William Aitken,* p. 34.

[93] *Northern Star,* 18 May 1839. For other accounts of this event, see PRO, HO 73/55, Mott to Poor Law Commissioners, 9 May 1839; *Manchester Guardian,* 8 May 1839.

[94] *Manchester Examiner,* 11 April 1848.

[95] *William Aitken,* pp. 29, 36, 31, 35.

[96] Hall, 'Work, Class, and Politics,' pp. 14-15, 262-64.

Selected Documents

Each Saturday for fifteen years the *Northern Star* was published in three editions. Wherever they lived, local Chartist activists looked forward to the appearance of their newspaper. Space might have been found for their own reports and poems; almost certainly there would be a new letter from Feargus O'Connor. For many Feargus' letter was their favourite part of the newspaper, and it was often read aloud. An edited version of one of Feargus' weekly letters is included in this selection of documents. Describing a lecture tour of Scotland in 1839, O'Connor emphasizes his hard work on behalf of the Chartist cause and triumphantly recounts how he saw off his – and his followers' – critics. The loyalty and love which O'Connor attracted is exemplified in a editorial written by Thomas Cooper for the *Midlands Counties' Illuminator*. Another Chartist who offered his view of O'Connor was Samuel Kydd. However, he had by the time of writing – soon after O'Connor's death in 1855 – set aside his Chartist loyalties for the Tory radicalism of Richard Oastler.

The commitment and confidence of local activists is reflected in reports in their local periodicals – such as the excellent *Commonswealthsman* – and in the *Star*. Addresses, reports and poems poured into the office of the *Star*. These reports told of lectures, camp meetings, welcomes for Feargus, Chartist schools and so on. The close rapport between the paper and the Chartist rank-and-file was reflected in the column 'To Readers and Correspondents'; some extracts from this column follow. Forceful editorials appeared in each issue of the newspaper; extracts from three of these are included in this selection, commenting on the Newport Rising of 1839, the strikes of 1842 and 'the people's last appeal', the great petition of 1848.

Vigorous, lively and indiscreet, the letters of Thomas Cooper – of which many hundreds have survived – offer real glimpses into the day-to-day work and personal feelings of an artisan politician and writer. Two letters from 1842 are reprinted here. The first letter vividly describes the Nottingham by election when, led by O'Connor, the Chartists gave physical support to the middle class politician, Joseph Sturge. Sturge, however, was defeated, the anti-Poor Law editor of *The Times*, John Walter, supported by J.R. Stephens, being returned. The second letter was written shortly before the outbreak in the Potteries, for which Cooper became a scapegoat, serving two years in prison.

This selection of documents concludes with two interesting letters from the *Star* concerning the petition and demonstration of 1848, and an extract from the little-known autobiography of the Aberdeen Chartist, William Lindsay. This volume intermingles recollections of book-reading, lecturing and mesmerism with passages on radicalism; Lindsay's appraisal of the events of 1848 and of O'Connor should be noted.

FEARGUS O'CONNOR

From the *Northern Star*, 19 January 1839:

To Moral Philosophers and Philosophical Radicals

Gentlemen … Your theory is that moral force is quite sufficient to effect all necessary changes. To this I subscribe, while I assert your want of moral courage, your want of energy and your denunciations of better men than yourselves, have made the words moral force synonymous with "bear patiently, wait submissively, endure slavery, turn not upon your oppressors" and the like …. In making my recent tour of Scotland and the north of England, I had two objects in view: firstly, I resolved to defend myself in person against the charges of some of your fraternity and, secondly, I thought it of vast importance that the public mind should be set right on the subject of Mr Stephens' arrest …. You will bear in mind that the Tory press, wishing to smother the question of universal suffrage, attributed Mr Stephens' arrest, and the whole of our agitation, to an opposition to the Poor Law Amendment Act. In this course I saw the seeds of dissension which were likely to be sown between universal suffrage radicals and the Poor Law Amendment party; and still further I saw the consequences which were likely to arise if our Scotch brethren imbibed the notion that English agitation was but for the purpose of repealing a law which did not affect them instead of ensuring a state of things which would prevent a recurrence of such an enactment …. After having worked for fifteen days without intermission in London, in Bristol and at Manchester, I proceeded on Saturday morning … from Leeds on my way to the north. I travelled to Berwick, a distance of 160 miles, without stopping. On Monday morning, at ten o'clock, started for Edinburgh …. At four o'clock arrived in Edinburgh, saw some of my friends and companions …. At eight o'clock proceeded to the Freemasons' Hall where from seven to nine hundred well dressed, respectable men and women had assembled at a soiree to compliment my humble self. I was cheerfully received and rejoiced that I merited the approbation of so many worthy individuals …. Mr Sankey, delegate for Edinburgh and Master of Arts of Cambridge, made one of the most classical and eloquent speeches I ever heard and produced upon all, your humble servant included, a most powerful effect …. Mr Leith, an operative of Leith, followed Mr Sankey, and quite astonished us, as well by his eloquence, as by his originality and cutting sarcasm. He, too, made a most powerful speech …. And now I come to the most important part of my tour. Dr. Brewster, a minister of the Scotch Kirk, resides at Paisley. He is the parson who … was most loud in his denunciation of myself, Stephens and the English radicals

.... Upon my arrival at Paisley I was met by the worthy working men and by large numbers from the spirited village of Barrhead and others in the neighbourhood. I was told a meeting was convened in the Philosophical Hall .... I accordingly went to the Hall and was received with deafening cheers – it was overflowing. Brewster was well backed by his friends, but the body of the meeting overawed them and, before I had spoken ten minutes, assigning my reasons for being there, Brewster and his crew, many of whom were the young Church Tories of Paisley, appeared thunderstruck. Hope gave way to despair and when Brewster, one of the most confident, insolent bullying-men in existence, rose to reply, I found that I had paralyzed him .... I remained with my friends at Paisley, about 120 sitting down to refreshment, till half past two o'clock in the morning, and then, having spent a delightful morning, noon and night, proceeded to Glasgow .... I had invited Dr. Brewster to Glasgow if he required a larger jury. He did come and now hear the result .... After the chairman had opened the meeting in an admirable and straightforward address, Brewster presented himself .... For several minutes it was impossible to restore order; repeated cries of "kick him out", "turn him out", "throw him out, the traitor" interrupted the proceedings till at length the storm so raged, Mr Moral Philospher Brewster retreated, without his hat, through the back door amidst the execration of assembled thousands. I then proceeded to enter on my defence and the defence of Stephens and the English radicals .... I was then entertained at an excellent supper .... I got to bed before half past two and rose at half past five to start for Carlisle, a distance of 95 miles and where a public meeting had been announced for that evening .... Within about fourteen miles of the borders of a village, the name of which I regret to have forgotten, the coach was surrounded by a vast concourse of persons, who had been deputed to watch the changing of horses in order to present me with an address which terminated thus, "and the tell the Rev. Parson Stephens, Sir, with our love, that if the tyrants attempt to hurt a hair of his head, we will retaliate" .... The meeting went off triumphantly .... I spoke for more than an hour and felt very weak; however, I got through .... I was glad to attend the meeting at Newcastle .... I was very ill on my return from the meeting, and was obliged to have a person sitting in my room all night; however, the spirit prevailed for I got up at half past five and started eighty miles on my way to Peter Bussey's dinner at Bradford .... On Tuesday I left Bradford for Leeds to beat Neddy Baines and the Whigs which, let them say what they may, I did most effectually. After the meeting I returned to Bradford, thence to Queenshead, where a dinner was given to me .... I left them at eleven o'clock, and the only drunken man which I have seen in my tour was a manufacturer, lying in the middle of the road with his horse standing over him. He is one of the electors. Thus, Gentlemen, ends my eight days' tour, during which time I attended nine public meetings, travelled over seven hundred miles, slept upon average three hours a night, and once again united the Scotch and English radicals in a union more lasting than brass .... You are advocates of moral force. I have set you an example of what moral force can effect, and to you, many of whom are more wealthy than myself but who nevertheless travel for the people as post horses for their masters at so much a mile, to you, Gentlemen, I say, "go and do likewise"; and then all thought of physical force will vanish.

Your obedient servant Feargus O'Connor

P.S. To my friends I beg to say that I am now fresh and ready for the winter's campaign when I shall be prepared to meet the friends of the people in council and their enemies in the field. I now conclude, returning thanks to God, that I feel better than I ever did in my life.

From the *Midlands Counties' Illuminator*, 17 April 1841:

Feargus O'Connor cannot fail to produce a strong impression on the mind of every genuine Chartist by every line he pens. Chartists know that there is no mistake about him: all the dodge and trickery and subtle insinuation of Whig hirelings and sham radicals cannot draw the people into disaffection towards their energetic and incorruptible champion. This is not the language of personal idolatry: it is simply a candid confession of proper and deserved attachment on the part of working men to their best human friend …. Working men feel an ardent devotion to the names of Vincent and Lovett, and Collins and O'Brien, and Moir and McDouall and Pitkeithly, and a host of others that might be mentioned; but, while they know how to appreciate the sterling honesty, the active intelligence, the indomitable perserverance, the glorious enthusiasm, in brief the true patriotic qualities which distinguish, severally, the individuals in the front phalanx of their army, in no one name do they discern a combination of qualities so commanding in their influence, so magnetic in attracting an unwavering attachment, as in their brave O'Connor. This discerning preference – without a grain of undervaluation for other deserving names – it is, which irresistibly rivets the attention of the great majority of Chartists on every word given to the world from his dungeon by the untameable Feargus; and thus his late expressions of thought on Teetotalism and other subjects have fallen like sparks amongst us …. We do not, after much reflection, think that his jealous dread of disunion being produced by Church Chartism and Teetotal Chartism and so forth results merely from a spirit of querulousness in the mind of Feargus – or is the effect of incarceration and unacquaintance with the actual state of Chartism. We fear lest events may prove that O'Connor, on this as on various other subjects, is possessed of greater political foresight than all the other leaders of Chartism put together.

From Samuel Kydd, *The History of the Factory Movement* (1857), II, pp. 130-1:

The late Mr Feargus O'Connor, the acknowledged head of the Chartist party, was a man of great energy; a rapid and ready speaker, he was in the strength of manhood, and possessed a commanding bearing. He was aristocratic in manner, the descendant of an ancient, honoured and persecuted Irish family; his influence over the working men was great, and rapidly on the increase. Mr O'Connor had been reared in the school of Irish agitation, and possessed that floating recklessness, which is, in part, inseparable from a political agitator; fed by the events of the hour, he was ambitious of popularity and not scupulous as to the sacrifices he made for its attainment. In passing it is just to observe that Mr O'Connor's intellect and stores of knowledge did not improve with his years. When first in the House of Commons he was checked by men at least his equals in talent and knowledge; and he had regard for his standing as a politician and gentleman. When he became the popular leader of working men, his popularity gave him the choice of colleagues who were, with rare exceptions, subservient to his desires and to none was his absolutism more injurious than himself, for not any man stood more thoroughly in need of that kind of training which conflict with equals and superiors can alone give. When Mr O'Connor entered on English agitation, he was far from being a vulgar demagogue; he was amongst the last of that class of Irish orators who made agitation a business and hatred of the English government a profession; he possessed that kind of oratorical talent necessary for successful platform speech-making and he seemed to rely on it to serve him on all occasions and for all purposes; as a writer he was irregular and diffuse but strong in denunciation which, with his readers, was the principal commodity in demand. He was frank and bold, and, under better training than an anti-tithe agitation in Ireland and a desultory political warfare in England, might have been in parliament a man of mark; to considerable talent and fine physical power, he inherited from his father a manly generosity of heart.

CHARTIST LOCALITIES

From the *Commonswealthsman*, 2 April 1842:

Dear Sir – I am very happy to inform you that we are getting on well at East Leak. We have an association of upwards of 30 members, and Chartism is growing very fast. We have crowded congregations both on Sundays and week nights …. Our greatest opponents are those who profess to be Christians. I was told the other day of a man who said that my doctrine would not stand above two months; but it has stood three already. This man's daughter asked her father what politics were, "Oh", said he, "something very bad, my dear". The parson had been trying to kill Chartism by saying he would make the preacher and the people all rue the day they had begun it. The woman that lives in the house where we preach asked him how he intended to go on. After a great deal of talk, the woman let him see the licence. The parson turned round and said, "It will do you no good" – and away he went! We have been much disturbed on meeting nights. One night there was a host of young people came with a whistle, a Jew's harp, a tin pan and other musical instruments. But just when they had got into action, a policeman made his appearance and the band was off in a jiffy! I have been told that a gentleman farmer of the name of Mr John Burrows had sent the policeman to protect us! There is a great deal of poverty and distress, and the tyrants increase it daily. The other day there was a poor man breaking stones on the road. One of the farmers went to him and said, "Do you break them small enough, Bill?" The man said, "I don't know". "Well", said the farmer, "you have got your gauge with you, and you must gauge them". "Gauge? What do you mean?", said the man. "Your mouth", said the farmer. "You must break them so that you can put them in your mouth and swallow them" .... I was at Kegworth last Sunday morning. I had a good company to hear the Chartist preacher at this place. The people seem to have confidence in the principles of the Charter. The longer I spoke, the more people came up. There are some active men at Kegworth. Let us unite for "the Charter and no surrender" – no, not a jot .... I subscribe myself, dear Sir, yours in the cause of Liberty, John Pepper, Normanton-on-Soar, 23 March 1842.

From the *Commonswealthsman,* 18 June 1842:

My dear Cooper – Isham is a little village with a Chartist churchwarden, and a most intelligent population; and a splendid, lively meeting we held in it on Monday evening; indeed all looks cheering through this part of Northamptonshire.... I lectured, on Tuesday and Wednesday evenings, in Mr Jenkinson's large room (built for the purpose) at Kettering .... Great enthusiasm was displayed -18 new members were enrolled and I formed a female Association. Democracy goes on here at railway pace. I lectured on Wednesday noon at Rowell – the meeting was large – say 400 present – I formed here another Associaion with every prospect of success. On Thursday evening I lectured in the market place, Northampton, to 1600 persons .... The attention was rivetted to the last. The town is now a stronghold of Chartism. Thanks to Dr. McDouall! I lectured to very attentive meetings in the market place, Daventry, on Friday and Saturday evenings. The cause here is much crippled by want of more frequent agitation -Webb and Ashwell keep the steam up. I preached to 2000 people last evening at Buckby Folly – and a better impression I never produced in my life. Parties came 12 miles to hear me; labourers, artisans, females and middle class men. Chartism has beaten down every obstacle in Buckby. All hail to the brave lads! ... I remain, yours ever faithfully, 'A Chartist from heel to crown', J.R.H. Bairstow.

From the *Northern Star,* 25 June 1842:

HANLEY – On Monday evening, June 13th, a public meeting was held in the market place, Hanley, to adopt measures for the relief of the Loughton colliers, now on strike, when upwards of 2000 people attended. The meeting was addressed by Messrs. Robinson, Oldham, Ellis and Mayor, when the following resolution was adopted without one dissentient – "That this meeting views with disgust and indignation the attempt of Messrs. Sparrow to reduce the wages of their workmen and pledges itself to support the workmen with all the means in their power in their struggle of right against might".

VALE OF LEVEN – All communications for the Vale of Leven Chartists are to be addressed to John Millar, bookseller, Bonhill, who is elected corresponding secretary for the ensuing six months. A meeting of the Vale of Leven Universal Suffrage Association took place in the Democratic Seminary on Saturday the 18th inst, when the meeting was addressed by Mr M'Crea.

BILSTON – A numerous and enthusiastic meeting, called by placard, was held on the large piece of building ground near the market place in Bilston on Monday last. A commodious hustings was erected on the occasion, which was ornamented in front with the beautiful banner of the National Charter Association. The meeting was called for the purpose of enabling the five thousand who signed the petition to hear and adopt (in the present alarming state of the country) the remonstrance advised by the late Convention, and also to memorialise the Queen to dismiss her present ministers from office and to call such men to her councils as know how to legislate for the country. Mr Richard Boglin was called to the chair. Excellent speeches were made by Messrs. Jones, Linney, Soar of Birmingham, Thomason of the Vale of Leven, Cook of Dudley and others. The remonstrance and memorial were unanimously passed, and the meeting manifested a most enthusiastic spirit.

From the *Northern Star*, 2 July 1842:

LONDON – The members of Walworth locality met at their large room, Ship and Blue Coat Boy, Walworth Road on Monday evening, Mr Shaw in the chair. Minutes were read and confirmed ... Mr Keen read the letter from the *Star* of Feargus O'Connor respecting Mason, when it was unanimously agreed that five shillings should be voted for his defence. The sum of ten shillings was voted as national tribute to the executive and several new members enrolled. The subject for discussion next Monday evening is 'can we obtain the Charter without the aid of the middle class?'

From the *Northern Star*, 9 July 1842:

HUDDERSFIELD – Mr Ross attended what is called a camp meeting on Sunday last on the summit of our famed Castle Hill. The labour and toil required to obtain so great an altitude is amply rewarded by the rich and varied scenery which presents the eye ... Swarms of people were soon wending their way to the place of meeting ... there could not have been less than fifteen thousand present. Mr Ross delivered a

most eloquent and impressive lecture in favour of the People's Charter.
From the *Northern Star*, 16 July 1842:

CAMPSIE – Chartism here is progressing steadily. The lot of poor Holberry has created a strong feeling of sympathy. On last Sabbath Mr Wingate, pastor of the Chartist Church, preached an appropriate and impressive sermon on the death of Samuel Holberry. A collection was made for his widow by the members present.

HUDDERSFIELD – At a meeting in the Association Room, Upperhead Row, it was resolved on Tuesday night that as many Chartists as can possibly attend shall meet on Tuesday 19th inst. at six o'clock in the evening in the above room to form a procession to meet Feargus O'Connor Esq. and escort him into town.

ABERDEEN – On Wednesday last Mr Henry delivered the first of a course of lec tures on land to the Female Association.

From the *Northern Star*, 16 August 1843:

STRATHAVEN – Wednesday week being appointed for a public examinaion of Mr M'Crae's Junior Seminary; at the hour of meeting the Universal Suffrage Hall was densely crowded with a respectable audience. The pupils seemed to be from five to twelve years of age; and, although Mr M'Crae has only been some seven months in Strathaven, yet the youths who have been under his care evinced a knowledge natural history, arts and sciences, reading and explanatory exercises on the Old and New Testament Scriptures far superior to many, very many grown adults. They also showed their acquainance with a political catechism complied by their teacher, being an exposition of the six points of the People's Charter. A variety of recitative pieces and songs that breathed a strong and genuine feeling for democracy were given, chiefly selected from the Chartist Circular. The whole of the interesting and instructive exercises of the day were concluded with an American dance or reel.

LETTER WRITERS TO THE *NORTHERN STAR*

From the *Northern Star*, 6 January, 20 January, 26 May 1838, 29 August, 5 September, 12 September 1840, 27 February 1841, 6 August 1842, 5 July, 6 December 1845, 10 April 1847.

Several poetical correspondents must excuse us, We cannot be so unmerciful as to crucify them before the world.

Legal questions must stand over, Mr O'Connor being in Scotland.

The address of Samuel Healey will subject both him and us to a prosecution.

James Bennett – Should any improper opposition be offered, the Northern Star will be at his service. He shall not be trampled on.

John Campbell thinks the powerloom weavers of Manchester would do well to set an example to all the powerloom weavers of Great Britain and Ireland by making universal suffrage, as well as resistance to the reduction of wages, the basis of their union. We think so too.

'Loyal Address of the Chartists to the Queen' declined.

Wm. Albister – His verses are declined.

T.R. is desirous that political knowledge should be spread in Ireland as well as in England, and thinks it would be beneficial to the cause of liberty for the men of England to collect a small fund for the charitable purpose of sending a confidential man into that degraded and insulted country to distribute useful political tracts. He sends, along with his letter, sixpence as his mite towards the expense.

A Constant Subscriber, Sheffield – The song won't do.

Samuel Simestur had better apply to a legal gentleman. We are no lawyers, and Mr O'Connor is locked up.

Hebden Bridge Radicals – We are sorry that our crowded space precludes the possibility of publishing their Address.

We cannot undertake to give legal advice. The rascals have robbed the poor of that privilege by locking up Mr O'Connor.

W.H. Turner of Deptford may read the *Chartist Circular* in the open air to as many as will listen without any fear of violating the law.

We frequently receive letters having the seals broken. It is not for us to say they have been subject to the process of Grahamisation or not. We merely wish our correspondents to see all is right ere they post their favours.

C.B., Fenton, Staffordshire – We never give advice in quarrels between members of the families of the working classes except for the purpose of uniting them and saving law expenses.

We have a cart load of "poetry" on hand; it is impossible to print a tithe of what we receive.

EDITORIALS FROM THE *NORTHERN STAR*

From the *Northern Star*, 16 November 1839:

Having no other grounds whereon to form a judgement of the insurrection in Wales than the reports of a press which we were justified in using sceptically, we were inclined last week to view the recent outbreak as the madness of a few, heightened by the colouring of government artists, but, from the evidence of some of the witnesses, we are now justified in giving the whole proceedings the stamp of reality. That it was a mountain torrent long pent up until continued oppression and mulitiple insult prematurely burst the dam, we now believe....The middle classes, who have now by the operation of machinery, turned man into a beast of burden, which may or may not be employed at their pleasure or convenience, and who may not even live except upon their will and bidding, hope to hold power and increase oppression by the bayonet, paid for by the people; but they are mistaken ... Let them look to Wales for a practical instance of what is sure to follow the putting down of the free expression of opinion ... The Star and its proprietor have already suffered much in this cause; however, despite further oppression, our motto still shall be "no surrender".

From the *Northern Star*, 13 August 1842:

The reductions now attempted to be made in the price of labour are the result of a conspiracy on the part of a class to overawe the government and to accomplish their own selfish ends at the expense of the community at large. Look well at the parties who offer these reductions! Who and what are they? Members of the Anti-Corn Law League! "Extension of commerce" advocates! Bawlers out for "cheap bread"! The very men who have been for the last twelve months dinning in our ears loud and wordy expressions of "SYMPATHY" for the distresses and privations endured by the working portion of the population! These are the men who try to alleviate the distress they so feelingly deplore by reducing the wages of the men they employ!... The great Anti-Corn Law masters are to reduce the wages of their workmen until they drive them into acts of outrage and riot; and then they will go to Sir Robert Peel and say to him: "Didn't we tell you this would happen? Give us repeal to quiet the alarming state of the country and afford the starving people cheap bread". Having by these means forced their measure from the Minister, they will turn round on the people themselves and put them down. They will join in yeomanry bands, in special constable bands, and in jury bands; and they will bludgeon, sabre, shoot, hang, transport and imprison the very men who have done the Leaguers' work for them by "rising" and "rioting" ... If the working people intend ... to frustrate one of the most horrible schemes ever hatched to subjugate labour, if they intend to defeat the wiles and strategems of their deadliest foes, if they intend to advance their own cause of right and acquire unto themselves power to establish the right of justice, THEY WILL BE PEACEABLE!... Every succeeding day furnishes additional proof of the villany inherent in the despicable middle classes, of their hostility to the interests of the masses, of their hatred of justice ....

From the *Northern Star*, 8 April 1848:

On Monday next the matured will of the producing classes of this country will be carried in triumph to the Senate and will be presented to the representatives of worn-out prejudices and exploded privileges – prejudices and privileges which allow the idle few to lord it over the industrious many and to live sumptuously upon the sweat of the producer. This mighty monster may be, and probably will be, rejected by those who feel strong in the posssession of power, but we warn them gravely and warn them in time of the fallacy and folly of any attempt to resist the flood of mind and fixed resolution manifested in this, the people's last appeal.... Great and dreadful will the consequences be if vengeance and despair should once possess the minds of the millions of free men who pant for liberty and the restoration of their long-withheld rights ... For a people to ensure their freedom, it is sufficient that they know their rights and dare maintain them. ONWARD AND WE CONQUER! BACKWARD AND WE FALL! THE PEOPLE'S CHARTER AND NO SURREN- DER!

THOMAS COOPER

From PRO, TS 11 /602, Thomas Cooper to Susanna Cooper, 3 August 1842:

I have but a few moments. We had a grand affair in the market place last night. The Tory waggon, with Stephens on it, was drawn up opposite ours. Our lads would not hear him. The Tory lambs, chiefly butchers, began to shew fight – when O'Connor leapt, like a lion, from our waggon crying "Now my side, charge!". He fought like a dragon – flooring the fellows like nine pins – was thrown – forty men upon him – sprung up again – seized a fellow by the leg who stood on the waggon – tore him down (Stephens and the rest had cut) and then mounted the Tory wag- gon! What a shout then rent the air, amidst throbbing hearts! McDouall & others then crowded the waggons, and it was dragged alongside ours – we stepped on to it, and, successfully addressed the meeting! All the Tories were driven from the ground, & we remained in possession of the market place – O'Connor only lost his hat. We all marched singing round the streets at night – thousands upon thousands. I have been talking at Carlton today – McDouall at Bulwell etc etc. Tonight we have another demonstration in the market place & round the town. O for a thousand of my own darling brigade here. I never wished so much for a thousand pounds as now – I would have a thousand of my own lads here on election day then. O'Connor says we will carry it – in spite of soldiers & police.

From PRO, TS 11/602, Thomas Cooper to Susanna Cooper, 12 August 1842:

I am afraid you will feel uneasy ere this reaches you. I could not possibly write yesterday. I was somewhat put about in getting off from Birmingham, and was set down from the omnibus at noon in the middle of 33,000 colliers at Wednesbury (Wedgebury, they call it). Arthur O'Neill, Linney etc were there, and I talked to them about 1/2 an hour, and then spent an hour indoors among their delegates, who were contriving plans for bringing out other collieries in the kingdom on strike. We got to Bilston – and there I addressed another outdoor meeting for about 2 hours at night: we enrolled 50 after dark at the room. This morning I walked on to Wolverhampton (3 miles) and addressed about 4,000 more colliers in the open air. I came hither (Stafford) by steam – and, if permitted to talk unmolested in the market place tonight, shall get off, by coach, for the Potteries tomorrow. Now do not be alarmed, my dear Love. If they take me a prisoner tonight, bear up, like a woman. Mason is in prison here: 150 colliers have also been imprisoned this week: two troops of foot soldiers came here yesterday: the town is all on an alarm – and I really do not expect to be permitted to talk in the market place without interruption. However, if I am told to desist – we shall go off quietly to the Common; but if they take me up, I cannot help it. I must speak the truth – although, if they will let me, I will tell it discreetly. Run away, I cannot. Latimer would not – Christ would not. My sweet Love will not expect me to act cowardly. I trust, however, all will pass off quietly – and that I shall be able to write my Love from the Potteries tomorrow – assuring her that I am still at large & well.

THE PETITION AND DEMONSTRATION OF 1848

From the *Northern Star*, 15 April 1848.

The following letter, testifying the devotion and enthusiasm of the people, has been received by Mr O'Connor.

We, the inhabitants of the village of Coalsnaughton, assembled in a public meeting on the 13th of March and adopted the national petition and ... chose a committee of twenty, determined to ... swell the petition. Next day we set to work, the population of the village amounting to about seven or eight hundred and every man and woman, electors and non-electors, signed the petition with two exceptions, the one a silly creature of a schoolmaster, the other a poor labourer. We next paid attention to the outskirts of the surrounding parishes, where no petition sheets had been distributed – the parishes of Alloa, Clackmannan and Dollar – and got every man and woman, with few exceptions, to sign, likewise the 'navvies' on the railway, we may say to a man. There are a few of the Old Guards belonging to this village, working at Forth iron works, a distance of ten miles away; they sent us word that there had been no names taken up there. We lost no time but set off with the petition sheets and set the Old Guards to work with ourselves, and the result was from thirteen to fourteen hundred weavers, which would have been all lost had we not repaired thither. We had a meeting … with the Tillicoultry and Alva districts and agreed to meet on Monday evening to choose a delegate to carry our sheets to Edinburgh, our number of signatures being … 4,350. Now, sir, as you have offered a reward of five pounds and the flag which is to surmount the petition as a stimulus for exertion in getting signatures, we are of the opinion that few can have done better; and if you think we are entitled to the reward, we, in public meeting assembled, do heartily agree that the five pounds remain in your hands, to be disposed of as you may think proper, but we would be proud to obtain the flag …. We remain your obedient children, John O'Connor (Chairman), Thos. Bennie (Secretary), Jas. Scotland, Alex. M'Ewan, Jas. Watters, John Hunter etc (Committee), Coalsnaughton, March 31 st.

From the *Northern Star*, 6 May 1848:

Several of the London daily papers, in their zeal to run down the demonstration yesterday, have today made a grossly untrue representation of the numbers on the Common. *The Times* and the *Chronicle* try to make their readers believe that not 20,000 were present …. The Common is about 500 yards long and 200 broad, giving an acre in square yards of about 100,000. Now, at one o'clock, the whole space was dotted over, the centre very dense and the outside rather thin and straggling. Assuming only one person to the square yard instead of nine, the usual calculation in a crowded meeting, we have 100,000 people. These at least were on the ground yesterday, independent of the crowds in the adjoining throughfares. I went expressly all around the Common to be satisfied with my estimate, which, had the meeting been for any more aristocratic party purpose, would no doubt have figured in the 'Thunderer' at 200,000 souls. Yours respectfully, TRUTH.

A CHARTIST MEMOIR

From William Lindsay, *Some Notes, Personal and Public* (Aberdeen, 1898), pp. 133-198

With most of the leading advocates of Chartist principles I became well acquainted, of whom I name the following: William Lovett, a cabinet maker, a man of great organising ability; John Collins, who drafted the first bill, so far as I am aware, for a system of national education; and Thomas Cooper, the proprietor of *Cooper's Journal* and author of many books on theology, politics and poetry, the *Purgatory of Suicides* being perhaps his best known work; Feargus O'Connor; Ernest Jones; Julian Harney; Robert Lowery; Abram Duncan; Samuel Kydd; Dr. M'Douall; Rev. Arthur O'Neill and Henry Vincent. Jones and Harney were men of marked literary ability and the others named here were, without exception, entitled to be ranked among public speakers of a high order. Henry Vincent was not merely a powerful and effective speaker, but was an orator whose platform appearances secured for him the highest reputation wherever he went. He possessed all the qualifications which go to make a great public speaker. His reasoning was clear, his language perfectly adapted to express his meaning; his power of humour, of banter, or of satire, was such as I have never known to be combined in an equal degree in any other man. With men of this calibre supporting its claims there need be little cause for wonder that the Charter, wherever proclaimed, secured public attention ....

In the month of April 1848 the Chartists held their second great Convention in London. This time the petition that they had been preparing, praying that the Charter might be made the law of the land, was to be presented to the House of Commons by Feargus O'Connor MP, backed by an imposing procession which was to follow him to the House of Commons .... The 10th April, which was the day fixed for the demonstration, arrived, and the working people of London mustered, it was said, to the extent of a quarter of a million early in the day. Their behaviour was most orderly. Sir Richard Mayne, then the Head of the London Police, sought an interview with Mr O'Connor. This resulted in O'Connor announcing to the vast assemblage that the Government had resolved to allow the meeting on Kennington Common, but not to permit the procession to the House. The vast concourse of people took this announcement good humouredly. The meeting on the Common afterwards took place, and was regarded by the Chartists as a great success. They claimed to have beaten the Government because they said that it was the right of public meeting that they had resolved at whatever cost not to allow themselves to be deprived of. This right having been vindicated, they were satisfied. This, the last great public act of the Chartists, although it led for months before it happened to the most gloomy forebodings, passed off without serious disturbance, and in a manner that greatly encouraged the Radicals, both in and out of Parliament, in the further prosecution of their objects ....

The Chartists were supposed to be divided into two sections, the one styled the Physical Force, and the other the Moral Force, party. I devoted some attention to this point, being myself utterly opposed to any form of physical force, my reading of history having led me to the conviction that the gaining of an object, even good in itself, by mere brute force is scarcely any gain at all. It is only progress worthy of the name when obtained through the exercise of enlightened reason. I never thought any considerable number of the Scottish Chartists either inclined to, or expected any benefit from, physical force ….

I have very pleasant recollections of discussions that took place among the Chartists during their agitation in Aberdeen. The local leaders of this party were men of no mean ability: John Mitchell, bookseller; James McPherson, comb manufacturer; Archibald McDonald, flaxdresser; John Legg, mason; George Ord, combmaker; Duncan Nicolson, woolcomber; James Strachan, shoemaker; John McDonald, gardener; George Smart, preserved provision manufacturer; Alex Ross, combmaker; James Shirren, tailor; and George Smith, plumber. Robert Campbell, wood merchant; George Thompson Jnr., shipowner; and James Hall, shipbuilder, also supported the movement. Mr Shirren was sent as the Aberdeen representative to the great Convention that assembled in London in April 1848. Many other names might be mentioned, but these were men of really outstanding ability, and each, after his own manner and fashion, did the cause of Parliamentary Reform great and abiding service.

The Aberdeen Chartists, although they hired halls in different parts of the town, where, for many years they held meetings almost nightly, conducted their agitation to a great extent in the open air in Castle Street, on the Inches, and under the shadow of the Broad Hill. I have witnessed many most stirring and animated scenes at these places. The meetings were invariably interesting because the speakers divested themselves of every form of conventionality and spoke naturally and with vigour, using the most ordinary, simple, but always telling comparisons and illustrations. Sometimes splendid pieces of natural humour enlivened those great gatherings. These large meetings did much to weld the working classes together, and led them to see clearly wherein their common interests lay.

There was a Chartist Church formed in Aberdeen in 1844 over which Mr Robert Lowery presided. The services were held in the old Relief Church in St. Andrew Street. Mr Lowery delivered, for two winters, a series of very able lectures which crowded the Church to overflowing. His discourses dealt cheifly with history and the Christian side of politics. Similar churches and schools were formed in Edinburgh, Glasgow and Dundee ….

In the Spring of 1852 delegates from different parts of Scotland were elected by radical associations to assemble in Edinburgh at a Conference, the main object of the gathering being to settle a policy for an Advanced Liberal Party …. I was appointed to represent Aberdeen …. Fergus O'Connor, then member for Nottingham and well known as a Chartist leader, was present. O'Connor originated and set agoing a land scheme about 1844. It had for its object the putting of as many working people as possible in circumstances to cultivate little plots of land and maintain themselves and families by spade labour. The scheme, although undoubtedly well meant, may be said to have been a failure from its very beginning …. It was felt by a great body of Chartists that this land scheme of O'Connor's militated against the Chartist Movement …. I had been appointed to move the resolution declaring the Scottish radicals adhered strictly to the six points of the Charter, and that their agitation in favour

of these must not in any way be prejudiced by the operations of the land scheme
… O'Connor, on landing in Edinburgh, had got information about this resolution
of mine. He called immediately at my hotel, and in the most excited manner, denounced both the resolution and me. I was extremely sorry for the poor gentleman.
With all his eccentricities, I knew he had rendered noble service to the democratic
cause and for that I respected him.… I put the resolution, however, that Mr
O'Connor so fiercely objected to, when the proper time came for doing so, and it was
carried unanimously; a delegate was unwise enough to congratulate me on having
been the first man that had carried a resolution in Scotland that Mr O'Connor was
opposed to. At this O'Connor got into a condition of the wildest passion and black-
guarded everybody and everything. In his paper, the *Northern Star*, on the following
Saturday, in dealing with me, he fell into quite a different vein. He characterised me as
a thin, fair haired Scotsman, who manifested a remarkable degree of tact and intelligence in dealing with public affairs. The Conference lasted three days, and wound
up with a political meeting in the Calton Convening Rooms at which I presided.

It came out afterwards that even before this time the condition of Mr O'Connor's
body and mind had been a source of great anxiety to his most intimate friends.
Mentally he continued to get worse and worse, his utterances in the House of Commons being frequently of the most incoherent description. In short a crisis soon
arrived when it became necessary to put the unfortunate gentleman under restraint
in an asylum … O'Connor's death took place shortly after … and so there closed
the career of one who, with a body of Herculean strength and a brain of great vigour,
had for twenty years, both by speech and by his pen, aroused all over the kingdom a
widespread interest in the political enfranchisement of the people.

Index

Other Titles in the Chartist Studies Series from The Merlin Press

Images of Chartism
Stephen Roberts & Dorothy Thompson

Seventy contemporary images of the Chartist Movement.

1998 0850364752 paperback £15.95

The Chartist Legacy
Edited by Owen Ashton, Robert Fyson & Stephen Roberts

Eleven essays by leading scholars.

1999 0850364968 hardback £25.00
085036484 paperback £14.95

RECENTLY PUBLISHED

Friends of the People
Uneasy Radicals in the Age of the Chartists
Owen R. Ashton & Paul A. Pickering

This study of six Chartist leaders portrays movements for democracy and social progress, and explores the role of the uneasy middle classes in movements for working-class rights.

Chartist Studies Series, Volume 3
2002 0850365198 paperback £14.95

FORTHCOMING

Reprinting Spring 2004

A History of the Chartist Movement 1837-1854
R.G. Gammage

A chronological history of the movement that campaigned
for democracy and the right to vote in Britain in the early
Victorian era. Gammage wrote from direct experience and
involvement in the movement. 'An essential document for the
study of the Chartist Movement'- *Times Literary Supplement.*

First published 1854, facsimile of the 1894 edition

Chartist Studies Series, Volume 5
085036213X paperback

Summer 2004

Chartism After 1848
The Working Class & the Politics of Radical Education
Keith Flett

Based on original research, a study of the campaign for
political and social democracy and for workers' education.

Chartist Studies Series, Volume 6
0850365449 hardback
0850365392 paperback

FORTHCOMING

2005

Papers for the People
A Study of the Chartist Press
Edited by Joan Allen & Owen Ashton

An original study of the role of the Chartist press in the campaign for democracy in Victorian Britain and overseas from 1838 to the late 1850s.

Chartist Studies Series, Volume 7
0850365457 hardback
0850365406 paperback

Other titles of Interest

Chartist Reprints Series

The Democratic Review
Edited by G. Julian Harney

A facsimile reprint of a Chartist journal, printed originally in 1849-1850. It provides commentary on contemporary politics in Britain, and on events in Europe after the revolutions of 1848.

1968 0850360986 hardback £30.00

The Red Republican & The Friend of the People

A facsimile reprint of two Chartist newpapers, originally published in 1850-1851, with news, letters and articles on poetry, politics, etc.

Introduction by John Saville

1966 085036096X hardback 2 volumes £50.00